Couples, Kids, and Family Life

Social Worlds from the Inside Out

Series Editors
Jaber F. Gubrium
James A. Holstein

Social worlds come to us through stories, conveyed to us both by members and through detailed descriptions offered to us by careful observers. It's through such narratives of experience that we come to know what's happened to members of particular social worlds, how they feel about themselves, what life is like under the circumstances, and what their prospects are for the future. *Social Worlds from the Inside Out* is a book series which explores this theme for various social worlds by way of compelling qualitative case material. It opens to view the everyday lives of those who, day in and day out, experience and contend with the social worlds that are the focus of sociology courses.

Couples, Kids, and Family Life

Edited by

Jaber F. Gubrium
James A. Holstein

New York   Oxford
OXFORD UNIVERSITY PRESS
2006

Oxford University Press, Inc., publishes works that further Oxford University's
objective of excellence in research, scholarship, and education.

Oxford New York
Auckland Cape Town Dar es Salaam Hong Kong Karachi
Kuala Lumpur Madrid Melbourne Mexico City Nairobi
New Delhi Shanghai Taipei Toronto

With offices in
Argentina Austria Brazil Chile Czech Republic France Greece
Guatemala Hungary Italy Japan Poland Portugal Singapore
South Korea Switzerland Thailand Turkey Ukraine Vietnam

Published by Oxford University Press, Inc.
198 Madison Avenue, New York, New York 10016
http://www.oup.com

Oxford is a registered trademark of Oxford University Press

Library of Congress Cataloging-in-Publication Data

Couples, kids, and family life / edited by Jaber F. Gubrium, James A. Holstein.
    p. cm. — (Social worlds from the inside out)
  Includes index.
  ISBN-13: 978-0-19-517791-6 (alk. paper)
  ISBN-10: 0-19-517791-6 (alk. paper)
  ISBN-13: 978-0-19-517790-9 (pbk. : alk. paper)
  ISBN-10: 0-19-517790-8 (pbk. : alk. paper)
    1. Family. 2. Family life education. 3. Couples. 4. Parent and child. 5. Divorce. I.
Gubrium, Jaber F. II. Holstein, James A. III. Series.

HQ734+
06.87—dc23

                                                                2005047299

Printing number: 9 8 7 6 5 4 3 2 1

Printed in the United States of America
on acid-free paper

CONTENTS

CONTRIBUTORS

Derek Ball is a marriage counselor in private practice.

Autumn Behringer is assistant professor of sociology at Weber State University.

Amy L. Best is associate professor of sociology at George Mason University.

Emily Fairchild is a doctoral student in sociology at Indiana University.

Daniel Farr is a doctoral student in sociology at the State University of New York, Albany.

Jaber F. Gubrium is professor and chair of sociology at the University of Missouri-Columbia.

Scott R. Harris is assistant professor of sociology at St. Louis University.

Ramon Hinojosa is a doctoral student in sociology at the University of Florida.

James A. Holstein is professor and chair of social and cultural sciences at Marquette University.

Peter Kivisto is Richard Swanson Professor of social thought at Augustana College.

Demie Kurz is codirector of women's studies at the University of Pennsylvania.

William Marsiglio is professor of sociology at the University of Florida.

Susan Walzer is associate professor and chair of sociology at Skidmore College.

Rebecca L. Warner is professor and chair of sociology at Oregon State University.

INTRODUCTION

Couples, Kids, and Family Life approaches the realm of family from the *inside out*. It offers a distinctive view of what the social worlds of family life might look like from the standpoint of "insiders"—family members. The book is organized around the theme that social worlds are not collections of facts and figures, but comprise intensely shared and personal constellations of talk and interaction. Family life is more complex and fluid than survey statistics make it out to be. Families are more than enumerations of household composition or demographic trends. Like all social worlds, family is comprised of ordinary actions undertaken in relation to others, in which meaning and communication are the working subject matter of everyday life.

Getting to know social worlds from the inside out—in terms of the meanings that transpire between people—takes a special method of procedure. The lives under consideration need to be described in their own terms, to highlight what things and events mean *for them*. In the case of this book, the contributors aim to convey what it means to couples, kids, and parents in the everyday context of domestic life.

The term "social world" has two important connotations. One refers to a set of experiences or way of life specific to a group of people. For example, we might say that preteen girls occupy their own social world, the implication being that they have their own unique interests and concerns, their own tastes and troubles, even their own vernacular. They might occupy their own territory—particular tables in the lunchroom at school, for instance. Social worlds in this sense refers to realms of experience with specific, identifiable characteristics. Sociology is full of stories about the worlds of people differentially located in society, such as the social worlds of the waitress, the cab driver, or the thief. The accent here is on internal organization, less on a particular outlook or orientation to life as a whole.

"Social world" also is used to refer to a working view of reality, in this case highlighting how members see and interpret life. Perspective is stressed rather than sets of experiences. A social world represents experience as it is apprehended from a particular vantage point. In this sense, a social world is a constellation of meanings assigned to experience, which of course takes its shape and substance in relation to ongoing social interaction. A social world is a comprehensive understanding that captures what life is like for those involved when they view it from a particular standpoint. This connotation suggests that persons occupying the same physical space and engaging in social interaction can easily inhabit different social worlds. The social world of the dentist, for instance, is quite different from that of the dental patient, even while they readily get on with their relationship. The dentist's social world is a realm of professional expertise, close examination, and precise craftsmanship. The social world of the dental patient, in contrast, may more closely resemble a torture chamber from his or her perspective. And, as any student knows, the social world of the school is vastly different for teachers and pupils.

Whichever the connotation and even when used in combination, the important point stressed by all contributors is that one needs to get inside a social world in order to understand it fully. Being inside means more than simply locating oneself in a particular physical space; it also means taking account of how those who occupy the space orient to themselves and to others. Through the accounts and stories conveyed by actual participants, we can learn about members' own ways of interaction with each other, how they view their experiences, and what their understanding of life is in part or as a whole. This book describes various social worlds by way of compelling qualitative case material. This material opens to view the everyday lives of those who, day in and day out, contend with the experiential challenges of domestic living, both in place and from distinct perspectives.

FAMILY LIFE AND SOCIAL WORLDS

Today, family life takes many forms. Increasingly, we have come to appreciate the points of view of various family members, including those of children, parents, and interested outsiders. As a result, any discussion of what is family, who is part of the family, or what particular types of families are like is bound to be complicated and even controversial. *Couples, Kids, and Family Life* deals with the issues in relation to this complexity. The contributors take account of the perspectives of a wide variety of family participants, providing richly descriptive material drawn from a wide range of perspectives. The trials and tribulations of divorce, for example, are explored not only from the separating partners' perspectives, but also through the eyes of children. The aim throughout is to show the experience of family living from the vantage points of an array of participants, whose configuration of social worlds differentially refract contemporary issues such as the meaning of marital equality, the difficulties of keeping tabs on teenagers, and the challenges of stepparenting.

Family life isn't a single experience. Because of the family's diverse forms and the multiple perspectives of members and significant others, we can no longer describe "the" family as if it were a uniform social object with homogenized roles, rules, and relationships. Even differences such as the viewpoints of older and younger siblings convey the various social worlds a single household can be. For instance, the oldest child in the family might experience home as a peaceful, supportive environment, with the parents cultivating and appreciating everyone's skills and accomplishments. In contrast, the middle child, who is a mere five years younger, might perceive a tense household with nary a word of encouragement for anyone from the parents. Family life, not "the" family, comprises multiple experiential realms—social worlds—that can be so at odds that it would lead us to wonder whether the members of a single household could possibly come from the same family.

To capture the richness and diversity of contemporary family life, the contributors underscore three aspects of its social worlds. The chapters discuss their subject matter by taking account of different *realms of experience* and *diverse meanings*, from the perspectives of the *participants themselves*.

Social Locations as Realms of Experience

The first aspect of family life underscored has to do with social location— that is, one's distinctive position in relation to others. Each contributor analyzes and illustrates how diverse social locations, such as being a father versus a stepfather, being a traditional versus an equalitarian couple, or being a first child versus being a child of the parent's later years, provide alternative challenges and understandings to those within them. Different social locations carry varied perspectives on domestic roles, domestic relationships, domestic sentiments, and how domestic activities unfold.

For example, think about how a brother and sister—let's call them Karl and Krystal—who are close in age view the way they've been raised by their mother and father. Being close in age, we might expect Karl and Krystal to see their parents in similar fashion. They grew up in the same household, and the small difference in age would hardly suggest significant disparity in how they would characterize family life.

Now, what if Karl had been born ten years before his sister? The difference in age could mean that Karl and Krystal were reared in two different sorts of households, reflecting different stages in their parents' career paths. If Karl was born when his mother was a stay-at-home mom, his experience of parenting could be quite distinct from Krystal's, whose "same" mother went back to work soon after she was born. We're not saying that this makes for better or worse parenting; rather, we suggest that the difference in these children's social location within this family's domestic life might lead to significant contrasts on how they view their parents' presence in their lives. Because Karl was born and spent his early years in a home with a working father and a homemaker mother, we might guess that his experience of parenting wouldn't parallel Krystal's, whose early years were spent with both parents working. For one thing, if social location affects one's experience, we might figure that Karl's location would lead to a different perspective on how he was raised than Krystal would have on her upbringing. He experiences parenting from within a different social world than his sister did. Attending to this multiplicity of perspectives, the contributors would argue that a single family can be a different set of social worlds for its members, even while the participants and their roles—father, mother, son, daughter—would seem to be the same.

Add gender to the mix and social location becomes even more complicated as it relates to social worlds. Not only are Karl and Krystal differentially located in the "same" family because they grew up in relation to different phases of their parent's careers, but gender also has a way of working its effects on how parents relate to their children. Not only is Karl the "oldest" and, for that reason alone, perhaps regularly used by his parents to set an example for his younger sister, but being a *boy* locates him differently in social life in general. In the context of the family, gender is likely to provoke the use of a different set of rules for conduct and misconduct within, and especially outside, the household. Again, the point is not whether this is good or bad, but rather that boys and girls find themselves occupying different *gendered* social worlds—even within the same households. If boys are subject to fewer rules and regulations, then in the context of this family, Karl's perspective on parental supervision is likely to stand in considerable contrast with Krystal's. Gendered standpoints can thus turn the "same" family into distinct social worlds for the two siblings, one being relatively free and the other being restrictive.

One way to think about social location is to figure that, while family members may reside in the same household for years, they don't necessarily relate to its domestic affairs in the same way. In the preceding example, Karl experiences family life differently from Krystal with respect to both his parents' career paths and the siblings' gender differences. Indeed, such factors can work together, or intersect, to exaggerate the difference in experience that would result from either one alone. Their intersection might lead Karl to view *both* parents as nurturing and supportive of his outside activities and lead Krystal to view her mother especially as "rarely around" and not at all encouraging of her outside interests. The point is not that things would turn out just this way, but that differences in these siblings' social locations are likely to make their "common" family lives distinct realms of experience, as contrasting social worlds.

Underscoring the way social location relates to the experience of domestic life offers a multidimensional view of the family. The contributors illustrate the many ways in which a family can be experienced by its members. On this count alone, after having read a chapter, we come away with a sense that references to "the" family do scant justice to the many things social life can be for family members, as different from each other as night and day.

Diverse Meaning

Diverse meaning is the second aspect of family life underscored in the book. Matters of meaning are closely related to social location and social worlds. A set of exemplary questions that highlight several important ways of thinking about meaning are: What does divorce mean to a husband as opposed to a wife? What does it mean to divorcing partners who both have thriving careers versus those where one partner has a career and the other has tended the household? What does divorce mean to partners with children as opposed to those who are childless? And what does divorce mean to the kids, who may have no say in whether their parents stay together, but who clearly feel the impact of the divorce process? Meaning is the key to each question.

Clearly, meaning can be problematic, even while members of the household might live in what seem to be the same circumstances. It's not unusual, however, for researchers and social commentators to ask about the impact of major events such as divorce, a child's death, disability, sudden fame, or a change in household location, as if their consequences were straightforward. They ask these questions as if a single set of meanings for things, actions, or events could be identified. The assumption is that when certain things happen, other things are likely to follow. This way of thinking tends to homogenize experience. It makes everything seem predictable, as if there were little variation from one family to another, as if "the family" or "family life" were uniform things subject to various events.

But as there are so many social worlds emerging from family life—with their attendant meanings—it would be simplistic to think in terms of straightforward causal relationships. When we take a family's various social locations and members' perspectives into account, we tend to "dehomogenize" the family. This permits us to consider how an event such as divorce affects, say, older as opposed to younger children, the husband as opposed to the wife, or the girls as opposed to the boys in a family. Family meanings ultimately are drawn through the prisms of the myriad social worlds in place.

It is important to recognize the way meaning is being characterized in this book. From our perspective, meaning doesn't emanate directly from things, actions, or events. Rather, it emerges out of social interaction—interaction between people as they relate to things, events, actions, memories, anticipations, and a host of other elements of social life. The contributors emphasize the interactional character of meaning, even as they appreciate the general bearing that events such as divorce have on family life. We know that divorce can have a big impact on members of a family, but that impact differs according to how the divorcing partners view their relationship to domestic life. It differs according to how children see each of their parents, how the parents get along after the divorce, and how families are rebuilt in the wake of divorce. The meaning of divorce is never completely straightforward. Despite the fact that family life is often viewed as a set of cause-and-effect relationships, such as the impact of divorce on family members' well-being, it's never that simple. Meaning makes all the difference in the world, as social location and its realms of experience come into play.

Getting Close

This leads to the third aspect of family life highlighted in the book. It follows closely from the emphasis on multiple perspectives, social worlds, and diverse meanings. The contributors work from the premise that to know varied social worlds and their diverse meaning, one must get close to, or inside, family life. A questionnaire survey of families, for example, would only skim the surface of such differences. In contrast, the chapters stress the importance of asking members themselves for their sense of the organization and dynamics of family life from their respective points of view.

Getting close is a method of procedure. It encourages researchers to minimize the distance between themselves and the people they study. Rather than prepare a set of questions ahead of time to ask each respondent, it is important to figure that the people being studied might have questions and concerns of their own to discuss. In trying to get inside a social world, a researcher shouldn't second-guess the people inhabiting that world. The point is to *understand* that world, not prejudge it. Researchers must take care to let respondents speak for themselves. Framing questions ahead of time tends to preclude the kinds of questions we might have asked had we become familiar with the experiences in which we're interested. A child or a teenager, for example, doesn't necessarily see the world in the same way we do because of our different social locations. The studies described in this book all orient to letting the people being studied convey in their own terms what their lives and perspectives are like.

The procedural bywords of getting close are to "go to the people" whose experiences are under consideration and "ask them" to convey "in their own words" what domestic life means to them. The authors of the chapters don't presume to know what's going on ahead of time. They draw their conclusions from what they see and hear from being up close. This requires that they become intimately acquainted with the organization and dynamics of domestic life in view. They leave themselves open to unexpected questions and concerns that arise in the interview process. In this kind of research, listening tends to override asking; the fewer "prepackaged" questions, the better. The object is to let the diversity of social worlds and their multiple meanings come through in whatever shape and form people actually experienced them.

THE CHAPTERS

The chapters are divided into three parts that take up conventional distinctions. For example, the division between Part 1 ("Couples") and Part 2 ("Parents and Kids") would appear to contrast distinct realms of experience, designating separate social worlds. But readers should be reminded that the social worlds represent differences in perspective as much as social locations. They never are as fixed as the conventional names for these parts of the book imply. As the chapters in each of the parts show, couples, parents, and kids occupy constantly changing positions in relation to each other and in relation to family life as a whole as they shift in social location and take up the meanings of distinctive social worlds.

Part 1, "Couples," focuses on married or soon-to-be married partners. While the section deals with the domestic partnership, it's clear that marriage as a relationship and the categories of husband and wife are not made out of whole cloth. They are more like a tapestry, woven from the myriad strands of interactions and meanings that comprise the varied social locations couples can occupy.

Chapter 1, by Emily Fairchild, is titled " 'I'm excited to be married, but . . .': Romance and Realism in Marriage." The author draws on in-depth interviews with women of various ages to explore women's experience upon entering their first marriage. The chapter hones in on the variable meaning of love in the context of marriage. Fairchild vividly demonstrates that women entering marriage don't completely buy into the view of romantic love highlighted in popular culture. Rather, their definition of marital love is judiciously constructed in terms of their varied perspectives on marriage. The chapter shows that the women do not reject the cultural ideal, but modify it to be consistent with their everyday experiences. Their "realistic" discussions of marital love are somewhat surprising, given that they are bombarded with a predominant culture of romantic love and a prewedding avalanche of romantic challenges.

Chapter 2, "Making Sense of 'Husbands' and 'Wives,' " by Autumn Behringer, takes up the meaning of the *categories* of husband and of wife. While these are single terms of reference applied to two different roles, it's evident from the in-depth interviews the author conducted that both husbands and wives interpret the roles in many different ways. The interpretations form a continuum, from those who view the roles traditionally, those who amend tradition, and those who express a desire for more tradition to those who desire more equality and those who see the roles as functionally equal or as a partnership. Some husbands and wives fall outside the continuum and are confused over the meaning of the categories. Once again, we see that while these roles might appear uniform categorically, in practice, they are assigned a wide range of meanings.

Chapter 3, by Scott R. Harris, is titled "The Everyday Meaning of Marital Equality." The author challenges the widely held view that marital equality pertains mostly to the equal division of household labor. Researchers, for example, often study equality (and inequality) in terms of the amount of time each of the marital partners devotes to various household tasks. In contrast, when Harris asked couples how they actually experienced equality and inequality, they talked about a surprising range of things. For some, the meaning of equality centered on simply hoping a spouse would take over a rather minor household task—a relatively small commitment of time and energy in the overall scheme of things. For others, equality had more to do with intellectual makeup. In a sense, equality turns out to be something in the eye of the beholder and not a one-size-fits-all standard.

Part 2, "Parents and Kids," turns to the perspectives of different actors in the family drama. It features adults in their roles as parents and children in their roles as, well, kids. The chapters are especially concerned with their different takes on common domestic challenges such as teenagers' whereabouts, using the car, and gender socialization. Meaning is again center stage as the diverse social worlds of parents and kids come into play. Yet here, too, the conventional distinction between parents' and kids' perspectives belies the many and varied social worlds that each category can put forth.

Chapter 4, "Being a Good Parent," by Rebecca L. Warner, uses in-depth interviews with fathers and mothers to get up close to what it means to be a good parent. Her point of departure is the conventional understanding that good parents are those who have happy, healthy, and successful children. Warner's interviews show that parents do speak in such terms, but they designate their meaning in terms of their children's specific trials and accomplishments. While any two parents might describe good parenting as a matter of raising happy and successful children, the meanings they assign to "happy and successful" can be as different as night and day. The lesson here is that the meaning of good parenting relates as much to the everyday vicissitudes of domestic relations as it is spelled out by common clichés.

Chapter 5, by Demie Kurz and titled "Keeping Tabs on Teenagers," takes up the continuing dilemma for parents of trying to protect their children, on the one hand, and "letting go," on the other. This is a particular challenge during adolescence, when teens want more freedom and parents are loath to go too far lest their children get into trouble or into harm's way. Parents see control over their children's whereabouts as essential to keeping them safe; at the same time, parents find this increasingly difficult to do. The chapter discusses the strategies that black and white parents of various backgrounds use to monitor their teenagers' whereabouts. Kurz shows that monitoring teenagers involves much more than the straightforward application of rules and regulations. Instead, parents and teens typically negotiate what the rules will be and how they will apply. Gender, social class, and race also play into the process.

Chapter 6, "Kids, Cars, and Family Life," by Amy L. Best, takes us into the volatile territory of teenagers, driving, and the use of the automobile. The chapter deals with how kids talk about cars, exploring what their talk reveals about the dynamics of domestic life. We are again presented with aspects of the dilemma about monitoring and letting go that Demie Kurz (Chapter 5) examined, but this time it's from the teenager's perspective. From in-depth and focus group interviews, the analysis illustrates how teens negotiate the borders of family life in relation to their outside interests. Best shows how the conventional characterization of parent-youth relationships as one of warring perspectives, while at times apt, in the end fails to explain the complexities of parents' and teens' management of their relationship. Car use and ownership is a quintessential part of teenage "rites of passage," and we learn much about the lives of both parents and teens from how they resolve their issues over cars.

Chapter 7, by Daniel Farr and titled "Sissy Boy, Progressive Parents," takes the relations between children and their parents in a different direction. Farr writes his chapter as an "autoethnography," which means that as a researcher he calls upon his own experience as a "sissy boy" growing up with progressive parents. His topic is gender socialization, but it's clear from his discussion that what it means to be a boy or a girl is not a simple matter of having particular gender characteristics. Characteristics such as toy preferences, pastimes, and intellectual interests have different meanings depending on the social worlds in which they are expressed. For Farr, being a boy at school is a far different matter than being a boy at home. Farr uses the concept of "magnified moments" to illustrate how certain occasions in his upbringing and schooling poignantly bring together the social complexities of being a boy or girl, man or woman. Farr's experiences at home and in school present some especially interesting questions regarding both gender and sexuality, and the relation between the two.

Part 3, "Rearrangements," deals with family change, in this case the process of divorce, remarriage, and stepparenting. The diverse meanings of the roles and relationships of domestic life are magnified and complicated by the challenges of uncoupling, recoupling, and building a new, blended family. Once more, the authors show how contrasting perspectives reveal the diverse meanings of domestic social worlds.

Chapter 8, by Derek Ball and Peter Kivisto, is titled "Couples Facing Divorce." It deals with the meaning of divorce from the perspective of couples that are facing the prospect of divorce. The chapter presents accounts offered by the couples in counseling sessions and suggests four different ways couples learn who they are as couples, what their marriages look like, and what their futures might hold. The meaning of divorce is refracted through the lenses of these four perspectives. We hear an intriguing range of explanations for marital troubles as we listen to the actual "divorce talk" of couples contemplating a breakup.

Chapter 9, by Susan Walzer, is titled "Children's Stories of Divorce." It takes a close look at how children interpret their parents' divorce. Once again, social location in the family makes for differences in meaning. The process of accounting for divorce is commonly studied from adults' points of view, so there is little research on children's perspectives. Walzer combines narratives, taken from interviews with a sample of children from 136 families, with autoethnographic material from her own family, to illustrate the various meanings that children assign to the uncoupling process. The chapter shows children interpreting their parents' divorce in ways that both reproduce and revise long-standing images of family, love, and marriage.

Finally, Chapter 10, by William Marsiglio and Ramon Hinojosa, is titled "Stepfathers and the Family Dance." The authors use dance as a metaphor for describing the stepfathering experience. This is apt imagery because stepfathers typically have to "get in step" with new households that are already choreographed as far as the roles, rules, and relationships of family life are concerned. The stepfather commonly finds that his new family dances to different tunes than those to which he's accustomed. His primary challenge is how to get in step with the existing rhythms of the household. Drawing upon in-depth interviews, the chapter discusses the complex interpretive work of adjustment, underscoring the active ways in which stepfathers navigate their new social worlds.

DISCUSSION QUESTIONS

Following each of their chapters, the authors provide questions for classroom discussion. While these are not taken up directly in the chapters, they suggest ways of approaching the key concerns of each chapter.

One way these questions relate to key concerns is to ask you—the reader and student—to use the material presented in the chapters as a basis for reflecting on your own family experiences. These are *empirical* discussion questions in that they ask you to compare experiences. Some of you are parents. Most are probably adult children. Virtually everyone has some experience in the domestic realm that may be brought to bear on the issues raised in the discussion questions. The questions ask you to think about how families and family members you've experienced—intimately or from afar—respond to events or issues such as getting married, marital equality, being a sissy boy or a tomboy, divorce, and stepparenting.

For example, as we noted earlier, Scott Harris suggests in Chapter 3 that marital equality may not just be a matter of the division of household tasks. Harris provides several illustrations from his research that encourage us to think in different ways about what "equal" means in practice. Two of the discussion questions provided at the end of his chapter ask you what equal means in the context of your own marriage or the marriages of others you know. In opening the term "equal" to broader definition and searching for its many meanings, Harris asks you not only to reflect on the conventional uses of the term, but to also search for meaning in the other ways equality presents itself in your experience. This is a way of getting close to what you know by comparing it with others and perhaps opening your eyes to what you may not have noticed before.

A second way the discussion questions relate to key concerns is to ask you to take the concepts presented and apply them to your own or others' experience. These are *conceptual* discussion questions in that they ask you to apply new ideas or frameworks of understanding to experience. Author Susan Walzer argues that divorce is not just something that couples go through, but a landmark experience for children as well. She highlights their social location and its perspectives on the issues. Children have their own sentiments and ideas about divorce's causes, its course of development, and its outcomes for both their parents and for themselves. In some of their discussion questions, Walzer and other authors ask you to consider how experiences associated with other social locations, such as that of being particular types of divorcing couples, relates to family life. Asking you to think about this, of course, relates to the idea that the meaning of familial events and issues depends on the social world in which it's embedded.

For example, in her chapter "Being a Good Parent," author Rebecca Warner provides several illustrations of attempts at good parenting. The illustrations show parents sorting out the meaning of good parenting in relation to various challenges their children present to them. Warner discusses a mother who worries about her son's sports success, a mother who is concerned about her daughter's sexual molestation, and mother and stepfather who talk about their son's alleged theft of a bicycle from someone in the neighborhood. At the end of the chapter, Warner asks you to consider what meaning the challenges and events described would have if the children in question were a different gender. It's another way of asking whether gender provides different frameworks for experiencing domestic life.

Taken together, the two ways of raising questions put you, the reader and student, in the analytic driver's seat. While the contributors analyze their own research materials, presenting them in terms of particular concepts or frameworks, you are given the opportunity to move beyond these materials to draw upon your experiential realms and social worlds. In this way, your own domestic lives become "data" for consideration, perhaps challenging the authors' arguments and interpretations, perhaps extending that into new realms of family experience. In doing so, domestic life and its social worlds will continue to reveal remarkably diverse senses of family living.

Part 1

Couples

1

"I'm excited to be married, but . . .":
Romance and Realism in Marriage

Emily Fairchild

Dear Janice,

You're getting married! This is a momentous occasion and I am so excited for you and Scott! We know your relationship has been strong for some time, but there is still great excitement when your commitment becomes "official." This next year will be busy (and stressful)! Remember that you're celebrating your love. This is the one time in your life when you get to revel in romance—trying on dresses, choosing flowers, and writing vows. I look forward to hearing all your details! You'll only experience this process once in your life, so have fun and enjoy it all! I hope you find that this is a time when all of your relationships—with Scott, your parents, and other friends and family—are strengthened.

Lots of love,
Eliza

This letter—from Eliza to her bride-to-be friend, Janice—virtually gushes with excitement, as Eliza encourages Janice to relish the new, exhilarating developments that engagement and marriage hold in store. In fact, Eliza uses a variation of the word "excitement" twice in the first three sentences! She enthusiastically touts the many delights that surround Janice's upcoming wedding, anticipating the emotional highlights of getting married.

The letter typifies the traditional sentiments surrounding a woman's engagement; it headlines many of the elements that are customarily associated with this "momentous occasion." Eliza urges Janice to celebrate and savor each aspect of the upcoming year—an adventure in planning, shopping, preparing vows, and building a new, strong relationship and family. "Revel in romance," writes Eliza, because romance makes even the most mundane activities burst with joy and excitement.

A CULTURE OF ROMANCE

In the contemporary United States, we typically assume that marriages are built on romantic love. Granted, not all marriages are the epitome of romance, but it is clear that men and women in the United States associate romantic love with marriage. When men and women are asked if they would be willing to marry a potential partner if that person "had all the other qualities you desired . . . if you were not in love with him (her)," they overwhelmingly respond that they would *not* marry such a person. Furthermore, they indicate that not being in love is reason for divorce; a couple should not stay married if they are not "in love" (Simpson, Campbell, and Berscheid 1986).

Even early childhood experiences contribute to the assumption among most girls that they will marry and that this decision will be based on romantic feelings. "Feeling norms" are widely enforced, whereby girls teach each other socially accepted ways of feeling that are consistent with the structure of marriage in American society. A girl is expected to have romantic feelings for someone of the other sex, she is not supposed to feel for a boy who is already attached, and she is to feel for only one boy at a time (Simon, Eder, and Evans 1992). These norms, which reinforce hetero-sexuality and monogamy, illustrate the cultural regulation of young girls' romantic feelings that guides them toward the goal of committing to one lifelong romantic relationship.

While peers are powerful influences in young girls' lives, media images regarding love and marriage also have strong sway. When I asked one of the women I interviewed in preparing this chapter why there was so much excitement surrounding getting married she responded, "I think it's because growing up you watch movies and you see TV programs where girls are going to get married and everybody's all jumping around and they're excited about it and you learn you're supposed to be excited about getting married." Like this woman, most of us can recount examples of such engagement-induced excitement drawn from personal experience or suggested by the mass media.

In her book *White Weddings* (1999), Chrys Ingraham refers to more than 350 movies that feature weddings or brides. This is in addition to the countless portrayals of weddings on television shows—from sitcoms to crime dramas to reality TV. The nearly constant bombardment of these images naturalizes the idea of romantic weddings. They are seen as inherent to the life experience, rather than as something we socially create.

As we will see in this chapter, while women have realistic perspectives on marriage, they also believe romance is important. They make sense of their experiences through the cultural view that getting married is romantic.

American culture draws a clear link between romantic love and marriage. Young girls learn the importance of romantic relationships from friends in school. Romantic wedding images are pervasive in the mass media. Marketing practices underscore the salience of romance in the transition to marriage. Each additional pairing of a romantic image with what is otherwise a legal and/or spiritual arrangement reinforces the notion that getting married is a romantic experience. The honeymoon industry, of course, glorifies the transition to marriage as the ultra-romantic experience, using rhetoric such as "images of ineffable bliss" and relying "on a vocabulary of romantic love" (Gersuny 1970:261, 260). To compete for customers, the honeymoon business provides hyper-romantic images, appealing to couples' desires to make their first vacation as a married couple as romantic as possible.

We see these images everywhere. Certainly the marketing of wedding products, such as gowns, jewelry, and reception favors, relies on romantic images; weddings are presented as occasions on which couples can splurge for luxurious items to have the perfect, magical wedding. The appeal of romantic wedding imagery, however, extends far beyond products related to the ceremony, reception, or honeymoon; advertisers use romantic images to sell everything from toothpaste to life insurance (Ingraham 1999). These campaigns are successful because they capitalize on the "magic" associated with weddings. The wedding industry is virtually ubiquitous; it's easy to see why it has been referred to as the "wedding-industrial complex" (Ingraham 1999).

THE REALITIES OF LOVE AND MARRIAGE

In a culture that portrays romantic love as the basis for marriage, we would expect people to abide by cultural standards and maxims. This should be especially true for women, who are the most frequent and direct targets of advertisers and cultural commercials. However, as this chapter will demonstrate, women near the time of their first marriage do not necessarily describe marriage and marital love as romantic in the conventional sense. Their presumptions and views are not as stereotyped as we might imagine. They are not completely "programmed" by cultural expectations. Instead, many hold what may be termed "realistic" characterizations of marriage and the love they want in their marriages. These realistic descriptions of marriage emerge from conversations with women who are younger or older, who are religious or nonreligious, and who have or have not lived with their partner before marriage.

Romance, however, is not lost on these women. Rather, the importance of romance is evident in the way they take their realistic descriptions and interpret them as romantic. In so doing, they are able to view the transition to marriage as a very romantic time in their life, even though they describe it in ways that are inconsistent with stereotypic cultural definitions of "romantic." The chapter suggests that women can sustain both realistic views of getting married and cultural visions of the romantic marriage, even if the latter are inconsistent with their own experiences.

I come to these conclusions after conducting in-depth interviews with women either just before or soon after the time of their first marriage. Interviews are especially good for this type of research because they provide rich, detailed information about the meaningful dimensions of lived experience (Holstein and Gubrium 1995; Agar 1996). In addition to learning what women think about love and marriage, the interviews delve into the processes through which women make sense of their marriage experiences.

Most of the interviews were a little more than one hour long and took place in my university office. I found most of my informants through letters sent to women who had applied for a marriage license or through flyers placed in bridal shops. The interviews were conducted as close to the wedding as possible so that the women would be likely to remember their experiences clearly. Women were eligible to participate if the interview took place fewer than six months before their wedding or during the first month after the wedding. The other requirement for participation was that the informant did not have children. With these restrictions, the sample is similar in terms of race and education to the population of women who live in the area in which the study was conducted. The majority of the women with whom I spoke were not yet married at the time of the interview. They range in age from twenty to thirty-seven. Although special efforts were made to find noncohabiting couples, the majority of the participants had been living with their fiancés before marriage, a trend to which we will return later in the chapter.

This chapter focuses on three key aspects of women's experience with love, romance, and marriage. First, the interviews provide rich descriptions of marriage, martial love, and the ways these are, or are not, necessarily "romantic" (or consistent with romantic cultural images). These descriptions illustrate women's sentiments that marriage may *not* be the romantic fantasy that American culture makes it out to be, but it nevertheless involves the sort of "everyday" love they want in their marriages. Second, the women indicate that they are aware of cultural connections between romance and marriage. They show that they know that their opinions differ from pervasive cultural images, but they resolutely avoid being pessimistic about love and marriage, even though they don't view them as necessarily romantic. Finally, the women I interviewed use familiar cultural notions to characterize their own experiences, casting their own realistic marital love as a necessary condition for marriage to be romantic. After exploring these three issues, the chapter will conclude with a discussion of the complexities of the cultural link between romance and marriage.

REJECTING THE ROMANTIC

"Romantic" love is often conceptualized as impractical, idealistic, or fanciful. The women I interviewed, for the most part, reject this definition. Instead, they present a much more realistic description of marriage. Rather than a romantic vision of exciting, idealistic love, these women hold the notion that marriage is something that demands constant attention. They replace the fantasy image of romantic marriage with one that is more pragmatic, grounded in the mundane realities of everyday life.

One of the interviewees, Maggie, exemplifies the rejection of the romantic when she says marriage is "not a fairy tale." Maggie is a professional woman in her thirties who has had considerable experience with relationships and has seen several of her friends get married. She contrasts the realistic view she has for her marriage with the rosy vision held by a couple she knew before they got married. Maggie explains that her friends thought everything would be fine after they got married—that their dating relationship would naturally turn into a *Leave It to Beaver* family upon marriage. She describes the couple: "I think that they thought that when they were married the whole world would be hunky-dory. It would always be sunny. . . . Just every time they talked about it they just had this really storybook view of it."

Maggie says that her friends actually are quite unhappy now, and she credits much of their unhappiness to what she sees as unrealistic expectations before marriage. Observing their experience, she says, has given her more realistic expectations. In her words, "I think [marriage is] a great thing and I'm excited to be married, but I definitely have a realistic view that it's not always happy and its not always perfect and that kind of thing." Maggie feels she is well prepared for married life because she does not expect that everything will be perfect—she expects difficulty.

Anne, like Maggie, was aware of the danger of unrealistic expectations before marriage. Anne is a twenty-one-year-old college senior who is particularly candid about her efforts not to succumb to the romantic fantasy machine surrounding marriage. She says: "We were really careful to go about it without being whisked up in the you know, the whole [excitement surrounding getting married], because it's not always—not always gonna be an easy thing, you know, it's not always the love story and the flame dies out." Anne realizes that it is possible to get carried away in the excitement of getting married and wants to be sure she and her fiancé do not incorrectly assume they are embarking on an everlasting fairy tale. In contrast, she acknowledges that there will be difficult times and that the "love story" may not really exist in marriage. Realizing this, and acting accordingly, she believes, will protect her marriage in the long run.

This is a common sentiment, as the women describe marriage as an ongoing challenge. Robin, a twenty-seven-year-old graduate student, says, "Marriage is something that you have to work at. . . . And I have learned that it is really important to set boundaries and not just assume that because you love each other that you're not going to have problems." Liz also comments on working to maintain the love: "Just because I feel this way now doesn't mean that I will forever if I don't make [sic] the time and effort into maintaining it." These women are not relying on the "magic" of love to support their relationships with their spouses; they believe that love exists, but that it is something the couple needs to nurture actively to reap its benefits.

Another woman, Cathy, struggles with figuring out how to have a lasting relationship. She states: "I did not grow up with good marriages around me. I grew up with—my mother was divorced twice; my father was divorced twice. So I have to learn it. I mean, I have to have faith that I can learn it." Cathy's comments about "learning" marriage reinforce the idea that marriage is not self-sustaining. Even before she was engaged, Cathy had been "studying" marriage. She sought a variety of marriage books and talked with her fiancé and a counselor about what being married meant and what they might expect as a married couple. These pieces of Cathy's story suggest that Cathy does not rely on the cultural notion that "love would keep them together." It was her experience that marriage was *not* a happy arrangement and that it could not succeed without conscious dedication on the part of both partners. Moreover, Cathy believes her own situation warrants particular care, since she had such negative experience with marriage when she was a child.

Interestingly, one woman I interviewed expected difficulties in marriage even though her relationship had been blissful up to that point. Ashley, one of the youngest women I interviewed (twenty-one), reports having had no troubles in her relationship. Her perspective is unique in that she identifies herself as optimistic about marriage, but she still emphasizes its difficulties:

> I have a very idealistic view of marriage. I don't know why. I think it's because we haven't really been in a situation where we've—we haven't had like a big problem where we've had big issues. So we haven't really had a lot of hard times. And I know we will once we're married. And its easy for me to sit here and say "Oh, it's gonna be so great and easy" but I know it's not.

The preceding quotations and descriptions attest to the fact that the women I interviewed are not under the illusion that their married lives will be easy, or even that they will be happy most of the time. They speak more realistically than romantically about the institution of marriage, but this does not mean that they deny the importance of love in marriage. Love does play an important part in these women's decisions to marry. All the women indicated that they loved their partners, and most said that a marriage without love was doomed to failure. Divorce, they said, was acceptable if love ceased to exist. Nevertheless, these women do not believe that loving one's partner guarantees a happy marriage. As Anne succinctly summarizes, "There are times in your marriage that you don't even—you can't even imagine how much of a challenge it is. But I think that's just part of it."

PRECLUDING PESSIMISM

The women I interviewed use a very interesting tone when rejecting the fantasized notion of marriage based on romance, one that acknowledges the dissonance between their experience and the cultural ideal. Ashley, the young woman who has had no problems with her relationship and is admittedly optimistic about its future, is the only participant who regards her view of marriage as idealistic. The other women believed their opinions were likely to be interpreted as pessimistic, even though they did not intend to convey negative views of marriage. For example, Maggie says:

> I'm not like a pessimist or anything like that, you know, I'm really excited
> about being married and all that kind of thing, but you know, I recognize
> from my parents' relationship, from my friends' relationships and everything,
> that it's not always fun and games. It's a lot of hard work and so I have that
> expectation, you know, we're not always gonna get along.

While Maggie says she is excited to be married, she qualifies her excitement in light of realistic expectations. She realizes she is contradicting the
romantic ideal, providing a less-than-glowing endorsement of marriage.

Similarly, Jill notes that her optimism has waned: "I just used to be very
optimistic. I'm not saying I'm pessimistic now, but, there's just, there's so
many people in this world. And I do believe in soulmates or whatever. But
even soulmates come with their problems, you know, it's not always going
to be perfect." Jill knows that the realities of a relationship can detract from
even the most perfect of marital matches. Like Maggie, she is uncomfortable with her less-than-glowing endorsement of marriage because she realizes that in the context of a culture of romantic marriage, her pragmatic views
can sound pessimistic.

Jill and Maggie are not jaded or discouraged, but they understand the
consequences of not embracing the romantic ideal. Being "realistic" in a
romantic cultural context is likely to lead others to view them as "down
on marriage." And, because the cultural influence is so strong, they do not
want to be seen as violating normative expectations. Talking about marriage realistically, not romantically, is likely to convey an overly negative
impression—more negative than they actually hold. At the same time,
however, they feel their realistic approach to marriage is likely to serve
them better than a "Pollyannaish" belief that marriage is all hearts and
flowers. Thus, the women struggle to reconcile their experiences and
realistic expectations with a cultural view in which they do not believe.
Caught in a cultural bind, they don't want to sacrifice their realism, but they
feel the need to repeatedly preclude that they are pessimistic or negative
about marriage.

RECASTING THE ROMANTIC

My informants also deal with this bind by portraying marriage in ways that
may differ from the idealistic romantic view, without completely compromising the romantic image. That is, they reconstitute what romantic
marriage might look like. This shift is best illustrated in the way the women
think about marital love. Rather than describing marriage in terms of

"fireworks," "stars," and "sparks," the women I interviewed suggest that they are seeking the "everyday romance" that grows as two people go about their lives together. In the words of one interviewee, "Love is what's left after the excitement's gone."

Romantic marriage simply isn't possible twenty-four hours a day, seven days a week. As Kelly says, "You don't want to be nervous in front of them forever!" Susan agrees: "Life can't be a constant high." Kelly and Susan each believe that romantic love is an important part of the relationship, but that it is not enough to sustain the relationship. They argue that it makes more sense for marital love to evolve into something that can be experienced in the course of everyday living rather than something that might disrupt "regular" life. Romance is there, but cast less idealistically.

In one segment of the interview, my informants dealt with this issue very directly: I read them a short description of a married couple and the type of love they held for each other. While the partners in the fictitious relationship said they loved each other, they were unhappy and felt they were "growing apart." In the scenario, the couple was worried that they might not have the right kind of love for marriage. Liz's response to this vignette is typical of my informants:

> If they're looking for the fireworks and the stars and all that kind of stuff, then perhaps they'll be disappointed, but it doesn't make it any less real or any less strong than other types of love and I think that what they might require is a reassessment of what they expect love to be like. And if that is what they want, the romantic fireworks stuff, then this [marital relationship] may not be for them.

While Liz undermines the romantic ideal of marriage, she is careful to uphold the importance of love. She simply broadens the understanding of what "strong" love might look like. In the process, she validates a less romantic, more down-to-earth view of marriage. Liz doesn't necessarily denigrate "the romantic fireworks stuff," but she does suggest that the couple in the scenario may not want to stay in their relationship because they aren't realizing the romantic ideal they seem to seek.

Mindy echoes some of Liz's sentiments regarding what a couple "should" feel in order to be married: "[Others may say], 'Well this is what I feel—what I should feel. Maybe I should feel something more, something different, something better.' And in a lot of cases there's nothing more, different, or better out there. It's just what you feel—what you are together." Mindy validates a nonromantic view of marital love and suggests that comparing one's feelings to an ideal (personal or cultural) may have harmful effects on the relationship. In making this comparison, Mindy acknowledges the powerful cultural images discussed earlier in this chapter. These images can lead people to expect romantic feelings and, in turn, to think their marriages are in trouble if such feelings do not exist, or fade over time.

The women I interviewed, however, expect the romantic love to wane. They think it is unrealistic to expect romantic love to be everlasting, as the ideal form might suggest. Consequently, they turn elsewhere to find romance, proposing the notion that the "ordinary" can be romantic. Jill compares the importance of conventionally understood romantic love to the ordinary qualities she believes are most important to a strong marital relationship:

> It's just being comfortable with a person. . . . Whether there are sparks or not, you have the commitment, you have like those years of being together, knowing each other on like, friendship, relationship or whatever people call it, and you have the comfort level of building your lives around each other. And that is more important in the long run than whether or not there's a huge passion.

For Jill, then, other things mean more to the relationship than conventionally defined romantic feelings. Daily interactions with the spouse create a kind of "comfortableness" she considers more important than the culturally prescribed romantic love.

To varying degrees, all of the women I interviewed focus on the importance of spending time with one's spouse. They indicate that everyday interaction supplies the unique bond that makes for a strong marriage. Consider Cara and Anne's remarks:

> *Cara*: I think a lot of it is just practicality and living together and day-to-day things. . . . I don't think it's like a, like a hugely like romantic thing as opposed to like, more of like a caring about each other, about each others' feelings and wanting to make the other happy.

> *Anne*: Just spending time together. It doesn't always have to be, you know, talking to each other or assessing your relationship and things like that, but I just think it's so important that you're in each other's company because there's this bond that you both have that you share. . . . I mean, I just think that since you're together everyday, that's your life, that if you can you should do things like go to the store together, little things, cause I think they build up and really matter.

These women believe that there is a particular type of love that should exist in marriage, but that love is intimately tied to realities of everyday life. As a couple lives together, they develop the qualities of a relationship that make their marriage distinctive and desirable. The ordinariness of the relationship leads to its uniqueness and strength.

Despite their current views, these women say they have not always held these opinions. Rhonda explains that there is an idealized image of getting married to which one is exposed early in life. That image, she suggests, is not realistic. One's notion of romance changes as one enters the "real world." Rhonda explains:

> You just have this idealized version of getting married, you know, everybody plays it up as so romantic and so wonderful and sweet. Now that I am married and now that I have gotten older and hit the real world I'm kind of like, "That's a load of crap!" . . . It's a lot more hands-on, you know, getting stuff done, hard work than it is that idealized romantic notion that you get as a girl—you meet your prince charming and everything's wonderful and you get married and it's all good. That kind of thing. That's not it.

For Rhonda, a relationship in which each partner helps the other accomplish his or her goals is romantic:

> We're not here on this earth to stand and look at each other and say "Oh, you're really nice." We're here to get stuff done and the point of marriage is that we do it together. . . . My idea of romantic is Brad staying up all night helping me study for my biology test the next morning. That kind of stuff. Practical stuff to me is romantic.

Rhonda argues that it is not realistic to focus on a notion of romance that is separate from the trials of everyday life. Instead, a married couple should treasure the support each provides and the ways in which that support makes them better individuals. She recasts "romantic" love in her own terms, thus sustaining a version of the romantic image while drawing her own experience under the romantic rubric. Similar to other women I interviewed, she both acknowledged the pervasive ideal of romantic love and located her own experience in positive relation to it.

DOES EXPERIENCE MATTER?

An obvious question arises: Do women get more realistic about love and marriage as they get older and more experienced? There is certainly a culturally promoted notion that romance is for the young. Idylls and passion are thought widely to fade with age. Similarly, we often think that experience tempers romance. For example, wouldn't women who have previously been married or lived with a partner also tend to view marriage more realistically, based on their own experience? Or, on the other side of the coin, wouldn't married life seem more exciting and romantic for those who have never lived together with a spouselike partner?

Contrary to what we might expect, neither age nor experience seemed to make much difference in the view of the women I interviewed. The evidence presented here came from women across a spectrum of ages, from women in first-time relationships to women who have been long-term cohabiters. For instance, Maggie and Anne both suggested that marriage is no "fairy tale," but they are very different in terms of characteristics that might affect their views on marriage. Maggie is twenty-six, is finishing a Ph.D., and has had several relationships and work experiences. Anne is twenty-one, is finishing college, has always lived with her parents, and has been with her fiancé since high school. Anne is not only younger than Maggie, but she also has had generally less life experience. Despite their differences, the two women expressed very similar opinions about what constitute healthy expectations about marriage.

I explicitly asked some of my informants if they thought they would have a more or less romantic view if they were older or younger. Interestingly, the woman guessed that younger women would view marriage more romantically. Liz, a woman in her late thirties, combined her opinion about the relationship between age and romanticism with a comment about the work required in marriage: "I don't think I would have had the energy [when I was younger]—I wouldn't have had the energy to make that kind of sustained effort that a good relationship requires."

Maggie used a particularly interesting metaphor in describing why she, at twenty-six, might be less romantic than a younger woman:

> I think the younger you are the more romantic your view is. I mean, I like the romance. I want it to stay and that kind of thing. But I think as you get older, you know, you take over your car payments, you take over your insurance payments, you buy a house, you get sick. I just think that you—at twenty-two my parents were still paying for everything. And it's a really nice way to be. You know, and so I think that now I just have a much more realistic view that when you buy something, you have to pay for it.

Maggie's realistic (and humorously economic) metaphor draws a stark contrast between the way she views her upcoming marriage with how she might have seen it four years earlier. Of course there is no way to know how Maggie might have actually viewed marriage four years prior. The point of interest here is that my informants generally believed that younger persons were more romantic, even as their own collective accounts proved this to be untrue. Similarly, the accounts and opinions of women who have and have not cohabited are strikingly similar. Among my sample of interviewees, age and experience did not drastically affect their views of romantic love and marriage.

CONSIDERING COMPLEXITIES

The women in this study are at a unique stage in life: the transition to marriage. Since marriage is associated with romantic love, and since a "culture of romance" surrounds those who plan to be married, one might expect their understandings of marriage and marital love to be fairly romantic. However, the women's understandings are more complex than one might have anticipated. They speak of the difficulties of marriage and describe marital love, as it *should* be, to ensure a successful, lifelong relationship. We are left, then, with some contradictions between popular romantic culture and the ways women make sense of their own lives. How might we explain the complex mixture of realistic and romantic visions of marital love?

One explanation might be that I have selected an atypical sample, that my informants are in some sense "hardened" and have lost the romantic ideal because of various life circumstances. I do not believe this to be the case. Although many of the women lived with partners before marriage—an experience that might breed more realistic understandings of the relationship—the cohabiters' views are strikingly similar to those of non-cohabiters. Moreover, because premarital cohabitation is increasingly common, my sample is likely to accurately represent the current population of women planning to marry.

Another possibility is that my informants simply are not aware of, or influenced by, the culture of romance. This is clearly not the case, however, since the women did talk at length about romantic ideals. Indeed, they indicate that romance is important to them in several ways. First, they are typically somewhat embarrassed that they don't agree with romantic ideals, often apologizing for being too negative. The women's insistence that they are not overly pessimistic about marriage clearly recognizes that they are resisting the cultural mandate. The women know that marriage is normatively characterized in romantic terms, and they are uncomfortable offering more realistic understandings. When this feeling is combined with the women's tendency to recast their own (realistic) experiences in romantic terms, it appears that the cultural ideal of a romantic marriage does influence these women.

The way the women innovatively cast their mundane experiences in romantic terms implies that aspects of the romantic ideal remain important to them. Were they not concerned with having romance in their lives, they could more easily describe their martial expectations in practical terms with fewer caveats and apologies. Interestingly, they manage to interpretively transform pragmatic images—which are, by definition, not romantic—into new visions of what being romantic might possibly entail. By understanding many mundane, everyday activities as romantic, the women accept the cultural prescription that getting married is romantic, even as they maintain their realistic visions of marriage.

It is not surprising that my informants accept some version of the romantic ideal. They are not immune to culture, so to speak. We should expect them to have internalized some romantic norms and expectations. Rather than living the romantic ideal, however, my informants seem to accept the idea of a romantic narrative that can be molded to the realistic circumstances of their own lives. A romantic narrative is a story line in which the protagonist confronts obstacles and emerges victorious (Jacobs 1996). In the lives of my informants, the challenges women have to overcome are the grinds of everyday life. Victory is having a successful, lasting marriage. My informants describe marriage in terms that allow them to construe their own actions and accomplishments as important, if small, everyday victories that collectively constitute a romantic success. Their romantic narratives are about the practical challenges of relationship survival.

In light of the endurance of the romantic image, then, how can we account for my informant's realistic views of marriage? The well-known "demise" of marriage and the family undoubtedly shapes they way women anticipate and experience marriage. As Charles Lindholm (1998) writes, our expectations and beliefs about love "clearly develop out of our unique historical trajectory and cultural background" (257). Three features of the contemporary social landscape may be particularly consequential for women's understandings of love: cohabitation rates, divorce rates, and economic independence.

The women I interviewed are in relationships during a time in which cohabitation is more popular than ever, placing them in unique social circumstances. Women marrying today (the majority of whom have lived with their spouses before marriage) have more marriagelike partnerships *before* getting married than did previous generations. Because of this, and as cohabitation increases, the meaning of marriage is changing. Perhaps those who are marrying today have more realistic expectations regarding marriage because they feel that marriage is serious business, not to be entered into lightly. There are, after all, more options available that involve less work and commitment. The women I spoke with are making a decision (to get married) that may be seen as more serious, and perhaps more real in its consequences. Therefore, their realistic expectations are warranted.

The fact that today people are marrying at a time when divorce rates are very high may also explain women's realistic conceptions of love. They may adopt a pragmatic stance because so many marriages fail. Seeing many couples divorce may motivate women to look ahead seriously—not frivolously or romantically—at marriage and to base their expectations accordingly, rather than relying solely on ephemeral cultural images. The realistic approach to marriage may be motivated by the very practical challenge of succeeding in an enterprise in which the success rate is perilously low.

Finally, the relative economic independence of men and women may help to explain my informants' realistic views of marriage. The study mentioned early in this chapter—in which men and women were asked whether they would marry a person without being in love—showed a historical increase in women's association between romantic love and marriage. The authors explain this increase by pointing to women's growing economic independence. As women became more economically independent, their concerns for finding a partner who would provide economic support diminished, to be replaced by a quest for romantic love (Simpson et al. 1986). While women's economic dependence on men has certainly declined, economic inequalities between men and women persist. Because many women anticipate that their husbands will be the primary breadwinners in their marital families, they may take this into account in assessing marital prospects, relegating romantic love to a lower rung on the ladder of marital success.

SUMMING UP

This chapter has investigated the ways in which women that are preparing to marry present their understandings of love and marriage. I found that these women, who are engaging in a ritual that has been greatly romanticized, do not speak about marriage and marital love in particularly romantic terms. This is surprising since these women are subject to both an American

18

culture that values romantic love and the prewedding culture of idealized romance. Women's conceptions of love and marriage, however, are complex; they both reject the romantic ideal and incorporate it into their realistic descriptions of love and marriage.

The women I studied are aware of the culture of romance, and they work to reconcile this culture with their own beliefs about what goes into a successful marriage. They do this by interpreting many of their own mundane experiences and expectations as "romantic" aspects of a successful marital relationship. We can make sense of this process by looking at the cultural imperatives and social circumstances that shape the women's visions of marriage. As American culture would have it, the women value romance, particularly at this time in their lives. However, social circumstances such as increasing cohabitation, increasing divorce, and residual economic dependence lead the women also to value very pragmatic aspects of a marital relationship. This leads to a more realistic focus, as women hone in on the everyday challenges of making a marriage succeed.

Finally, women reconcile the contradictions between their romantic notions of marital love and their realistic appraisals of what marriage is like by recasting their anticipations and experiences as elements in a romantic narrative. They interpretively transform everyday, realistic aspects of marriage into highly significant, romanticized keys to marital success. In this way, women adhere to the cultural prescription that marriage is romantic even though they are skeptical of the romantic ideal.

REFERENCES

Agar, Michael. 1996. *The Professional Stranger*. San Diego: Academic Press.

Gersuny, Carl. 1970. "The Honeymoon Industry: Rhetoric and Bureaucratization of Status Passage." *The Family Coordinator* 19 (2):260–66.

Holstein, James, and Jaber Gubrium. 1995. *The Active Interview*. Thousand Oaks, Calif.: Sage.

Ingraham, Chrys. 1999. *White Weddings: Romancing Heterosexuality in Popular Culture*. New York: Routledge.

Jacobs, Ronald. 1996. "Civil Society and Crisis: Culture, Discourse, and the Rodney King Beating." *American Journal of Sociology* 101:1238–72.

Lindholm, Charles. 1998. "Love and Structure." *Theory, Culture, and Society* 15:243–63.

Simon, Robin, Donna Eder, and Cathy Evans. 1992. "The Development of Feeling Norms Underlying Romantic Love Among Adolescent Females." *Social Psychology Quarterly* 55 (1):29–46.

Simpson, Jeffry, Bruce Campbell, and Ellen Berscheid. 1986. "The Association Between Romantic Love and Marriage: Kephart (1967) Twice Revisited." *Personality and Social Psychology Bulletin* 12 (3):363–72.

FURTHER READING

Holland, Dorothy C., and Margaret A. Eisenhart. 1990. *Educated in Romance: Women, Achievement, and College Culture.* Chicago: University of Chicago Press.
Ingraham, Chrys. 1999. *White Weddings: Romancing Heterosexuality in Popular Culture.* New York: Routledge.
Otnes, Cele, and Elizabeth Hafkin Pleck. 2003. *Cinderella Dreams: The Allure of the Lavish Wedding.* Berkeley: University of California Press.
Paul, Sheryl. 2000. *The Conscious Bride: Women Unveil Their True Feelings About Getting Hitched.* Qakland, CA New Harbinger Publications.
Radway, Janice. 1984. *Reading the Romance: Women, Patriarchy, and Popular Literature.* Chapel Hill: University of North Carolina Press.
Sprecher, Susan, and Sandra Metts. 1999. "Romantic Beliefs: Their Influence on Relationships and Patterns of Change over Time." *Journal of Social and Personal Relationships* 16:834–51.

Discussion Questions

1. This chapter contrasts "romantic" and "realistic" visions of marriage. How "romantic" is your view of marriage? How would you define a "romantic" marriage? What experiences do you think have influenced this view?

2. This chapter discussed cohabitation rates, divorce rates, and relative economic independence as social circumstances that might contribute to women's realistic expectations for marriage. What other factors might influence women's views of romantic love and marriage?

3. Are men's visions of marriage similar to those held by the women in this study? How might gender affect the way a person views love and marriage?

2

Making Sense of "Husbands" and "Wives"

Autumn Behringer

Every couple gets married a bit differently. When I was a bride, I wore a simple white dress and ballet slippers, skipped the veil, had photographs taken in a garden, and served filet mignon to the guests. When my friend Dawn was married, she wore a black dress and carried dead roses, and the guests came in costume since it was Halloween. I have another friend who wants to get married by a judge atop a mountain in Oregon, and still another planning a posh, black-tie, wedding "event" in downtown Chicago. I have sat through Catholic weddings, Jewish weddings, and half Catholic/half Jewish weddings. I have seen ceremonies with no attendants and those with a dozen; I have seen women as groomsmen and mothers as bridesmaids.

The wedding ceremony itself may not be universal in content or structure, but the marital labels we receive afterward certainly are. The wedding ceremony has been described as a ritual of transformation, one that furnishes each bride and groom with a new status (Freese 1991; Scanzoni 2000). Even though weddings themselves may vary, every married couple has one thing in common—when the ceremony is over, the labels of "husband" and "wife" have been bestowed upon them.

Married persons orient in various ways to the words "husband" and "wife." Despite the diversity of marriages, and the possible resistance to particular identity labels, these tags are cultural challenges for all married people to understand who they are as couples. Of course, if vivid differences exist across marriages, then equally colorful variations may surface in spouses' interpretations of these marital labels, even within marital dyads. After marriage, the identities of individuals are personally and socially transformed when they suddenly find themselves considered a husband or a wife. These terms, although ordinary and seemingly commonplace, can be interpreted in vastly different ways and can convey radically different understandings of what it means to be married.

Understanding meaning is crucial to social life. Meaning determines how human action proceeds. Individuals act based on the meanings they assign to physical objects, living things, situations, institutions, other human beings, statuses, and abstract concepts (Blumer 1969). Meanings, however, are not universal. "Snow" has different meanings to a northerner and a southerner; "cow" has different meanings to a vegetarian and a rancher; "operation" has different meanings for a surgeon and a patient; "religion" has different meanings to an atheist and a Catholic; "parent" has different meanings for a six-year-old and a sixly-five-year-old; "patriotism" has different meanings for war veterans and war protesters.

Marriage is not a new subject of inquiry for social scientists. For centuries, scholars have investigated marital trends, laws, and policies. But researchers often neglect to ask those presently living in marriages what the experience means to them. To understand the meaning assigned to the roles of married individuals, we must probe the ways in which husbands and wives make sense of the terms "husband" and "wife" in general and in relation to each other. This chapter first explores how married individuals understand the meaning of these terms, then looks at how closely spouses' definitions match. As we'll see, while the labels are commonly bestowed at marriage, to those in question the labels vary considerably in meaning.

THE INTERVIEWS

To answer these questions, I conducted qualitative, in-depth interviews with married individuals. Both the husband and the wife participated. To generate a diverse cross-section of couples, I relied on multiple methods of subject recruitment. For example, I recruited interviewees by posting fliers around a medium-size midwestern city, making announcements in classrooms at a large public university, and placing advertisements in city newspapers. In the end, twenty-seven couples participated, resulting in fifty-four interviews equally divided between the wives and the husbands.

Participants ranged in age from twenty-two to ninety-four. The average length of marriage was thirteen years, although the duration of marriage ranged from just four months to seventy-two years. Generally, husbands tended to be older than their wives, and the age gap between husbands and their wives was as great as eighteen years. Participants tended to be white (87 percent), and all seven of the respondents who were of a racial/ethnic minority were married to a white spouse. The educational background of interviewees was relatively diverse. Although 50 percent of respondents had obtained a bachelor's degree, over one-fourth had a high school degree or some college experience. Nine individuals had advanced degrees. Financial status also varied, with yearly income ranging from none (unemployed or stay-at-home parent) to over $200,000. Over half of interviewees associated with some branch of Christianity. Approximately one-third, however, could be classified as "other," including those with no current religious affiliation, agnostics, atheists, Taoists, and Pagans. Eight couples were involved in a second or third marriage, and 48 percent had children living at home. Among these, four were living with stepchildren.

During the interviews, I asked a variety of questions concerning marital identity: What does being a good wife/husband mean to you? How would you describe your husband's/wife's role in the marriage? How does your spouse define the terms "husband" and "wife"? I first compared the responses of individuals and looked for patterns in the answers provided. I then compared the responses of each husband and wife couple to see if they had compatible (or incompatible) interpretations of the marriage roles.

THE MEANINGS OF HUSBAND AND OF WIFE

I categorized the various ways husbands and wives understand the labels "wife" and "husband." I then created a typology of spousal labels that includes seven varieties of marital identity. As seen in the accompanying figure, six of these categories form a continuum of spousal identity, moving from traditionalist notions of marriage on the left to more egalitarian ones on the near right. The seventh category, "role confusion," lies outside of the continuum and is reserved for those who convey uncertainty about the meaning of the terms as it applies to their marriage.

Traditional	Amended	Desire for More Traditional	Desire for More Tradition	Functional	Partnership	Role Confusion
			Equality	Equality		

[_____]

Traditional Meanings of Husband and of Wife

When asked about the meaning of wife and of husband, many interviewees drew on long-established distinctions between husbands and wives, men and women in general. This was the most popular type of response, with sixteen out of fifty-four interviewees interpreting marital labels through a traditional perspective. I labeled this category "traditional" simply because so many respondents referred to marriage in this just this way. Some respondents even declared their marital arrangement to be an outdated model.

Quotations from Brach and Betty illustrate how spouses in this category prefer the conventional definitions of husband and wife despite an awareness of more contemporary marital ideas. (In the quotations, ellipses are used to indicate omitted talk.)

> *Brach* (thirty-one, married two years): I'm the leader, the manager. I'm responsible for things like bookkeeping, finances, vehicle maintenance, bills, insurance, everything. If we lock ourselves out of the house, I'm the one who has to break the door in and get in. . . . Betty tries to fulfill the traditional role. When I say traditional, I mean old-fashioned role of wife. Cleaning, cooking, laundry.

> *Betty* (twenty-two, married two years): We're pretty old-fashioned. So, I pretty much take charge of the household, just pretty much taking care of him and myself. . . . I think he's more financial . . . and I'm like more household and the old-fashioned wife duties.

This "old-fashioned" conception of marital roles was expressed by young couples, older couples, newly married couples, and couples with long marriages. Though the boundaries between work and family have been blurring steadily since the 1950s, it is evident that many spouses still equate marital identity with historically persistent gender roles. When defining the term "wife," respondents frequently used words such as "cooking," "cleaning," or "childcare," while definitions of "husband" often included words such as "provider," "finances," or "breadwinner." Descriptions in this category clearly make an association between household responsibilities and wife and see a connection between financial responsibility and husband. For these interviewees, the meaning attached to spousal identity appears directly linked to a "separate spheres" ideology in which women's roles dwell in the private household domain and men's roles occupy the public realm.

Additionally, individuals in this category drew on conventional notions of masculinity and femininity when defining the words "husband" and "wife." For example, definitions of "wife" frequently contained references to shopping or decorating, while definitions of "husband" often referred to aptitude for mechanics or yard work. Donna and Daniel captured how a separate spheres ideology and an ideology of gender difference shaped the meaning of marital roles:

Donna (forty-five, married twenty-one years): I don't see myself primarily as a career woman. . . . I think of myself first as a wife and mother. . . . We have different roles. My role, I do more of the music with the kids. . . . I do more with the homework and keeping the kids on task. . . . I still do all the cooking and the groceries and stuff like that. I'm a pretty good cook. I'm a pretty good Mom. . . . He does most of the breadwinning. . . . I really think that Daniel is that head of the household if it comes right down to a decision, but I'm not a weak person.

Daniel (forty-seven, married twenty-one years): I'm the primary bread-winner. . . . I'm the trash taker-outer, the recycling taker-outer, heavy lifting, mechanical kinds of things, a Mr. fix-it. Donna is a good cook and she likes to cook and she likes to do things in the kitchen. So that's kind of her role to do the cooking, meal planning, shopping.

The most common feature of those who fit the traditional category may be their use of gender difference to demarcate meanings of husband and wife. For instance, familial responsibilities such as "nurturance" and "discipline" appear to be gender-based for most of the traditional couples, but more antiquated gender stereotypes, such as "male dominance" and "female subordination" are not present for all traditional couples.

Nonetheless, for some traditional women, such as Candice or Betty, wife does indeed symbolize deference or subservience to one's husband.

Candice (twenty-four, married four years): Well to me, being a wife means being the supporter, supporting my husband and what he's wanting to do. Letting him run the family, you know? Letting him make the decisions and stuff. A wife should be submissive to her husband but also able to give her opinions and what she thinks or whatever, but ultimately the decision is his on certain things. . . . When we disagree sometimes I'll just be like, "Go ahead and do whatever you think" because he'll be like, "I know I'm right" and I'm like "OK." I just kind of go with the flow I guess.

Betty (twenty-two, married two years): . . . And him, he plays the role of, well, kind of, all-around-take-charge person, and I just kind of go with his lead. I'm more of his little follower. . . . He's solely the decision-maker.

The presence or absence of marital power undoubtedly influences the connotations of wife and husband for some couples. Inequality is not inherent within traditional definitions of spousal labels, however. (See Chapter 3 for further discussion of marital equality.) Though gender difference permeates the responses of all of these interviewees, difference does not necessarily translate to unfairness. In fact, aligning household and childrearing responsibilities with wives and financial and outdoor duties with husbands may signify a celebration of gender differences and relatively easy means by which two married individuals can make sense of each person's place within the relationship.

Amended Traditional

The language used by spouses in this category generally mimics that of the aforementioned group, but seven interviewees altered the traditional definition enough to warrant an additional category, which I called "amended traditional." For this category, gendered characteristics and responsibilities continue to serve as the basis for the labels of wife and husband. As the category name suggests, however, interviewees in this group slightly amended the traditional definition of spousal labels, presumably because their particular life experiences were a modified version of the traditional arrangement. With the exception of one or two variations on the traditional theme, those in this category have a philosophy on spousal roles that matches those in the traditional category. Take, for instance, the responses of Han and his wife, Haley.

> *Han* (twenty-eight, married one year): I think that probably the first thing I would say would be we have more traditionalist roles. . . . She's very talented in many of the traditional areas, in terms of cooking, sewing, baking, things of that nature. Although I'm not the handiest of men I'm working towards that way in trying to be more of a traditional male role in fixing things, taking care of the car, yard, mechanical things. I would probably say that ultimately I would have the final say on things. As far as financial things, I would probably say it's joint. We both watch the finances and do the bill paying and things of that nature because obviously for a number of years we've been taking care of our own money and Haley is actually a CPA.

> *Haley* (twenty-eight, married one year): I do more of the, I guess, traditional wife things, like the cooking and cleaning. He takes the garbage out and tries to learn to fix things. But finances, paying bills, keeping the books, that's a bit more my responsibility and I think it's going to become more that way.

Clearly, Han and Haley have adopted a traditionalist view of marital roles, but because of Haley's experience and expertise in accounting, the couple's finances, which, according to the traditional definition should be handled by the husband, are instead a shared responsibility. The following quotes from Ingrid and her husband Isaac further highlight how individuals modify the traditional meanings of husband and wife in order to be compatible with their particular marital/familial experiences.

> *Ingrid* (thirty-six, married five years): First of all [being a wife] means taking care of my son, providing for my son. I think I have a fairly traditional role within my marriage, to my husband, since I'm the one who provides the meals. I do all the shopping. . . . So I think that there's fairly traditional roles there as far as I'm the one who's primarily responsible for our son . . . and just making sure the house is taken care of, the laundry gets done, there's dinner on the table, and things like that. . . . But I really do have quite a bit of freedom . . . because I work. . . . I work almost every weekend . . . and he takes care of our child on the weekend. So when it comes to our son, I think we work really well together as a team.

> *Isaac* (thirty-six, married five years): The finances, I cover all that. Pretty much make the decisions on how and what activities [our son's] involved with. I pretty much have the final say . . . and we don't have disagreements on that. There can only really be one true chief in the family. . . . Both of us [care for] our son. Because I take care of him on the weekends, and she takes care of him during the week. . . . Every weekend I have [our son] and it works good because he doesn't get too much of one parent.

For Ingrid, the word "wife" appears to be synonymous with carrying the bulk of household and childcare responsibilities, yet her employment provides her with slightly more freedom by reducing her childcare load. For Isaac, the word "husband" connotes some degree of authority or ultimate control, but it also signifies fatherhood and refers to the days on which he is the primary caretaker of his son. For Ingrid and Isaac, traditional conceptions of the terms do not suffice since both spouses are actively participating in the childrearing process. In the amended traditional group, therefore, the meaning of wife and husband may slightly deviate from conventional marital ideology, but still largely upholds a traditional marital configuration.

Desire for More Tradition

Individuals in the category labeled "desire for more tradition" conveyed a strong preference for the traditional version of marriage and family, but felt that either they or their spouse fell short of actualizing the traditional model. When asked the meaning of husband and wife, these six respondents underscored their desires and ideals rather than defined terms based on the existing marital situation. For instance, Jack and Jennifer both expressed dissatisfaction with Jack's present fulfillment of the husband role, implying that the ideal situation would be one in which Jack acted more like a traditional married man.

Jack (thirty, married four years): Well what being a husband means to me, I suppose, is the stereotype of what I've always read or seen. I'm supposed to be the one to bring to bring home the bacon, you know, the provider. The disciplinarian in the family, which doesn't always work that way with stepchildren. . . . That's what I think my role *should* be, but I tend to put things off on her though. I don't really do it on purpose, but, like, if I can't get through to the kids, then I'm always like, "You deal with it." . . . I see myself as trying as hard as I can [to be a good husband], but I don't think I live up to that expectation as much as I should, but I try. That's why I'm wanting to go back to school, to *be* more. To better myself and my situation, so she doesn't have to depend so much on having to pull twice as much of her weight than she needs to. . . . I let her deal with stuff I don't want to, and she doesn't like that aspect a lot. She would rather I be probably more the person who handles the business and handles financial needs, but like I said, I'm still learning to do that.

Jennifer (thirty-seven, married four years): I think I'm the stronger person in the relationship, period. . . . I am the stronger person, covering a lot more areas than he does. . . . I think I get resentful [because] he knows as long as I'm there, maybe he doesn't have to do anything because I'm the stronger person. I take care of business. . . . I think the only strong point I can say is he goes to work every day. He does make sure that he provides for us . . . but sometimes I get frustrated that it's not enough. . . . He relies on me too much . . . from simple things to the more complex, he relies on me to solve problems.

Clearly, both Jack and Jennifer feel that Jack needs to become a more "take-charge" husband, adopting the more traditional role of family leader, rather than leaving Jennifer to tackle the majority of problems. In a sense, spouses who desire more tradition regard the marriage as too egalitarian. For them, the boundaries between the spouse's roles and identities have eroded too much, and a return to tradition is in order.

Jennifer and Jack are unique in two notable ways. First, both spouses identified a need for more tradition. In other marriages, only one spouse discussed "shortcomings" in the fulfillment of traditional marital roles. Second, Jennifer is the only female respondent to fall into this category. While some male respondents pinpointed their own inadequacies in performing traditional roles, such as a wish to be a better provider or stronger disciplinarian, in other cases men in this category wished their wives would show more interest in observing tradition. When asked the meaning of "husband" and the meaning of "wife", Viktor, for example, stressed his desire for traditionalism.

> *Viktor* (thirty-one, married two years): I like to see myself as pretty traditional, conservative. I like the traditional masculine roles of provider, protector and that sort of thing. . . . It's kind of interesting, because I would like to have a traditional wife, one that takes care of the house—that would be nice—if I'm out working. Takes care of the house, takes care of the kids. Like my mom was raised to be a traditional wife, an old-school wife. You serve your man, that's kind of how my mom was. I've never really seen Vanessa as that.

In sum, for those wanting more tradition, the word "husband" or "wife" symbolizes something they desire either in themselves or in their partner, but has yet to become a reality. Additionally, the quest for more traditional, gender-based, distinctions appears to be much more common among husbands than among wives.

Desire for More Equality

While many husbands communicated a need for more tradition, the desire for more equality resided exclusively in three wives. These female interviewees made important distinctions between who they are in their marriages as wives and who they want to be, and similarly who their husbands are in the marriage and who they want their husbands to be. These women felt that they had taken on a traditional role in the relationship but expressed displeasure with the arrangement. Zelda, for example, had clearly internalized the notion that household duties were women's duties, but was frustrated that she'd adopted this view.

> *Zelda* (thirty-one, married two years): When I get up in the morning, I'm very concerned about what we need for breakfast [*wondering*]: "Did we pack a nutritious lunch?" and "What are we going to eat for dinner? and "Do I need to prepare anything before that?' Whereas for Zachary, he's like, "Well I'd rather just sleep an extra twenty-five minutes and not really worry about that". . . . I feel like I should do those more domestic things. And I feel like I should, you know, if we need food, go to the grocery store and make sure we always have this and that and always do the laundry and stuff like that. . . . I just feel that I *should* do that, but I don't like thinking that way. . . . I don't want to say he does nothing. . . . He's just much more laid back, so a lot of the things that I feel I should do, I probably don't *need* to do, but

I just do them first . . . but I feel that they need to get done. . . . I feel that all these little chores need to get done and if they don't get done the world's going to end. . . . I don't think he focuses so much on those little, daily, day-to-day details.

Zelda is unhappy with her adherence to traditional gender norms within marriage. On the one hand, she seems to feel that completing household tasks is a requirement of a good wife; yet on the other hand, she would prefer to abandon this stereotype, eliminating her compulsion with household chores and creating a more even-handed division of labor. How she and her husband behave aligns closely with tradition, but she would prefer them to have a more egalitarian marriage.

Zelda is experiencing a tug-of-war between tradition and equality. Interestingly, she assumes all the blame for inequities in the marriage. Zelda highlights how it is her own conception of marital roles that is to blame for the unsatisfactory arrangement. She feels responsible for her own frustration. Other wives, however, identified their husbands as the main culprits. Yvvone, for example, described how her husband, Yao, fails to pull his own weight, which has caused her to modify her ideal definition of wife.

Yvvone (thirty-four, married ten months): What does being a wife mean? I have to do *everything*. Everything. I have to take care of myself, and the house, and I have to make sure that Yao does what he's supposed to be doing. . . . Making sure that he makes his doctor appointment and that he's called the insurance agent about car insurance. . . . It gets to be kind of a hassle. . . . I'd like him to take a little bit more initiative than he does with things that need to be done. . . . He doesn't want to take responsibility. . . . I think he thinks that he does just as much around the house as I do . . . but if I didn't clean the bathrooms, they wouldn't get cleaned. . . . He wants me to take care of everything. . . . My mom said, "You just have to realize it's 80 percent on the wife and 20 percent on the husband. If Yao needs you to call and make his doctor's appointment, you got to do it. Just do it." And I'm like, "He's a big boy. He's thirty-four years old. He can call the doctor himself." . . . I feel like I'm barely getting along taking care of myself and making sure that I'm doing all the things that I need to be doing an a day-to-day basis, why should I have to do everything that Yao's supposed to be doing too? . . . But I cave and just do it. I get tired of waiting for him to do it.

Like it or not, Yvvone takes primary responsibility for her own welfare, her husband's welfare, and the welfare of the household. Like the other wives in this category, Yvvone would prefer a more equitable arrangement where neither tradition nor gender delineates marital responsibilities and roles. Yet, if one spouse desires equality in marital roles but does not perceive equality in the couple's everyday life, aggravation with either one's self or one's spouse is the likely result.

Functional Equality

The category "functional equality" is so named because these individuals divide their domestic responsibilities in a functional manner, typically supporting some semblance of gender equality in the marriage. When defining the roles of husband and wife, these six individuals consider efficiency more than tradition. These interviewees spoke in terms of logically carving out tasks and roles based on individual likes or dislikes rather than relying on gendered divisions of labor. Loretta and her husband, Lamar, captured the practicality that underscores these conceptions of husband and wife.

> *Loretta* (fifty-six, married thirty-three years): I would describe us both as, well, I think it's pretty much of a 50-50 thing. Over the years our roles of what we've done around the house and what we're responsible for has changed with our situation. When we were both working—we both worked the same length of time and both retired basically at the same time—so there were always two working people. So you knew that you sort of have to divide up tasks and everything, and after awhile we figured out who was better at doing what. I started out paying the bills. The gas company or somebody threatened to turn off our gas, so we figured out maybe Lamar should take the bills! So over the years we've figured out who's better at doing what, and sort of just divide things up that way. Neither one of us is, I would say, autocratic. . . . We try to be pretty democratic.

> *Lamar* (fifty-four, married thirty-three years): There's probably a lot of *typical* roles that in most marriages the husband plays it or the wife plays—but in ours, I think we have some *different* roles. I've always done the dishes, 'cause she always claims she doesn't know how to operate the dishwasher. . . . So, I always clean up the kitchen, but she typically cooks. But I typically bake. . . . We try to divide things up equally so she's doing tasks that she likes to do and I'm doing tasks that I like to do. And then there's stuff like toilets that neither one of us like to do!

Like those with traditional notions of marriage roles, spouses defining marriage in terms of functional equality tend to make sense of the terms "wife" and "husband" by reflecting on their division of labor. Unlike traditionalist couples who use gender to divide responsibilities, these couples partition tasks based on personality, preferences, and competence. In many ways, spouses in this group organize their marriage on principles of effectiveness, taking into consideration each person's predilection for assorted tasks. Krystal highlights how couples blend efficiency and inclination, achieving a kind of symbiosis.

> *Krystal* (twenty-four, married four months): We figured out that if I wash both of our laundry, and he puts away both of our laundry, everything gets done faster [because] I hate putting away and he hates washing.

The meaning attached to these marital labels derives from couples' life circumstances. As marital, familial, or work conditions change, so might marital identity. For instance, Kevin discussed how, at the time of the interview, he was the only one employed and thus technically was the primary breadwinner. Because his wife was a student, she spent considerably more time in the home than Kevin and, consequently, she was largely in charge of home care. However, he was quick to clarify that these roles were currently the most feasible and by no means permanent.

> *Kevin* (twenty-four, married four months): I don't see a whole lot of distinction between the husband and wife. They both serve equal sides of the same joint relationship. At the moment my roles are different than hers because I am the one going to work and she's the one going to school. After she's done with school those roles will switch, when I will probably go back to school and she'll be working. Actually before we were married *I* was in school and *she* was working. . . . They just keep flip-flopping. Back and forth. I don't think there's any real distinction.

In these instances, spouses with marriages characterized by a functional equality convey ideas about the roles of husbands and wives that work best for their current circumstances. The roles may approximate a traditional arrangement or a nontraditional one; they may remain fixed for long periods of time or be swapped regularly. Though the marital setting may be vastly different across groups, what unites those in this category is that they pay no heed to gender stereotypes when characterizing their marital identities. Those with a functional equality look to efficiency, logic, desire, and skill when making sense of their place within the marriage. As Whitney sums up, "I'm kind of proud of our relationship in that the roles that we play into are often the roles that are best for our marriage. They're not sex-determined."

Partnership

The second most popular response when asked to define "husband" and "wife" was that the notes should be a partnership. When asked what the role of husband or wife meant in their marriage, the responses of these twelve individuals tended to be couched in a language of support and team-work, and all of these individuals used the word "partner" or "partnership" frequently. Interestingly, spouses in all of the aforementioned categories reflected on their division of household labor when contemplating the symbolism of the words "husband" or "wife." Spouses in the partner-ship category, at times, would reference housework, but customarily these individuals conceptualized the terms "husband" and "wife" in broader ways. That is, they looked beyond "who's cleaning the toilets" and "who's taking out the trash" toward more intangible aspects of marriage. For example, for Stephan, the labels of husband and wife carry a sense of mutual assistance.

> *Stephan* (twenty-nine, married three years): What does a husband mean? I don't really have a quick answer for that. I don't know. I think part of it's supporting Sasha, and I mean that more in the emotional sense than the financial sense. . . . Encouraging her and helping her and encouraging *us* and helping *us*. It's a partnership. . . . Her role as wife? I'd say the same thing.

For these individuals, marital identity is not wrapped up in the allocation of chores such as making the bed, responsibilities such as taking a child to the doctor, or statuses such as being the breadwinner, but rather is viewed as a collaborative endeavor in which each partner shares each facet of the relationship. Nora's comments exemplify this view.

> *Nora* (forty-three, married twenty-one years): We've always had a very easy sense of give and take. There is no specific job, detail, chore, responsibility that he has taken on or that I've taken on. We've always shared both in raising our children, both in household chores, both in finances. We've always worked on everything together. Neither one of us have ever taken full responsibility for something.

As another wife, Olga, put it, people who view husbands and wives as equal partners, "don't have 'him' and 'her' things." The marital labels of husband and wife are essentially indistinguishable for these interviewees because each term carries with it the same requirements of encouragement, cooperation, and commitment. As Zachary explains:

Zachary (thirty, married two years): Being a husband or a wife means being there to support the other person. It means being the other half. Ideally, what each should strive for, would be that you're the support of that person. You're the other half of the team, so to speak. You're going to be there for the other person no matter what.

Melanie highlights the "teamwork" mentality common to those in the category:

Melanie (twenty-three, married three years): I think [being a wife] means just being a partner in general. . . . I think my role is to be a friend, to be a confidante, to share in the responsibilities of the household, to be committed to the relationship, to make decisions with him, whatever needs to be done. . . . I would describe his role in the exact same way. . . . I think it's about having a good partnership. I think there's a lot of teamwork.

Olga added another dimension, saying that spouses should be "partners, partners even in the roughest of times." The following quotation from her husband, Oscar, provides some context for understanding how spouses uphold a partnership during challenging times.

Oscar (forty-six, married twenty-two years): Being a husband? It's part of my identity. It's who I am. I am in the most meaningful partnership I can imagine two humans being in. This relationship means so much to Olga and I both that it's worth working for every day. I'll tell you how I see myself as a husband. At night when I pray and I run through the list of all the people that I should pray for, when I get to me the first thing I think about is being a husband. That means believing in Olga, believing in our marriage. . . . I've tried to be a good partner, even when I was going through a pretty traumatic period wrestling with my male ego because I felt hugely devalued in being a stay-at-home-dad. . . . I felt, you know, I'm the man and I'm not contributing to the family's finances. It was a very tough time for me emotionally. But that was part of the partnership, I supported our daughter so Olga never had to worry, and Olga was hugely supportive of me and what we were doing. Partnerships of any nature require hard work. But if it's important to you, it's worth it.

Those in the partnership category clearly conceive of marriage as a joint effort. They don't see a stark differentiation between roles of husband and wife. Rather, the word "spouse" symbolizes assistance, sacrifice, sharing, teamwork, commitment, and camaraderie. Whether egalitarianism is the root or the result of these perceptions, in most cases an equitable marital atmosphere appears to exist.

Role Confusion

The category "role confusion" falls outside the continuum. Though confusion surrounding marital identity was present for only two couples, their situations are worth mentioning. These couples display the malleability of marital roles and show how marital identities are subject to change.

Quentin and Quella are newly married, but each has been married before. In addition to negotiating the terms of a second marriage, each spouse came to the marriage with children from their previous unions. When asked what it meant to be a husband or wife in their relationship, Quella and Quentin each explained that they were still in search of an answer to that question.

> *Quella* (thirty-three, married one year): It's been *really really* difficult for me because I haven't really defined my role yet in this marriage and in this new family . . . you know, with new kids, different kids that aren't my own kids. What does it mean to be a mom to his children? It's the same for him. What role does he have as a father to mine?

> *Quentin* (fifty-one, married one year): It's interesting that you ask about roles because that's the hardest thing. I mean what role am I supposed to play? Before we got married we underestimated what it would be like to merge two families together. We're still trying to find the roles and how you blend a family and all that stuff 'cause it's—well, that's *tough*. Without a doubt, it's the toughest challenge in our marriage. I guarantee you she'll say the same thing. I don't think she has an established role yet in the marriage either.

For Quella and Quentin, the meaning of "husband" and the meaning of "wife" remain undecided. As their marriage develops, their identities will likely undergo several transformations as they navigate the blending of two preexisting families and settle into a new, second marriage.

Rena and Ryan have been married fifty-eight years. For most of the relationship, both adhered to the separate spheres ideology. Rena was in command of the private domain and knew her role as a wife required cooking, cleaning, and childrearing. Ryan was in control of the public domain and was well aware that he must ensure the family's financial security to fulfill his role as a husband. These marital identities were sufficient and very agreeable for decades—right up until Ryan retired from his job. The arrangement began to dissolve rapidly when Ryan permanently left the public domain and he and Rena had to share the private domain of the home full-time.

When asked to define the roles of husband and wife, both spouses indicated that they were in the process of reworking what these terms mean in their new circumstances. As Rena summarized:

> *Rena* (eighty-two, married fifty-eight years): I think everything was as smooth as it could be for about forty-five years. It was heavenly. I relate it to the fact that I had my job, and my husband had his job. My job was running the house and the children, and everything just seemed so smooth. Then, after retirement, for about the first five to ten years we traveled quite a bit because we were like free spirits. Then, after that, we were constantly together at *everything*, which is probably not good. . . . After twelve years or so after retirement I found him sort of telling me too many things, to "Do it this way." I had done it my way for so many years and had been so successful, and I firmly resented it! He'd come into my kitchen and tell me I was cutting an onion the wrong way! Got to be done Ryan's way.

Ryan reiterated his wife's sentiments:

> *Ryan* (eighty-two, married fifty-eight years): Retirement changes the whole picture. . . . Up until this time, Rena had her job and I had my job. I brought home the bacon and she took care of the kids. We had our responsibilities. Now when you go into retirement . . . we found ourselves bickering over things to a point that we'd get really upset with one another. . . . Life does change after retirement. That's where I learned the fact that there's got to be consideration and compromise in marriage. Took me a long time to learn that. It took me a long time to consider the fact that she has been doing things her way for all this married life without my help. I better consider the fact that with regards to how she's doing it, she's comfortable doing it, so butt out. That's where I learned the fact that I was wrong by not considering what she did, what she liked to do, and why she liked to do it. Being an engineer, analytical, I would say, "If you would do it this way it would be easier. If you would do it that way it would be easier." I'm sure you're familiar with the onion-cutting story. Here's a man that's coming into the house, which had been the domain of the woman, and this is when things get squeaky.

The challenges facing Quentin, Quella, Rena, and Ryan are certainly not the only trials to result in role confusion. It is not beyond reason to believe that one's interpretation of the terms "wife" or "husband" will bend and shift over the life course, and may even require a complete overhaul. The connotations of these labels may be transformed as people enter and exit the workforce, as children come and go, as partners age, or as couples relocate. Countless marital, familial, or life experiences can produce uncertainty in one's sense of the meaning of husband and wife, leading individuals to question who they are in their marriage.

CONSENSUS, COMPLEMENTARITY, AND CLASHES

My second concern has been to consider whether partners have similar interpretations of the terms "husband" and "wife." The accompanying table pairs each husband and wife and then lists the category into which each spouse's identity falls.

TABLE 1 Do "Husbands" and "Wives" Agree on Marital Identity?

Consensual Definitions

Wife/Husband	Classification of Spousal Identity	Age of Interviewee	Length of Marriage
Andrea and Amos	Traditional	25, 33	1 year
Betty and Brach	Traditional	22, 31	2 years
Candice and Carmine	Traditional	24, 35	4 years
Donna and Daniel	Traditional	45, 47	21 years
Elena and Eric	Traditional	48, 51	29 years
Flora and Fredo	Traditional	92, 94	72 years
Gladys and Gregory	Amended traditional	22, 23	7 months
Haley and Han	Amended traditional	28, 27	1 year
Ingrid and Isaac	Amended traditional	36, 36	5 years
Jennifer and Jack	Desire for more tradition	37, 30	4 years
Krystal and Kevin	Functional equality	24, 24	14 months
Loretta and Lamar	Functional equality	56, 54	33 years
Melanie and Monty	Partnership	24, 23	3 years
Nora and Nathaniel	Partnership	43, 43	21 years
Olga and Oscar	Partnership	46, 46	22 years
Patty and Peter	Partnership	46,46	26 years
Quella and Quentin	Role confusion	33, 51	1.5 years
Rena and Ryan	Role confusion	82, 82	58 years

TABLE 1 (Continued)

Complementary Definitions

Wife/Husband	Classification of Spousal Identity	Age of Interviewee	Length of Marriage
Sasha	Functional equality	26	3 years
Stephan	Partnership	29	
Tabitha	Traditional	37	13 years
Trevor	Desire for more tradition	34	
Uma	Traditional	24	1 year
Ulysses	Desire for more tradition	25	
Vanessa	Traditional	26	2 years
Viktor	Desire for more tradition	31	

Clashing Definitions

Wife/Husband	Classification of Spousal Identity	Age of Interviewee	Length of Marriage
Whitney	Functional equality	22	2 years
Warren	Traditional	23	
Xena	Partnership	34	12 years
Xander	Amended traditional	38	
Yyvone	Desire for more equality	34	10 months
Yao	Partnership	34	
Zelda	Desire for more equality	31	2 years
Zachary	Partnership	30	
Adrianna	Desire for more equality	34	14 years
Arnold	Desire for more tradition	37	

CONSENSUAL DEFINITIONS

As seen under the heading "consensual definitions," the majority of couples (eighteen out of twenty-seven) agreed on their understandings of their respective marital roles and identities. Andrea and Amos, for instance, both spoke of husband and wife in a traditional manner, whereas Jennifer and Jack both indicated a preference for more tradition. While these eighteen couples may differ from one another, it is inspiring and somewhat reassuring that so many spouses saw eye-to-eye when it came to defining their identities within the marriage.

Not only were the majority of husbands and wives in sync with their partners, but in many instances, spouses literally echoed each other's words when discussing the meaning of wife and husband. Elena and her husband, Eric, are a perfect example of the uniformity that existed between some spouses' perceptions. When asked about the roles in the household, Elena stated:

> *Elena* (forty-eight, married thirty years): Well, our roles are kind of traditional. Eric says that I bring in the softer side to the family. There's three guys and me. So I try the special touches that men wouldn't do. I mean if they lived in a house it would be all stainless steel. So, bringing in the color. . . . He is the leader. Spiritually, physically, mentally. I mean, he's the protector of the family, the provider, and he takes that very seriously. . . . I see him as the provider, the spiritual leader.

As evidenced here, the meanings that wife and husband hold for Elena coincide with those of her husband:

> *Eric* (fifty-one, married thirty years): We each have our forte, OK? . . . I would be a stainless steel and concrete person, OK? She's the one who adds color. She's the one that holds the brush to it, you know? I would say that I'm a provider. That's very male, I think. . . . I have been the spiritual leader in the family. . . . So, she brings a softness into the family. I hope that I bring some order.

Complementary Definitions

Four couples in the sample had similar, but not precisely identical, interpretations of their marital situation. I have classified these couples as having "complementary," rather than consensual, views of marriage roles. Sasha, for instance, described the terms "husband" and "wife" by explaining the utility and purpose of their equal division of labor. Her husband, Stephan, on the other hand, defined those same terms in a more theoretical manner, amplifying notions such as encouragement and teamwork. Though Stephan and Sasha did not necessarily duplicate each other's responses, they seem to approach marriage from similar, rather than divergent, standpoints. Furthermore, the categories of functional equality and partnership are adjacent to each other on the continuum of traditionalism, and both accent standards of equality.

Curiously, the other three couples with comparable, but not identical, views of the labels of husband and wife were couples in which the wife felt the marital roles were sufficiently traditional, but the husband wanted more tradition in the arrangement. In two cases, husbands desired self-improvement and felt they could better fulfill the stereotypical male role in marriage by such actions as earning more money, working harder, controlling the finances, and being sterner with the children. In one case, however, the husband wanted a more traditional role for his wife (who, incidentally, saw herself as a traditional wife), but not for himself. While these couples technically disagreed about the *level* of tradition present in their marriage or the amount of tradition necessary to be a good wife or husband, all three couples agreed about the *necessity* of tradition in marital roles.

Clashing Definitions

Finally, five couples provided descriptions of marital roles that I have termed "clashing." When asked what being a husband or wife meant, each spouse supplied me with a definition that contradicted that of his/her partner. Xena, for example, dismissed notions of gender imbalance and championed the concept of partnership. Her husband Xander, however, believed there were marked differences in spousal roles.

> *Xena* (thirty-four, married twelve years): What does being a wife mean? I don't know. The question has some subservient undertones. If you go by the structure of society, the wife is obviously subservient to the husband . . . and that isn't me. . . . We make up a sliding whole. . . . Sometimes I have to be the bad guy [with the children] or I have to do more, more I guess, on a daily basis, but sometimes he does. So I think we're still a whole even if the line isn't 50-50 all the time. It's a partnership.

If Xena gives an impression of egalitarianism, her husband Xander provides a colorful analogy that emits a strong sense of traditionalism.

Xander (thirty-eight, married twelve years): My role is being a leader. . . .
It's like in a movie. She plays the supporting role. I guess I'm the leading
actor. . . . Now, keep in mind in the movie, every now and again she'll try to
steal the starring role. I'm like, "Wait a minute. What are you doing? You've
got your lines. Stick with your lines."

Significantly, in three of the five couples with clashing perceptions of marital identity, the wives communicated an intense desire for more equality.
Interestingly, the husbands of Zelda and Yyvone (discussed in the earlier
section, "Desire for More Equality") alleged that principles of partnership
already guided their marriage. Both Zachary and Yao used egalitarian
rhetoric when defining the terms "husband" and "wife," yet their wives
saw things differently. For various reasons, Zelda and Yyvone were both
performing activities associated with traditional wives and were frustrated,
since these traditional actions did not conform with their visions of what a
wife should be.

Possibly the most problematic situation occurs when two partners wish
to shift their marital identities in opposite directions. Adrianna, for instance,
wanted more equality, whereas her husband, Arnold, wanted a more traditional marriage. For this couple, marital tension and conflict have resulted
because of their extremely dissimilar interpretations of marital roles. Currently, Arnold and Adrianna share the breadwinner and caretaker roles.
This system is less than ideal for Arnold, who would prefer a major switch
back to a traditional marriage arrangement, where women are nurturers and
men are breadwinners. When asked to describe the meaning of husband and
wife, Arnold answered:

Arnold (thirty-seven, married fourteen years): You know when you get
married you think about what is really possible. For example, I was in the
military. I had this delusion . . . this idea that I might have a spousal camp
follower. You know, somebody who will clean your stuff up and get you
packed up for the next day. Someone to shine your boots. . . . I've seen some
people and *their* spouses do it. . . . I guess I would expect the woman would
have some expectation the man would . . . go out and have a decent job and
try to be some sort of a provider. I keep the family organized. I bring in probably right around half or a little bit more than half, of the family income. . . .
I don't think that, for most people, the idea that you can totally reverse the
roles, where the guy just sort of stays at home and minds the kids—that
doesn't work. Maybe you know of some situations where that works out,
but I can't think of any. I guess I would look at those cases as odd when
they actually do work. Some structure seems necessary. Some tradition.

Traditional roles *do* tend to work out. For me, it creeps me out to have to sit at home and mind the kids for a long, long time. It causes my stress to raise quite a bit more than my wife's. She's much better being able to take care of the kids for long periods of time than I am. I like taking care of the kids—in *small* doses. Couple hours here. Couple hours there. Couple of days? Kind of a stretch.

Recognizing her husband's push for traditional marital identities, Adrianna explains her displeasure with his tendencies to create a less-than-equal environment:

> *Adrianna* (thirty-four, married fourteen years): I see myself as a mother, as a wife, but also somebody who can function separate from that, and hold down a job, and take care of things all by myself. . . . [I would describe my role] in terms of nouns. Mine: housekeeper, nanny, wage-earner, or wage-earner partner. Cook. My husband: manager, director, standard-setter, handyman. He'll be like, "You need to dust the front room" "You need to, (telling our son), you need to change out the laundry." "You need to do the dishes." "You need to . . ." There's a lot of, "you need to's" instead of doing. He sort of gives out the tasks rather than doing any of them. . . . There has not been a lot of compromising on his part. It's not the full partnership that I would like it to be. . . . In a lot of the ways that he behaves, he would much rather it be the 1950s. . . . He wants to be the breadwinner and he wants to have the house clean and me do the dishes and everything else, everything. Fortunately, with our paychecks we have to wait until taxes come out to see who makes more. . . . So he can't claim to be the breadwinner. I'm not a stay-at-home mom, . . . but he doesn't do well when he's with the kids twenty-four hours a day. In fact, our son was six years old before my husband had him twenty-four hours in a row!

I have used these lengthy quotations from Arnold and Adrianna to demonstrate the discord that can exist within a marriage, especially when spouses are pulling toward opposite ends of the continuum. Not all spouses have synchronized perceptions of the marital reality, and when spouses disagree on foundational elements of the relationship, such as the meanings of "wife" and "husband," the result may be a marital tug-of-war.

SUMMING UP

Let me summarize by saying that couples may opt for a traditional arrangement, may choose an amended traditional arrangement, or may desire more tradition in the marriage. Some couples may downplay the role of gender

and accentuate partnership, divide household labor functionally, or desire
more gender equality in the relationship. Still, other men and womens in
couples may be at a loss as to their place and identity within the relationship, and they experience role confusion. While various conceptions of the
terms "husband" and "wife" exist, the ways in which spouses define their
marital identity affects what they view as appropriate behavior within the
relationship. Perceived marital identity not only shapes the ways in which
spouses act but also influences the ways in which spouses think about and
behave toward their partners.

The majority of husbands and wives in this study expressed convergent
definitions of their marital roles. It appears that many married couples share
similar views when characterizing the husband and wife roles. Though this
harmony does not render couples immune to marital strife, having consensual viewpoints may reduce the number of quarrels or level of conflict
in the marriage. Without a shared definition of marital roles, divergent
perceptions of marital experiences may result, leading to agitation or anger.
For instance, if a husband favors the traditional style of marriage, when his
wife leaves him a list of household chores to complete, he may perceive her
act as disrespectful, selfish, or offensive. Similarly, if she considers both
spouses to be equal partners, when her husband leaves her a list of household chores to complete while he is out playing golf, she may perceive his
act as disrespectful, selfish, or offensive. Each perceives the other's conduct to be a violation of marital norms—as he or she views them.

REFERENCES

Blumer, Herbert. 1969. *Symbolic Interactionism: Perspective and Method.*
    Englewood Cliffs, N.J.: Prentice-Hall, Inc.
Freese, Pamela. 1991. "The Union of Nature and Culture: Gender Symbolism in
    the American Wedding Ritual." Pp. 97–112, in *Transcending Boundaries:
    Multi-Disciplinary Approaches to the Study of Gender*, edited by P. Freese and
    J. M. Coggeshall. South Hadley, Mass.: Bergin and Garvey.
Scanzoni, John. 2000. *Designing Families*. Thousand Oaks, Calif.: Pine Forge
    Press.

FURTHER READING

Blumstein, Philip, and Pepper Schwartz. 1983. *American Couples.* New York: Simon and Schuster.

Coltrane, Scott. 1989. "Household Labor and the Routine Production of Gender." *Social Problems* 36:473–90.

Coontz, Stephanie. 1992. *The Way We Never Were: American Families and the Nostalgia Trap.* New York: Basic Books.

Gerstel, Naomi, and Sally K. Gallagher. 2001. "Men's Caregiving: Gender and the Contingent Character of Care." *Gender & Society* 15:197–215.

Hochschild, Arlie Russell. 1989. *The Second Shift.* New York: Avon Books.

Discussion Questions

1. What do the terms "husband" and "wife" mean *to you*? Do your definitions of these terms align with any of the categories described in this chapter? If not, what other categories would you add to the continuum? Based on your views, are there additional categories that fall beyond the continuum?

2. To what extent does gender affect one's identity within marriage? Does social class also affect how people conceive of their place in marriage? What role might religion play in deciding marital roles?

3. How might the definitions of husband and wife influence a couple's interactions, marital satisfaction, or marital problems? How can a husband and wife ensure that they are "on the same page" regarding marriage?

3

The Everyday Meaning of
Marital Equality

Scott R. Harris

Most single college students imagine that they will someday be married or in a committed relationship. But what will that be like? Is a happy marriage or partnership in your future? A loving one? An *egalitarian* one?

That last possibility has been the focus of much research and discussion over the past several decades, as scholars have attempted to identify the factors that promote "fair and balanced" relationships, so to speak, as well as those factors that lead to unequal, exploitative, or hierarchical relationships. Most people assume that good marriages—unions that are mutually satisfying and rewarding—tend to be equal (Haas 1980; Schwartz 1994; Stapleton and Bright 1976). True equality may be rare and difficult to achieve, scholars have recognized, but they argue that the benefits for husbands, wives, and their children are tremendous. Thus, this is one area of sociology where the writings of academic researchers have attracted nonacademic audiences, since many persons are interested in having successful close relationships.

But what is an equal marriage? How do you know if you have one? That's the tricky part—or, at least, that's the tricky part on which this chapter will focus. It looks closely at the meaning of marital equality from an interpretive perspective (Blumer 1969). Interpretive sociologists focus their attention on how ordinary life provides meanings of its own for our relationships. I will argue that it's worthwhile to examine critically scholarly conceptions of everyday phenomena and to think about how those

My research and writing have been supported by a Charlotte W. Newcombe Dissertation Fellowship from the Woodrow Wilson National Fellowship Foundation, a Research Support Grant from the University of Oregon's Center for the Study of Women in Society, and a SLU2000 Research Leave from Saint Louis University.

definitions might overlap with, or differ from, the ideas by which people live. My thesis is that equality in marriage, while a laudable goal and an important principle, can have distinctive meanings in practice for married individuals.

DEFINING AND MEASURING EQUALITY

In books such as *The 50/50 Marriage* (Kimball 1983), *Peer Marriage* (Schwartz 1994), and *Halving It All* (Deutsch 1999) and in numerous journal articles (Haas 1980; Risman and Johnson-Sumerford 1997), scholars have identified several dimensions of marital equality and inequality. An equal marriage is said to have the following elements:

1. *A fair division of labor.* Husbands and wives should share responsibility for breadwinning and (especially) housework and childcare.

2. *Shared decision-making.* Spouses should be partners who have equal "say" in deciding where to live, what car to purchase, how the children should be raised, and so on.

3. *Nonhierarchical communication practices.* Neither spouse should dominate in terms of interruptions or speaking time, or be authoritarian or dismissive of the other, or fail to reciprocate attentiveness and active listening.

4. *Egalitarian sexual relations.* The physical relationship should be satisfying to each spouse. Partners should share responsibility for the success of their sex lives, in terms of initiating, being creative, and so on.

5. *Mutual respect and affection.* Egalitarian spouses should not view their partners as inferiors or treat them as if they were casual roommates. In an equal marriage, husbands and wives admire and care deeply for each other, usually more than they care for their friends, their extended family, and even their children.

Of course, not all researchers agree with the entire list. Among social scientists, there has not been a sustained, collaborative effort to develop a coherent conception of marital equality that all researchers hold in common. Usually, different researchers simply investigate one or another component of equality. Scholars are rarely as "comprehensive" as Gayle Kimball (1983) and Pepper Schwartz (1994), from whom this five-part list derives much inspiration. Instead, most researchers specialize in either the division of household labor or power and attempt to identify the factors that promote or inhibit equality, as well as the costs and benefits of overcoming inequality.

While an interest in "marital equality" can lead a person in different directions, I would like readers to think critically about the definition of that concept. To do so, just take any of these dimensions of equality and ask yourself, "But what does that mean?" That simple question is one of the main resources in the conceptual toolbox of interpretive sociology, which, I noted earlier, puts "the meaning of things" at the heart of inquiry (Blumer 1969).

Consider the division of household labor. Probably the main issue raised by social scientists when they hear "marital equality" or "marital inequality" is the degree to which husbands and wives share housework and childcare responsibilities. For years, scholars have been concerned (and perhaps rightly so) that women have been doing more than their share of work around the house. Arlie Hochschild (1989) famously described the situation as a "second shift," while others have called it "role overload" (Pleck 1985). In recent decades, wives have tended to increase their participation in the paid workforce, while husbands have not reciprocated by increasing their contributions on the home front. Study after study has found that husbands don't do their "fair share" of housework and childcare (Shelton and John 1996).

Nevertheless, one can question how such findings were assembled. How do researchers determine whether husbands and wives fairly divide the household labor? What does "fairly dividing the labor" mean? After looking closely at a number of published studies, I found that "equally sharing the workload" means different things to different researchers (Harris 2000).

Probably the most frequently used strategy for measuring equality has been to ask a sample of respondents (either by means of an interview or a paper-and-pencil questionnaire) to answer the question "Who does what?" regarding a small number of household tasks. This strategy requires the researcher to develop a brief scale that touches on a (presumably) representative collection of crucial chores or duties. For example, respondents may be asked to choose "husband always," "husband more than wife," "husband and wife about the same," "wife more than husband," and "wife always" in response to questions such as "Who washes the dishes in your household?" and "Who does the yard work?" Then, researchers assign numerical values to these answers, add up the scores respondents give to all the questions, and determine the degree of inequality in those marriages. Of course, different researchers have used different kinds of tasks in their scales, but the general format has been reproduced repeatedly.[1]

But what would it mean, for example, if a wife usually washes the dishes while her husband usually does most of the yard work? What if washing the dishes takes an average of seven hours a week and the yard work takes an average of one or two hours? Is that equal?

In response to measurement problems like those, some researchers have preferred to count up the *hourly* contributions that husbands and wives make to housework and childcare. Respondents are asked to estimate how much time they spend on housework in general or on certain tasks in particular, or they may be asked to keep detailed records of their daily activities so that analysts can later calculate spouses' hourly workloads.

Still, we might wonder, if a husband and wife were each to spend twenty hours on housework per week, would that necessarily mean that their division of household chores was egalitarian? Is it really true that "an hour is an hour is an hour"? Is an hour of cleaning the toilet really equivalent to an hour of cooking dinner or making school lunches? How can we know if one person's twenty-hour workload is "really" equivalent to another's?

To further complicate matters, there's also the issue of where to draw the line between what is "close enough" and "not close enough" to be classified as equal. That is, what if a husband were to do eighteen hours of housework compared his wife's twenty hours? Would that be "close enough" to be equal? What if he does sixteen hours? Or fourteen hours? When does an egalitarian division of labor end and an inegalitarian division begin?

In short, the underlying issue in these studies of household labor is the question of *meaning*. Researchers sometimes presume that meaning is a constant, but is that a fair presumption? The fact is that meanings vary in everyday life; they depend on the context of consideration and whose relations are in question, among a host of other matters of interpretation. Let's turn to everyday life and listen for the variations.

---

[1] Rebecca Warner (1986) has called this the "relative distribution method" (180). For examples of its use and elaboration, see Ross, Mirowsky, and Huber (1983), Smith and Reid (1986), and Twiggs, McQuillan, and Ferree (1998).

STUDYING MARITAL EQUALITY ON ITS OWN TERMS

If we take a moment to think about it, we can expect that the same sorts of dilemmas that complicate research on the division of household labor will also apply to other dimensions of marital equality. In general, it will be problematic to assign numerical values to indicators of "power" or "satisfaction," for example, add them up, and draw a boundary between what scores would be "close enough" and "not close enough" to be egalitarian (see Harris 2000).

However, rather than devising increasingly sophisticated surveys and scales to deal with these recurring measurement dilemmas, I have chosen to use open-ended interviews to inquire more directly about what things mean to married people themselves. To examine how the issue of marital equality enters the experiences of married people, I don't think we should ask whether an hour of "this chore" is equivalent to an hour of "that chore." Instead, we might ask whether, in the lives of the couple in question, the "the division of labor" is relevant at all. What if the issue isn't important to respondents? What if they present contrasting definitions of what constitutes an "equal marriage"? Since different researchers have chosen to focus on different dimensions of marital equality—such as the division of labor, power, or other conventional categories—it's likely that different married people may also focus on different dimensions.

Moreover, the actions, objects, and events of everyday life can be variously interpreted by different people (or by the same people in different situations). Consider, for example, a situation where a husband tucks in his children at night and reads them a bedtime story. Would that be experienced as a household "task"? Maybe it would, if the husband had a difficult day or the children were reluctant to sleep. But it could also be defined as a privilege, a pleasure that he enjoyed while his wife was occupied with a less attractive activity (perhaps washing the evening dishes). Tucking in the children could be interpreted in a variety of ways—as a sign of love, responsibility, "being there," sacrifice, conformity, and selfishness, among other things—both as the action was being performed *and* years (or hours or days) later, as the husband reflects back upon it. This is a matter of interpretive work—the work of making "sense" out of household activities, which is the work of making meaning.

To examine this interpretive work, I interviewed a small sample of married individuals who already considered their relationships to be

egalitarian or inegalitarian in one way or another. I distributed announcements and placed advertisements in the newspaper that began with the line
"Do you have an equal marriage?" or "Do you have an unequal marriage?"
I then explained that I was writing a book on marital equality and requested
that interested persons call me for an interview. By the end of my study
I met with thirty individuals, fourteen of whom responded to solicitations
for persons in unequal marriages (seven male, seven female) and sixteen
of whom responded to solicitations for equal marriages (eight male, eight
female).

In restaurants and occasionally at their offices or homes, I asked my
respondents to tell me about the equality or inequality in their marriages
in their own words. I avoided presenting them with the predesignated
dimensions with which most researchers start. As they spoke, and later
as I analyzed my tapes and transcriptions of the conversations, I listened
for how my respondents conveyed their own meanings of the equality or
inequality in their marriages. I noticed that some of my respondents did
seem to dwell on conventional sociological understandings, such as the
division of labor or power. These familiar-sounding responses invoked
common scholarly themes to construct coherent understandings out of their
marital biographies. Other respondents, however, drew on unfamiliar themes
as they assembled their marital woes and joys into contrasting patterns.

ELABORATING FAMILIAR THEMES OF MARITAL EQUALITY

Let's turn first to those who highlight familiar themes of marital equality,
themes that resonate with existing research. Still, as familiar as these are,
notice that respondents elaborate upon them in idiosyncratic ways.

Lucy's Account: *"If he would only do the things I can't."*

At the time I met her, Lucy was a thirty-seven-year-old homemaker who
had been married to her husband, Sam, for fifteen years.[2] As a full-time mom
to her two teenage children, Lucy described herself as busy but fairly happy

---

[2] I have given pseudonyms to all of my respondents and their spouses. I should also
note that in the excerpts that follow, I use bracketed elipses ([. . .]) to indicate that
I have deleted portions of the conversation, regular elipses (. . .) to indicate
pauses, and dashes to indicate abrupt stops and starts.

with her marriage. There were definitely things that frustrated her about her relationship, however, and those things took center stage during the interview. Lucy told me at the outset that she had "really strong feelings" about the "jobs and responsibilities" held by men and women. This let me know that her marital tale would likely be one about the division of labor. She immediately confirmed what she had told me on the phone, that her marriage was "pretty unequal." As she put it in the interview:

> My husband works really hard, he's a carpenter. And he's always worked— he has a physical, hard job. And I understand but . . . I have a physical hard job and uh, an emotionally kinda hard job. When he comes home from work he says "OK I want, I want a little time to myself" and regroup and whatever, and I never get that.

Right away Lucy framed her marriage as an unequal partnership because of her and Sam's respective workloads. Sam earned money outside the home; she took care of the household. While Lucy characterized both roles as demanding, she also implied that hers entailed an emotional component that was absent from Sam's. Lucy further claimed to "never" get any time for herself, while Sam was more or less off duty once he came home from his carpentry job. Teenagers are not like two-year-olds, she explained, because you can't "lock them in a room" or give them a "time-out." Thus, as Lucy constructed a comparison of her and her husbands' workloads, she simultaneously articulated an ad hoc evaluation of mothering younger versus older children: Because raising teenagers is as tough or tougher than raising two-year-olds, she argued, her nonstop workload was tougher than her husbands' was.

Lucy proceeded to describe some of the various ways that Sam could have contributed more around the house. She suggested repeatedly that while Sam put out a great deal of effort at his carpentry job, as soon as he returned home he was virtually on holiday. Making dinner, doing the laundry, cleaning the bathroom, chauffeuring the kids around town, help- ing with homework—in all of these areas Lucy found Sam's contributions to be missing or deficient. Lucy even went so far as to doubt whether her husband even knew the dates of his children's birthdays. While this might signal many things, in the context of her account it was cast as yet another example of Sam not doing his part around the house. Eventually, Lucy focused on an area where she felt her husband really ought to help more. She discussed home improvements requiring his special skills, as in this quote: "He's a carpenter but our house is like falling apart. Our house is the very last house on the list. He does this all day long, and I can understand that. But I can't paint the house, you know. I mean I can mow the lawn but I can't paint the house."

On and on Lucy's story went, with one after another task taking its turn as the source of her ire. For example, Lucy suggested it had been five years since Sam had cleaned a bathroom, then contrasted that example with his tendency to "lay around all weekend and watch TV and drink some beer." When I asked Lucy what specific improvements she would like to see in her marriage, she reacted pessimistically about the prospects for change. Then she returned to her husband's refusal to apply his special skills to his own home. Lucy was especially bothered by one of their bathrooms, which Sam had torn apart two years earlier but had never finished remodeling.

> He's a skilled carpenter; he's like the best, the best in his field. So why is my bathroom unfinished? You know, because he doesn't use—we have two bathrooms. We have a down—downstairs bathroom, we have an upstairs bathroom. He uses the upstairs the bathroom. The kids use the upstairs bathroom. Nobody wants to use that [downstairs] bathroom, you know? And I'm like . . . It would probably take just a weekend to finish it. A weekend, a full weekend of work, you know, of getting it in gear and doing it. And there's things that . . . that I can't do, I can't do that. Because I don't know how to put a floor in. [. . .] I would be really happy if I, if he just did those type of jobs I can't do. I mean the daily, the daily grind is not that bad. [. . .] If he would just do things around the house that I *can't* do. [. . .] Oh that would be, I would be happy. That would be it, that would be it, you know?

In the context of Lucy's account, then, the idea that "an hour is an hour is an hour" did not seem to apply. Some hours of housework can mean a great deal more than others, Lucy seemed to tell me. If Sam were to spend a weekend cooking and cleaning, it would not be nearly as helpful—nor bring their relationship as close to equality—as would a weekend of bathroom remodeling.

Meg's Account: *"Just take them bills!"*

Another respondent, Meg, also told me a story about her marriage that seemed to invoke the conventional theme of "sharing the labor." A mother of three children (four, seven, and eleven years old), Meg's days were certainly full. She not only worked as a certified nurse's aide but also sold Mary Kay products in her spare time. When I met her, Meg and her husband Chuck (a car wash manager) had been married for thirteen years.

As with Lucy, Meg argued that her marriage was less than fair and that her husband could contribute much more around the house. Unlike Lucy, however, her biggest complaint revolved around their finances rather than carpentry or home improvement.

Meg seemed to arrive at our interview ready with a mental checklist of her husband's unfair attitudes and behavior in her marriage. Initially, these centered on the division of household chores. Meg quickly rattled off a series of tasks that Chuck either neglected, avoided, or outright refused to do: changing diapers, cleaning the house, and hiring babysitters. At the beginning of their marriage, Chuck had even expected that Meg would make his lunch every day; he had also expressed a desire to have recreational time by himself, without having to look after the children. Neither of these expectations seemed fair to Meg, since no one made her lunch and her time off always included supervising the children.

When I asked what it would take for her marriage to be more equal, Meg's answer again revolved around Chuck's contributions to, and his mindset toward, the household workload. On the face of it, this resonates with a familiar theme in current research. Meg said she wanted Chuck to be more "active," in the sense of doing more and not waiting to be told what to do. What would be nice, Meg suggested, would be for Chuck to take the initiative and say, "This is what I've planned for us to have for dinner" rather than relying on her all the time. Usually, she suggested, when Chuck got home from work, he stopped moving while she kept going and going. "He lays down, plops, and dies" was how she put it.

Eventually, Meg honed in on one particular way that Chuck could have been a more active household participant. She was adamant that Chuck could do much more to assist her in managing their finances. While some scholars and laypersons might view "controlling the money" as a privilege and a sign of power, in Meg's account it was framed as an overwhelming and unwanted responsibility. The following excerpt is illustrative:

> I feel like I have the weight of the world on my shoulders. [. . .] I'm the one who worries about when they get paid—sure he's helping pay for them, but I'm the one that gets "Oh God, I gotta pay this bill by this date, I gotta pay this." It's just like when he hands over his check, he's handing over all the responsibilities of worrying about what goes where, and how much, and this and that. [. . .] Because I got all this stuff. You know I've got all the bills, and going and talking to the landlord, and making sure the car payments and the bills are paid, and then on top of that "What are we having for dinner?" the kids are "Aaaahh!" [*makes a screaming noise*], you know, it's like "Aaaahh!" [*Meg makes another screaming noise for herself and pulls on her*

hair.] I want to take it [*makes a gesture as if throwing something away*] and say that's enough. You take over for awhile. But I think he would pop. I personally don't think he could handle the stress of paying all the bills. It scares me. It scares me to—I would be afraid to death to hand him my paycheck and say "Here. Take care of the bills." [. . .] I would be stressed out, I'd be going "Oh my God, are the lights gonna be on tomorrow?"

Meg was in a real bind. Handling the finances was a tough chore that she desperately wanted to share with her husband, but that option was out of the question because (according to Meg) Chuck was both uninterested and incapable of correctly paying the bills and balancing their accounts.

I don't want to give the impression that Meg was *only* interested in the division of labor. Our interview lasted well over an hour and covered an array of topics. Meg explained that Chuck didn't permit her to go shopping alone after dark, but suggested that he was not nearly as controlling as many other husbands and boyfriends she had known; she told me that she had been physically abused in a past relationship, but she was confident this would never happen with Chuck. And she (rhetorically) asked me why men seem to feel that it's acceptable for them to wake up their wives in the middle of the night in order to make sexual advances, but get cranky whenever their wives do the same to them.

However, the division of labor did seem to be the subject that most preoccupied Meg, and within that area the task of "paying the bills" seemed most prominent. She repeatedly stated or implied that she envied Chuck's "freedom," his ability to "just come home and sit back" and relax. She wanted to periodically share in the comfortable feeling that "everything's paid for, everything's taken care of." In fact, at the conclusion of the interview, Meg helped wrap up our conversation by summarizing her thoughts on her marriage in this way:

MEG: The main thing that sticks out in my head is them bills. "Take them bills. I don't want to see 'em. I don't want to see 'em. None of 'em. You get the mail, you pay the bills, you worry about it for a while—"

SCOTT: You think that's like the biggest inequality in your marriage or . . .

MEG: I think so, oh definitely. I mean that's just kinda petty, but to me, you know, when you've got numbers in front of you, and you're trying to figure out what he's making, you know, that you got to put it with yours to get it, I'd just—I'd like to just take forty dollars out of my pay check, stick it in my pocket, say "Here ya go honey. Take care of the bills for this month." But then again that scares the crap out of me.

Lucy and Meg both offered accounts that centered on the division of labor, though the experiences they highlighted within that theme were somewhat idiosyncratic. Lucy lamented the unequal contributions her husband made around the house, but suggested that her relationship would have been "close enough" to equal if her husband would have just done one category of tasks: work that she couldn't do but that he was trained by trade to do. Sam's reluctance to apply his carpentry skills to their own ailing home overshadowed all the other tasks with which she wished he would help her. Meg's account also depicted an unfair division of chores, but she seemed most concerned with monetary challenges. Meg didn't claim that Chuck was earning or spending more than his fair share of income; it was that he left it up to her to ensure that all the bills were paid on time and that their accounts were all in order.

Lucy's and Meg's views show that two individuals can share a common concern with "equality as sharing the workload" even though the theme takes on distinct subjective meanings in each case. These meanings can be distorted by a research methodology that merely counts up the total number of hours that husbands and wives spend on housework and childcare.

ELABORATING UNFAMILIAR THEMES OF MARITAL INEQUALITY

While Lucy and Meg centered their discussions of inequality on familiar household matters, less familiar themes also emerged from my interviews. I talked to respondents who held quite unexpected views of what constituted inequality. In the following accounts, for example, Alicin and Michael offer portraits of the equality and inequality in their marriages that seldom appear in scholarly discussions of equality. These also deserve attention if we want to respect and understand people's diverse marital experiences.

Alicin's Account: The Importance of Being Erudite

Housework, power, and communication are mainstays of social scientific views of marital equality, but the horizon of everyday life concerns is virtually limitless. One of my respondents, for example, claimed—quite seriously—that the main form of inequality in her marriage was her spouse's inferior intelligence. Alicin, a thirty-five-year-old social worker and mother of two children, told me that the difference between her and her husband's mental acumen was both substantial and consequential. She argued that it was a constant source of dissatisfaction and the leading cause of a number of other problems that had undermined her marriage. Regardless of how a conventional researcher might classify her relationship, in Alicin's account of her marriage, the most worrisome inequality was based on IQ. She was reasonably bright, but her husband, Kevin, was simply not a smart man.

I met Alicin after she responded to my newspaper advertisement that asked to speak with women who felt they had unequal marriages. At the outset, Alicin informed me that she had recently separated from her husband and that her relationship was going downhill fast.

> It's probably something that never should have started but you know, you get into it and then you start having kids and it's hard to back out once you get heading down that road but . . . um, the inequality that we have is um, . . . I think uh, probably it's mostly intellectual inequality, and then everything else just kinda stems from that. Um, because we have earning inequality and . . . you know other basic differences but that's something that has caused him insecurity from the beginning, because he's always said "You're smarter than I am" and, you know, "Are you gonna leave? What's gonna happen?" And so that I think made him a little bit suspicious sometimes, which would really bother me. You know, if I got home fifteen minutes late [he would ask] "Where were you?"

Alicin causally connected Kevin's intellect to other relationship troubles, in particular Kevin's "insecurity." Though some might suspect there were issues of "power" or "control" in Kevin's suspicious questioning ("Where were you?"), Alicin chose to interpret her husband's behavior as a consequence of an insecurity that grew out of his awareness that she was more intelligent than he was.

As the interview continued, Alicin told me more about the financial troubles in her marriage. Because of Kevin's "limitations," his income was consistently lower than Alicin would have preferred. Moreover, Kevin occasionally *cost* them money through his failed enterprises as a contractor and a carpet cleaner. Though Alicin tried to be "the supportive wife," she secretly had her doubts about his ability to achieve his career goals. Those doubts were apparently realized because "he really didn't have the knowledge to make it work." There were reportedly some years where Alicin "made the money and he lost half of it."

Alicin did mention other troubles in her marriage. For instance, she characterized Kevin as having a problem with drinking. She also suggested that his (initially meager) contributions to housework and childcare had improved over time. But these issues seemed either causally connected (i.e., she said alcohol only further impaired Kevin's thinking) or subordinate to the principal form of inequality she noted. Intelligence was the main theme that Alicin used to organize the indeterminate elements of her failing marriage to Kevin. Listen to what Alicin said when I questioned whether she ever compared her relationship to other married couples she knew. As usual, her response focused on the role of intellect in her marriage.

> I compared our marriage for example to some friends that we had. Um, neighbors who had I thought a pretty equal marriage. They were really just equal in so many ways. And I, and I was envious of that. You know. They enjoyed each other's company so much more than my husband and I, and so I really did envy that. And same thing with my dad, he remarried, he remarried somebody who had so many more um, things in common with him, and equal in terms of education and, you know, the types of jobs that they do. [. . .] I wish we had something like that. And honestly I wish I had someone I could take and, and . . . you know, take and meet some of my other friends and be able to have a group conversation, but instead I—and I'm kind of ashamed of this, but I was—I was embarrassed to have him around. [. . .] Even if some—something as simple as, you know, one night we went to some friends to play Trivial Pursuit and it was painful to watch him play, for everyone in the room.

From start to finish, then, intellectual inequality was the dominant theme running through Alicin's account. Seemingly aware of the potentially negative connotations of claiming to be "superior" to Kevin, Alicin remarked near the end of our interview: "I hate to have it sound like it just boils down to that, but I really think that that was the root of most of our problems."

Michael's Account: Turf, Belonging, and Acceptance

In contrast to Alicin's resolute tale, some unfamiliar stories I heard were more complex, nuanced, and multifaceted. Michael, another informant, actually provided me with a succinct statement of what he thought "marital equality" meant. His succinct definition, however, emerged in the latter portion of our discussion, after much talk about his early relationship and living situation with his wife, Kathy. Unlike Alicin's pet peeve about unequal intelligence, Michael's vision of equality wasn't fully formulated from the start. The definition materialized as a subtle way of characterizing the many ways that Michael and Kathy had come to recognize their roles and spaces in their marriage.

Michael was selected from those respondents who claimed to have equal marriages. He described himself as a twenty-eight-year-old black male who was sixteen years younger than his white wife. As a registered nurse with two children of her own from a previous marriage, Kathy was already established with a house that felt like home when they met. Hence, when it was finally time to move in together, Michael explained, he found himself living alongside people who already "had gotten their roots into that house" (see Marsiglio and Hinojosa, this volume). The decorations, the clutter, the routines and norms—much of it seemed slightly odd to Michael. He felt out of place, yet as a newcomer he didn't feel he had legitimate grounds to complain. To achieve a fuller sense of equality—both in terms of having an equal "say" and in terms of feeling he equally "belonged" there—Michael said that he and Kathy eventually needed to move into a new home together, to live by themselves with their newborn child. Michael depicted his marriage as much more balanced and happy after they had established their new home.

Well into our interview, however, Michael suddenly articulated a shorthand definition of marital equality. I had asked him for his advice on how to conduct my future interviews, as another way to probe his thoughts and encourage explanation. In response, Michael emphasized the importance of "acceptance" to marital equality in general and to his life in particular. As a graduate student, middle-school teacher, and musician who worked part-time for low pay, Michael said that Kathy's acceptance of his life and career choices was central to the egalitarian marriage they had built together.

MICHAEL: I can tell you what *I* think equal is, an equal marriage. Cause it's gonna vary, couple to couple. . . . Equal marriage is when . . . two people accept each other for who they are, and can live with it for the rest of their lives.

SCOTT: OK. . . . What do you mean by "accept," like not try to change 'em?

MICHAEL: Not try to change 'em. . . . [. . .] If you start trying to change people, it doesn't work. And I tried to conform, I mean . . . you know, sometimes we get—I get down, and I say, "You know, I wish I was an accountant. Then I could play golf. I wouldn't do this music crap." [*laughs*] I wish I wasn't driven to do music cause it's almost like a curse sometimes. And then she probably wouldn't have [*laughs*] liked me if I hadn't been this way. It's like these earrings. I drove into Portland, got my ears pierced. Didn't tell my wife. Came home. "What do you think?" "She just goes 'You need bigger ones.' " [*laughter*] So that was pretty cool.

In light of his definition of equality as "acceptance," Michael claimed to feel fortunate in comparison with his friends, whose partners were not so tolerant of their work habits and artistic sensibilities. Michael didn't think that he was as demanding or difficult as "the heroin kind" of musician might be, but he still appreciated the fact that Kathy "put up" with him. "I *am* a musician," he said, and Kathy did not have a problem dealing with it. He explained:

> Like I'm working on a project. Everything's iffy. It's this big thing for MTV. [. . .] So every bit of spare time I get I'm working on the MTV thing. And she is *so* cool with that. She's so cool with me going to the studio and spending . . . hours, you know. Some nights she won't even see me. I just call and say "Yeah I'm at the studio." And she's really cool with that. And uh . . . I know a lot of—a lot of my friends aren't that lucky.

Along with supporting her husband's career aspirations, Kathy apparently also had been accepting of his educational pursuits. According to Michael, Kathy had even offered to move thousands of miles so he could pursue his graduate studies in another state. As he put it:

> Um . . . she's been cool about my uh . . . graduate studies. 'Cause right now we're talking about um . . . possibly going to another state. 'Cause I found a school who'll actually just pay my way to finish my degree. And that's like a big deal. It's an okay university, it's not the greatest but . . . [. . .] I want to go and get [my degree] done and um . . . maybe . . . go for a college gig or something, I don't know. Right now . . . um . . . I mean she sacrifices a lot cause she has put down roots. Oregon's been her life. She grew up here . . . and she owns a house here. But she's—If I decide to go and finish my degree . . . and uh . . . you might say that that's not equal [*laughs*]. She—she has sacrificed a lot for me.

At the end of this excerpt, readers might notice (as I did at the time of the interview) that Michael seemed to recognize that his description of his relationship could potentially be interpreted as a story about *in*equality. When I asked him a somewhat "politely phrased" question that subtly challenged his portrayal of marital egalitarianism, it prompted him to quickly assemble evidence that he really wasn't describing a sort of inequality.

SCOTT: Do you feel—it sounds like you might feel guilty a tiny bit that she's willing to give up so much.

MICHAEL: Oh yeah. But she also realizes that . . . See I'm from the South. two thousand miles away [from Oregon]. And uh . . . if I'm lucky I'll

see my family once a year. She knows um . . . we—we've gotta find a—
a middle of the road kind of spot [*laughs*] that we can go and visit our
families. 'Cause right now my mom is just really wanting me to move
back . . . 'cause of her grandkid. This is her first granddaughter.

Thus, Michael anticipated and attempted to deflect the potentially inegalitarian implications of Kathy's offer to move by suggesting that he had
already made sacrifices by living with her in Oregon. He implied that in
the future, to maintain a sense of equality, they had to find "a middle of the
road" location in between their families, so visiting home would not be an
unfair burden for one or the other. As it had in the beginning of the interview, the importance of "turf" found its way into the end of Michael's
account, augmenting (and complicating) his deceptively simple definition
of marital equality as mere spousal "acceptance."

SUMMING UP

"Do you have an equal marriage?" That was the simple question I asked
my interviewees. It's an issue that marital researchers have been studying
for decades. Yet, as I have argued in this chapter, standard research practices that predefine the meaning of equality can obscure or distort the
ways that married people themselves understand and depict the equalities
and inequalities in their relationships. There are drawbacks to methodo-
logies that predefine an equal marriage as being primarily about relative
amounts of household labor, power, communication, or other conventional
category(ies).

Some individuals may define their marriages in ways that are fairly
unconventional—as in Alicin's concern with intelligence or Michael's
interest in acceptance. The meanings these persons give to equality don't
fit very well with the ways social researchers choose to look at marriage.
But even when an individual does interpret his or her relationship using a
conventional theme, the "dilemma of meaning" is still present. Lucy and
Meg both invoked the idea of equality-as-a fair-division-of-labor, but they
selected and weighed their respective household "tasks" differently. The
most crucial chore for one person was not the most crucial for the other
because of their divergent circumstances and orientations.

The point is not to ignore statistical analyses of marital equality or the
division of labor more specifically. Many researchers and their audiences
have found these reports of marital equality to be informative and useful.

Rather, the lesson to take from this chapter is that it is also important to pay attention to the subjective meanings that married people give their own relationships, to see them from the inside out. Since people live and act based on what things mean to them (Blumer 1969), respecting and studying people's own views of equality seems an effective strategy for understanding them in the broadest terms possible.

Part of the appeal of interpretive research on social life is it can increase our ability to imagine how the world might look to someone else. Simultaneously, such research can help us reconsider how the world looks to ourselves. For those of us who plan to enjoy happily egalitarian marriages of our own, an important skill to develop is the capacity to think critically about the criteria and meanings that we, our spouses, and others use to identify equality in the first place.

REFERENCES

Blumer, Herbert. 1969. *Symbolic Interactionism*. Englewood Cliffs, N.J.: Prentice-Hall.

Deutsch, Francine. M. 1999. *Halving It All: How Equally Shared Parenting Works*. Cambridge, Mass.: Harvard University Press.

Haas, Linda. 1980. "Role-Sharing Couples: A Study of Egalitarian Marriages." *Family Relations* 29:289–96.

Harris, Scott R. 2000. "Meanings and Measurements of Equality in Marriage: A Study of the Social Construction of Equality." Pp. 111–45 in *Perspectives on Social Problems*, Vol. 12, edited by J. A. Holstein and G. Miller. Stamford, Conn.: JAI Press.

Hochschild, Arlie, with Anne Machung. 1989. *The Second Shift*. New York: Avon Books.

Kimball, Gayle. 1983. *The 50/50 Marriage*. Boston: Beacon.

Pleck, Joseph H. 1985. *Working Wives/Working Husbands*. Beverly Hills, Calif.: Sage.

Risman, Barbara, and Danette Johnson-Sumerford. 1997. "Doing It Fairly: A Study of Feminist Households." *Journal of Marriage and the Family* 60:23–40.

Ross, Catherine E., John Mirowsky, and Joan Huber. 1983. "Dividing Work, Sharing Work, and In-Between: Marriage Patterns and Depression." *American Sociological Review* 48:809–23.

Schwartz, Pepper. 1994. *Peer Marriage: How Love Between Equals Really Works*. New York: The Free Press.

Shelton, Beth A., and Daphne John. 1996. "The Division of Household Labor." *Annual Review of Sociology* 22:299–322.

Smith, Audrey D., and William J. Reid. 1986. *Role-Sharing Marriage*. New York: Columbia University.

Stapleton, Jean and Richard Bright. 1976. *Equal Marriage*. Nashville, TN: Abingdon.

Twiggs, Joan E., Julia McQuillan, and Myra M. Ferree. 1998. "Meaning and Measurement: Reconceptualizing Measures of the Division of Household Labor." *Journal of Marriage and the Family* 61:712–24.

Warner, Rebecca L. 1986. "Alternative Strategies for Measuring Household Division of Labor." *Journal of Family Issues* 7:179–95.

FURTHER READING

Deutsch, Francine M. 1999. *Halving It All: How Equally Shared Parenting Works*. Cambridge, Mass.: Harvard University Press.

Harris, Scott R. 2001. "What Can Interactionism Contribute to the Study of Inequality? The Case of Marriage and Beyond." *Symbolic Interaction* 24:455–80.

Harris, Scott R. 2005. *The Meanings of Marital Equality*. Albany: SUNY Press.

Hochschild, Arlie, with Anne Machung. 1989. *The Second Shift*. New York: Avon Books.

Schwartz, Pepper. 1994. *Peer Marriage: How Love Between Equals Really Works*. New York: The Free Press.

Discussion Questions

1. Can you think of any couples you know who have fairly equal relationships? How about unequal relationships? What behaviors or criteria led you to classify them as equal or unequal? In other words, what is your definition of an equal marriage?

2. Review the five criteria of marital equality discussed early in this chapter. Can you think of any other dimensions of equality that this omits, besides the dimensions highlighted by Alicin and Michael? What else could make a relationship equal or unequal?

3. Do you agree with the way that Lucy, Meg, Alicin, and Michael evaluate their own marriages? Given the information contained in their accounts, can you argue that their relationships are actually more equal or unequal than these individuals claim? Consider your divergent interpretations in relation to what the author of this chapter says about the "dilemma of meaning" and the "interpretive work" it takes to make sense of everyday life.

Part 2

Parents and Kids

4

Being a Good Parent

Rebecca L. Warner

INTERVIEWER: What are your goals for your children?

PARENT A: You know, I've actually written them down. It is to have them be happy, ah, self-confident, polite, and pleasant people so they are successfully integrated into society as a whole. I want them to have fulfilling, rewarding lives—whatever path they take to do that. I want to be there to help support them and guide them and try to help save them as much pain as I can. That's my goal for them.

PARENT B: Well, I guess I want them to have a happy family. I want them to have a safe, healthy life, and that I would be supportive of them in whatever they feel they need to do. I want them to be able to make life decisions—good decisions—by themselves. I want them to know who they are.

Good parents do whatever is necessary for their children to reach their goals (Garey 1999). The parents just quoted tell us that good parents are those who have happy, healthy, safe, and successful children—things that common clichés would suggest. When I examine the research literature I am told that parents can achieve their goals by engaging in certain kinds of activities that help children develop skills necessary to navigate their social worlds. For example, parents can promote skill development by enrolling their children in enrichment programs. Parents can prevent problems by keeping track of their children's whereabouts and establishing safe boundaries (see Kurz, this volume). Such parenting practices are referred to in the literature as "family management" (Furstenberg et al. 1999).

While the parents quoted here recognize that they have a role in family management, their comments suggest that children have something to say about it, too. "Whatever path they take" and "whatever they feel they need to do" are phrases that recognize children's agency—their active

65

participation in, and management of, the process of growing up. Like parents, children themselves are important managers of family time and planning (Thorne 2001). For example, children who are active in extracurricular activities may ask their parents to help in organizing transportation and events. Children with special medical needs can require extra time and attention from parents. Even when parents actively engage in helping their children to succeed, they can't always anticipate what the children's specific needs or desires for success might be. Children often need to initiate that help.

But what does all this mean in practice? Parents learn about their children's needs through direct interaction and observation. Good parenting is not something that can be spelled out ahead of time. The meaning of being a good parent grows out of the give-and-take of lived experience. Daily contact at mealtimes, playing games, or watching their children at school events—all give parents clues about what their children's needs and desires are. Children's lives also unfold away from parents and domestic settings. Such experiences can come to parents' attention as unexpected news, and can be good or bad. Parents learn a great deal about themselves as parents in response to unplanned and/or unwanted news about their children.

This chapter examines parents' stories about parenting, especially in relation to unplanned events in their children's lives. As parents describe their responses, we glimpse what being good parenting means in practice, which is far more complex than the literature and good parenting clichés would lead us to believe.

HEARING FROM PARENTS THEMSELVES

Several years ago, I began a research project to explore the everyday meaning of parenting. I wanted to hear from parents themselves how they went about parenting activities and what role they felt their children played in shaping those activities. I posted a call for participants in places where parents and children congregate, such as at churches, preschools, and recreation facilities. When I received a response, I set up an interview, typically in the parent's home. When there were two parents, I scheduled separate interview times for them. I spent one to three hours conversing openly with the parents about the parenting process.

I began the project with three broad questions: (1) What were your plans for family life? (2) What are some of the current issues you are dealing with? (3) What are your goals for your children? The first question elicited information about parents' own upbringing and their perspectives on raising children. It might reveal the broad ideas and beliefs about parenting that were heard through education and from the media. The final question was a way of encouraging parents to sum up their experiences. For most parents, it reassured them that their children were on their way to being productive members of society. The second question was really the heart of the interview. It helped me to discern and to understand what good parenting meant in relation to the ongoing challenges of domestic life. It was from responses to this question that I learned how much of what being a good parent related to matters well beyond what clichés about building safe and happy lives suggested.

The chapter focuses on interviews with just a few of the parents. Their accounts are especially rich in revealing what parents view as the everyday meaning of good parenting. The accounts show that good parenting is intricately embedded in daily living, learned as much from concrete events and unplanned interactions as from what is understood beforehand or generally accepted. Background characteristics of parents and children, such as their social class or their gender, also shape the way parents think about parenting and how they behave as parents. As we will see, parents do reiterate clichés such as "all I want is for them to be happy," but the practical meaning of such generalities relates to the give-and-take of their lives with the children, making for surprising nuance in the meaning of good parenting.

WANTING THEM TO BE HAPPY

As we get to know children, it becomes easier to detect when they are unhappy. Frowns, tears, staying in their rooms with the doors closed, or dismissing questions are signs of something amiss. Rachel, one of the parents I interviewed, is a single, divorced mother with a seventeen-year-old son, Mark. During the interview, it was clear that Rachel cares deeply about Mark's happiness.

Rachel is very proud of Mark and thinks he has a good chance of getting into college on a football scholarship. Mark is six feet, five inches tall and weighs over three hundreds pounds. He plays offensive line for his high school football team and has received a couple of letters from regional colleges. In her interview, Rachel told me that Mark is

> very popular at school. His yearbook is always full of nice, sweet things. And when we went on an out-of-state weekend with the youth group from church,

there were all these girls, who are drop dead model gorgeous, and they are "Mark, oh Mark!" They are hugging and kissing him and you know, dancing with him.

She went on to qualify her comments. She didn't think any of these relationships were more than friendship—"he's everybody's buddy"—that, in fact, Mark had just gone on his first date two weeks ago. He left with one group but returned with a different set. The news about the date was not good.

They all went to dinner together at another friend's house and she [the date] drove to the dance in her own car and then left. So when Mark came home that night, he was with a bunch of other guys and I said, "Well, did you have fun?" and he said, "We'll talk about it tomorrow." And they all went away and did the guys-spend-the-night-out kind of thing.

The next day, his closest buddy brought him back over and I said, "Well, what happened?" and he said, "Well, she left half way through, but you know I think she had a good excuse because it was her friend's birthday and she had to go to this birthday party." And his friend said, "Well, didn't she tell you when you were eating dinner?" and Mark said, "Well, no, but you know, it was like her friend's birthday." And I said, "Well, her excuse is that she's just trash!" and then I realized that, you know, me saying that was making it worse.

And so I just don't know how . . . I mean, in one way when we went to buy the corsage at the florist and I just paid for it because, at that point, he didn't have any money on him. So, you know, the woman showed us that we could get a little nicer one for four dollars more and I offered to buy it and he said, "Nah." So maybe he didn't really care. I mean maybe they really were just buddies and it wasn't that big of a deal, but I think that it did make him . . . I mean he did say that it made him look bad. And so I look at it and my heart just bleeds for him and then I think, because I remember high school and I think, do I want my child's star to shine in high school? Are you going to reach the epitome of where you're at in high school? I mean, if he were thin, just tall but thin, he would be so handsome. And I think, what a jerk he might have ended up being. How much am I going to let that go to his head?

Making friends and fitting in are important components of children's social lives, things for which many parents hope. Most of us have memories of how we struggled to find our place among others. Children tease one another about how they dress or what their bodies look like. However, much of this doesn't make it home for parents to hear. When it does, parents can feel awful ("my heart just bleeds") and they want to do something to help their children be happy. But the good-parent clichés only go so far in this regard; everyday life complicates its meaning, as the muddled news of Mark's "unsuccessful" date suggests.

For Rachel, there are many challenges to helping Mark. Her son's height and weight have always been a problem. Both have shed tears over clothes shopping and the inability to "look like everyone else." We see this in the preceding excerpt, in the connection that Rachel makes at the end between Mark's weight and the bad date. Then again, Rachel surmises, if Mark were thin, he might not be any happier. He might have been a jerk, someone who himself could have left a girl alone on a dance date, the kind of son she would not want to have.

Researchers refer to the accomplishment of successful family management as encompassing both "promotive" and "preventive" parenting strategies (Furstenberg et al. 1999). Promotive strategies include attempts to help children develop social competence, the ability to act independently in their social worlds. This includes enrolling children in recreational, education, spiritual, and health-promoting activities. Such strategies are targeted at children's safety and may involve talking to them about what to be cautious of, teaching them how to make good judgments, and establishing rules for appropriate behavior.

Aware of challenges that could result from Mark's size, Rachel took up both types of parenting strategies. Adhering to a preventive strategy, Rachel said that they always ate healthily: "I didn't use, like, cookies and treats to make him feel better and we didn't keep a lot of that kind of stuff around the house." Rachel encouraged Mark to work out with the wrestling team when football was not in season. But since the largest weight class for wrestlers is 275, Mark was not allowed to compete. However, being permitted to just work out with the team helped to keep him in good physical shape all the same. Promotive strategies included getting Mark involved in Cub Scouts and in youth group activities at their church.

At other points in the interview, it became clear that Rachel views her financial status as an insurmountable obstacle to her son's happiness and, in turn, her successful parenting. Rachel is a single parent. She was married to Mark's father for four years when he was involved in a serious car accident, causing brain damage. Their relationship fell apart as the damage led to violent outbursts. The ex-husband now lives across the country and there is little contact with him. As a single parent, Rachel is left to handle things on her own. She is employed full-time, sharing two jobs with other employees at a large company that provides good health benefits. But she is not upwardly mobile and has found it difficult to provide for Mark in the way she would like. This comes into play as Rachel continues to talk about parenting goals and responsibilities, and how she feels about herself as a mother. Rachel's comments point to the challenges of being a single parent bereft of what she figures are the economic resources needed to achieve her goals.

> He did the Cub Scouts for a brief time but that got to be sometimes sad because I've always been a person that I know that for everything that your child is involved in, you either have to give money or volunteer. Well, I never had the money, so I would have to volunteer and sometimes he would be irritated because it was like I was the "assistant person" or whatever, and he'd say, "Why is it always you, Mom? This is supposed to be a guy and dad thing." And I'm, like, it hurt my feelings and I would realize that's another thing, you know, when you have an only child and particularly if you don't have a strong relationship or a partner, then when you get mad or upset, then you share that with a child more than you would have . . . it's so sad.
>
> But, um, we've been going to the Congregational Church since he's been three. I grew up going to church, but then I did the typical out of high school [thing]. "Oh, you're all just a bunch of hypocrites." And then in college you don't go and then you have your own kids and you recognize that you want to have that foundation, that safe place for your kids. So I definitely got back involved. We do group activities together and, ah, it feels good to be involved in things. It's like fun. We never do any, like, theological things, just activities. We've traveled to Mazatlan where we did a building project. But to do that, we had to work the concessions at the college football games to raise money. They aren't so much fun but they are things we can do together.

Rachel grew up in a middle-class family. Both of her parents graduated from college and Rachel had also attended college. The way she talked about childrearing reflected her middle-class upbringing (Lareau 2003). She spoke of the importance of having her son involved in activities that transmitted life skills, and that were fun besides. Because of her financial status, she was not able to pursue middle-class goals in the traditional fashion, simply arranging activities for her son and driving him there. She was forced to limit the number of events in which Mark could participate and had to engage in fundraising so that they could do things together. There were times when she would send Mark off to sports or church camp alone, referring to these as his "vacations." Her own "vacations" consisted of "staying at home while he went to summer camps."

Despite the disadvantages, Rachel put a positive spin on her efforts. Referring to the dance incident, she explains that Mark really wasn't "invested," so it wasn't a big deal. After all, he didn't go for the corsage upgrade. Still, "he did say that it made him look bad." A shift of focus to the future centers on Mark's strengths. Taking the opportunity to provide a happier ending, Rachel specifies the particular meaning of good parenting in the context of her surprisingly articulate son.

> Here's a story I wanted to tell you about. We were having a discussion in our high school youth group at the church about zero population growth. One of the other leaders is really into how that will solve the problems of the world. And I actually come from the total opposite spectrum on that and one of the things that Mark said was, "Isn't it incredibly pathetic to think that we can't do the one thing that we are biologically predisposed to do, which is to come here and have a child? You know we weren't put on this earth to create plastic toys." And he says, "I'm not saying we were put here just to propagate like rabbits or something, but, you know, the whole survival of the species means that you have a next generation. And shouldn't we be able to figure out how to have everyone have that ability to have their next generation without getting to the point where people are saying the problem is too many people in India or Africa . . . or in any place other than where we're having them." And so I was really proud of him taking that stance. And I was just blown away that he brought it to that level of where he was coming from. I figure I've done my job as a parent, I mean, if he can come up with something like that.

Rachel takes pride in good parenting, the evidence of which is quite subtle. Her pleasure here involves something miles away in meaning from just "wanting them to be happy." Her pride is in her son's ability to communicate a clear position in relation to a public issue, which turns out to be that much sweeter because she shares the position with her son. Rachel later expresses confidence in her good parenting skills as she returns to the challenges of parenting a very large child. She's done her job, she is a "good parent," and Mark will be fine. This, the narrative details reveal, is evidence of good parenting.

At the end of the interview, Rachel touches on another point raised at the start. Children can alter parents' behaviors and ideas as well, mediating the meaning of good parenting on their own. Good parenting is built on two-way streets, in other words. Both mothers and fathers in my study spoke of how having a child made them become more responsible, how it made them stop and think about things more. Not only do children bring about

the challenging situations that elicit protective parenting, but they also
present opportunities for parents to experience social worlds they never
imagined. Mark loves football, and Rachel claims she never really paid
much attention to the game. But things have changed, in no small part
because of Mark.

> That's another thing about how having a child changed me. It opens you up
> to whole worlds that, if you choose not to enter those worlds because you
> don't like them or are not interested in them, then you are just closing off a
> path to spend time with your child. So football was nothing I ever paid atten-
> tion to. My parents took us to games when I was a kid. I would go to games
> when I was in high school because it was all just a social event, and that's all
> it meant, getting some free food from your parents, you know, a pennant
> or something. Now I'll go to games in the pouring rain. I wouldn't miss it.
> You know, ten years from now I imagine that Mark would be out of college
> and working. And whether it was his dream of going to the NFL or working
> someplace else that he wouldn't be going anyplace else but home for
> Christmas, or that he'd pick up the phone and ask me about a sports headline
> or want to dissect a game that we'd just watched on TV.

For Rachel, such are the everyday contours of "wanting them to be
happy." They are found in the way she has helped her son deal with his
weight, enjoying a game with her son when she'd never really been interested in the game before, and taking pride her son's ability to take part in
public debate. All of these things comprise her roadmap of how she might
help her son be happy.

WANTING THEM TO BE SAFE
AND HEALTHY

Today, we generally assume that parents, especially mothers, are responsible
for creating a safe environment for their children (Hays 1996). While
physicians do check-ups and professionally manage sickness, it is up to
parents to monitor children's day-to-day environments for safety and to
keep track of basic health needs.

The parents in my study, like those in others, shared concerns that
related closely to the public discourse about the dangers of childhood
(Best 1990). School shootings, child abductions, drugs, and gang violence
have been important media topics in the past several years. Few parents
I interviewed had serious experiences with violence and drugs. Perhaps this
was the result of my sample selection; parents having encountered severe

parenting troubles may not have volunteered for my study. In addition, those who did participate may have wanted to put the best face on their parenting. But for those few whose children were affected by unsafe situations, parenting became a matter of serious self-scrutiny.

One of these parents, Ann, grew up in Hawaii. She became pregnant at fifteen but was able to stay in school because "the teen pregnancy rate at my high school was high enough that they had a program to support teen parents and their children." Not long after giving birth to her son, Bane, Ann's own mother left the islands and Ann decided to move in with Bane's father and his family. This Filipino family was large and extended, and few of the members spoke English. Feeling isolated, Ann wrote to her mother "pleading" for a plane ticket to the mainland. Although Ann imagined she would someday return to Hawaii and marry Bane's father, things didn't work out that way.

Once on the mainland, Ann worked to earn her GED and then took "clerical update" training at the local community college. Completing the training, she worked a temporary job and eventually became a full-time office worker in a county social service agency. She began attending church, where she met her husband, Kevin, who was youth pastor at the time. They married and had two daughters. The relationship was fragile; Kevin was verbally and physically abusive with Ann and Bane, and he was away from home for long periods of time. Before Kevin finally moved out and took up with another woman thirty-five miles away, Ann discovered that her eldest daughter, Cindy, age eight, had been sexually molested for the third time.

I think the first time was actually when she was like three-and-a-half and our next-door neighbor boy who was seven years old and he was doing more of, kind of like an experimentation, but I mean it wasn't hurtful for her. He was like "blah!" and I think that just freaked her out so much that it made her blur her boundaries and so she didn't know how to say no. So it opened her up to, and I was concerned at the time and my husband was like, "Oh, you make such a big deal out of it."

But because of this incident, I really believe that she doesn't know how to say no anymore. So she ended up getting molested by an eleven-year-old boy like a year and a half later. This time she tells me about it and the extent of it. Kevin and I were separated at the time, so I called him and told him and had the police involved and we had to go through a social service agency which deals with young children who have been abused and then we were dealing with that, had her in private counseling. And then right in the neighborhood, um, this gang of boys, well, she was just playing with them and it was so weird. Well, anyway, I was at work. Kevin was at home watching the kids for the summer. Well, it turns out that they molested her. So we had to have the police involved again and by this time I'm thinking that I'm a horrible parent because how could this happen so many times?

So now she has to stay in the front yard and then she doesn't understand because she, well, and it's like then we had her in group therapy with other kids. We, Kevin and I, were in a parenting group, which he hated. I mean I think a lot of stress of this is why our marriage broke up. And so all of us went to family therapy. And even to this day, like we'll have to watch her because it's like she tries to wander off and then I have to find out why she's not in the front yard. I know that is because of the molesting, because of some of the things that she says. She never, she dresses like a boy now, she tries to act tough.

Ann doesn't convey the meaning of being a "horrible parent" completely in her own terms. While the interview comments are hers, of course, and the specifics are unique to the events recounted, she borrows from the language of counseling to make her points. The entire family had been in counseling since the second molestation. In Ann's account, we virtually hear her therapist speaking (see Gubrium and Holstein 2002). Ann says that the molestations made Cindy unable to "know how to say no" anymore. Ann learned that when young children go through such experiences, it "blurs their boundaries." Borrowing from what she had heard in therapy, Ann applies the language of counseling to make sense of what happened to Cindy. Still, while feeling "horrible" as a parent, she nonetheless plans to protect Cindy in the future, needing to watch over her and helping her to "reestablish boundaries." The meaning of good and, conversely, "horrible" parenting is constructed out of a mother's unwitting contribution to an unhealthy environment, this time in relation to a therapeutic framing of events.

Ann believes that Cindy's experience of being molested may have exaggerated her marital problems. She feels that Kevin has not been very helpful in coming to grips with things ("Oh, you make such a big deal out of it") or in planning for the future. There are also the mixed messages with which she's had to contend. Within the past month, she has heard that Kevin was moving with his girlfriend to another state and did not want to see the children any more. She's also heard the opposite—that he planned to move to the city where Ann is living so he can be closer to the children: "And it's always been like this. 'I love you, I don't love you,' that kind of thing. And I just realized, maybe I'm being paranoid, but I realized that I don't want my kids to have to know all this."

As I continued with the interview, Ann moved away from the family context of abuse to talk about her plans for the future, especially in relation to her children's safety. Again, the meaning of a safe and healthy life for children is particularized in the context of everyday life, this time in terms of her mission and getting over the "hurt of marriage." It's clear that good (or bad) parenting is not something one arrives at, period. It's a shifting issue and concern of daily interaction between parents and their children.

ANN: We're in the process of this huge transition. I had originally planned to take a leave from work to go to college at the University of Hawaii, but they [her employer] said no. And once they said that, I started thinking that I could either be married to this job forever or I could take a rest and do what I know is right in my heart and in reality. So I have applied, I have the application all filled out and everything. And I just came back from the doctors today so I got all my tests done and everything and if I get accepted into the program, we'll be leaving in July. We'll need three months to get the kids settled and in classes and then I'll start school.

INTERVIEWER: What type of program is it?

ANN: It would be a mission, actually. It will be outreach through the church. It would be helping whatever community we're put to live in [in Hawaii]. Maybe we'll help with orphanages, just a variety, whatever that community needs. They have a grade school on campus and then, oh man, I would not have Bane and Cindy go to a public school in Hawaii for anything. They're horrible. I mean, they are a hundred times worse than here. There is a lot of prejudice. Now Bane would probably do okay [being half Filipino] except that I know how terrible it is because I lived there. They would try to get him into drugs and that's just what they do between classes is smoke marijuana. I'm not going to do that to him. Well, it turns out that they have K–12 programs now because there are so many people coming from all over the world to get in. My classroom gets out at the same time as theirs so it will be easier to have family time. There are usually about fifteen families in the program and all the meals are served cafeteria style and you get to know all the other families. You all have actual jobs from 3 to 5 [o'clock] that you do, like work in the kitchen or whatever for the kids so they get to hang out together, but then the evenings are free. It would give us an opportunity to really be together and it would be good for me.

I think my goals are not to be stuck, you know, where it's like day-to-day nightmares where I think, "If I can just get this done tonight, I'll be good!" But I also want to get over the hurt of marriage, although I'm not there yet. I want to be able to be a good mom and to be able to enjoy my kids and help them to be able to have fun.

The plan is to address a number of Ann's concerns regarding her failed marriage and problematic parenting. The transition will allow her to re-establish boundaries for her children, as their time will now be structured from morning through evening. The meaning of good parenting is linked with the expectation that responsible adults will always be present. Ann will be in a family environment where the children can see positive adult relationships, helping her to heal from her bad marriage. The children will have the opportunity to learn the values of work and responsibility.

According to Ann, having her children go to school within the church program will avoid the dangers of public schooling. Because Ann grew up in the area, she has had firsthand experience in the high school drug culture. She's convinced that the peer pressure would be too much for her son. She also worries about her daughters with respect to race/ethnic relations at the school. She believes that the prejudice against whites will be detrimental to their learning, paralleling what children of color experience in much of the United States. Racism and discrimination can create unsafe environments for children and families, and parents can serve as buffers between their children and the negative imagery in the broader society (Collins 1994).

WANTING THEM TO BE INDEPENDENT

Another cliché of good parenting refers to raising socially competent children. Social competence includes the ability to navigate social worlds effectively and develop independence. Part of this entails being able to face ambiguous situations and make good decisions: What should you do if a stranger offers you a ride? What about when a friend offers you the answers to the final exam in your science class? Parents can be proud of their children when they say "no" in these situations. Parents can feel perplexed, too, as children make the wrong decisions, implicitly impugning their parenting.

Two of the parents interviewed, Tina and Jon, have lived together for eleven years. They've been married for the last eight. Both have bachelor's degrees and work in science labs affiliated with a university. Two sons

—Zack, seventeen, and Tyler, twelve—from Tina's previous marriage live with them. Jon's own sons—Jason, fifteen, and Jeremy, thirteen—from his previous marriage live with them every other weekend and during holidays and school breaks.

One afternoon, Tina received a call from Zack, who reported that he'd been assaulted by a group of boys while he was walking home from high school.

> This boy who is a year younger than Zack comes up to him walking home and starts yelling, "fag," and pushing him from behind. And Zack just kept walking, you know. He stumbled but he kept walking away from him towards the elementary school. And for, like, two blocks this guy is just cussing at him and calling him a faggot and all this stuff. And Zack tried to cross the street and the other kid crossed the street after him and he kept pushing Zack and stuff. Then, while he was crossing back, some friends of the jerk came up in a car and kind of blocked his way and then he kind of pushed Zack onto the car. Zack kind of bounced and rolled off around the car and he kept going across the street. When he got to the yard across the street, the kid slugged him in the head and when Zack kind of spun around, the kid hit him in the eye. And he was swearing at him and this older woman in the yard was yelling "not in my yard." And the kids in the car are like pulled into the parking lot across the street and were like cheering. Then that kid walked off across the street and they all high-fived each other and Zack got up and kept walking and walking to the elementary school.

Had this been the whole story, Tina might have focused entirely on the assault and how to protect her son from violence. However, as she learned more about the incident, she was challenged to do more than simply keep Zack safe. What she learned raised questions about Zack's judgment, especially his ability to take responsibility for his actions. This, in turn, implicated her own parenting skills.

The background to the assault relates to the time the summer before when Zack brought home a bike and told his mother that he had received it as a gift from his biological father. Tina questioned this, as Zack's father did not have much money and Zack had bought a new bike the month before anyway. Zack said he thought his father might have stolen it, so Tina said to take it to the police. "So the bike went away." Sometime later, Zack had the bike again, explaining that the police gave it back because no one claimed it. He made some changes to the bike and sold it to another boy. The problem was, the boy to whom he sold it was the bike's original owner. After the parents of the two households involved in the situation had a discussion, Tina decided to let the police settle it. She still believed that Zack had been given the bike, but she didn't want the situation to escalate. This was the day before the afterschool incident.

> So when the police arrived [after Zack was attacked], I said, "Zack, you gotta tell what you were doing. It's really coming out." So with the police chief there . . . you know he's a really nice guy, and I'm on the city council so I know the police chief . . . we all know each other. And I say Zack may have gotten the bike from his father. I mean, it could have happened. I just don't think Zack took it because it seems really stupid to take a bike from a rack and think that you could get away with it. He's never done anything like that. And he may have, but it's more likely, I believe, he could have found it and not stolen it. He ended up having to take a lie detector test and his test was not as black and white as he would like it to be. But it was more believable than not. So they, they concluded that, yes, he probably did find it and, yes, he blew it by not turning it in.
>
> You know, if he took it, he deserves to deal with the consequences. So, it was very good. He, he had to pay me back for the bike. We had to buy a replacement bike for the other family. So he is doing some part-time work, yard work, and things like that. He's also working at a local café once a week doing dishes. He has to pay for his own car insurance, which is only forty dollars a month, and we don't let him drive around as much.

After the "truth" emerged, Tina was determined to find a way to help Zack be more responsible. This style of parenting is typical of middle-class parents, who focus on the "concerted cultivation" of their children's upbringing (Lareau 2003). To become socially competent as middle-class adults, these children are encouraged to independently think through situations and make good decisions. Punishing Zack by grounding him or by yelling at him would not have moved him forward toward social competence, in Tina's view. Instead, Tina reports that she talked with him about how to make things right. She feels that she has been a good parent because Zack is now working to pay her back and take responsibility for his actions. She also maintains a positive public image of herself among her friends in the community by having guided him to the right decision. Again, good parenting rests in the particulars and ebbs and flows in the give-and-take of family interaction.

Interestingly, another complicated situation further specified the meaning of good parenting. It happens that both of Jon's biological sons, Jason and Jeremy, witnessed the entire assault incident. They had been walking some distance behind Zack on their way home, but neither of them did anything to stop what happened. This was a major disappointment for Tina and Jon. Tina explains:

> They never even walked up to him. Which, really, you know, I think Jeremy would have helped if he was by himself, but Jason I don't know. It really hurt my heart that he didn't do that because we have been together so long. It just, it was really a good thing for Jon to see how Jason keeps himself distant. Because that was really cruel.

In a separate interview with Jon, the incident takes on additional meaning, leading him to view his biological sons' failure to help Zack as a problem, issues concerning his own parenting skills. Jon's parenting skills are questioned as they bear on his son's independent decision-making.

> We had this long saga not long ago, and I'll give you just the bare bones about it, where Zack ended up finding a bike and it was stolen and he got in trouble with the police and stuff. But as that unfolded, the owner of the bike stalked him and attacked him. It was in this old yard while walking home from school. The kid gave him a black eye, but Zack was passive and walked away. We had warned him about this before and told him not to get involved with these kids, you know, just walk away. So they're calling him every name in the book and shoving him. My two biological sons witnessed it from about a block away and, um, they ended up going to court to testify and the aggressor was punished lightly, but you know, punished. So the episode with the bike resolved itself and they accepted Zack having found the bike and, you know, his crime was not turning it in.
>
> So I think that was a real demonstration of his maturity, knowing that wasn't a good time to lose his temper even though being unjustly, you know, punished for it. And then on the flip side of that, like I told you, my sons did not help him. And that was really bad. I think that is sort of an, ah, empathy or awareness type of thing, you know? And granted they were afraid they might get hurt . . . and then in court a lawyer for the bad kid started saying stuff about trying to get my other sons . . . but still they should have helped in some way. I talked to them about that, but it's not something that you can make someone do.

Being a good parent extends to stepfathering. Negotiating the role of stepfather can be difficult (see Marsiglio and Hinojosa, this volume). Social science research on stepfathering suggests there are a number of factors involved in establishing relationships with stepchildren (Marsiglio 2004). These include the age of the children, the presence of the biological father, and whether or not the stepfather has biological children of his own. Jon became a stepparent when Zack was six, so they have lived together for a long time. Entering the family when the children are younger tends to help foster stronger relationships. However, Zack's biological father still has a presence, as we saw when Zack said the bike was a gift from his father and that it might have been stolen. Tina had noted that it was "kind of sad that Zack blamed his father" and suggested that this was an indication of how tumultuous their relationship was. There also was the presence of Jon's two biological children. William Marsiglio's research with stepfathers shows that having biological children can give stepfathers a clearer sense of how to be involved with stepchildren—how to be a good stepparent as well as how to be a good parent. Jon claims he has worked hard to develop good relationships with all four boys. He takes them camping and fishing, and they all play on a family Frisbee team. There is a common division of labor in blended families, where parents take separate responsibility for disciplining their respective biological children, while working with all of the children to promote social competence.

Jon's account of the bike incident put Zack's judgment in a positive light. He did not follow up with any discussion of what Zack's responsibility might have been or how he would need to pay his mother back for replacing the bike. Instead, Jon focused on trying to contextualize his biological sons' behaviors, pointing to the possibility of danger to them as a contributing factor to their noninvolvement. At another point in the interview, he returned to an account of how he was trying to help Jason deal with his anger, which I assume was another part of the explanation for why Jason did not want to help his stepbrother, Zack, during the assault. Once more, the details convey the hugely complex practical meaning of good parenting, how the meaning of good and bad shifts with social interaction.

JON: So my biggest challenge with Jason is to parent with consciousness, I guess. I have a lot of guilt about divorce stuff and I think that, I feel that Jason is a lot like me. And I think that sometimes I get a little protective and Tina and I constantly clash. We have this triangle thing, you know, where she thinks that Jason and I gang up on her. It's kind of the dominant theme around here that we can almost count on with Jason and Tina and me.

INTERVIEWER: So how are you working on that?

JON: Well, we have a really nice counselor. She's wonderful. We all see her and Jason has been seeing her for about four months now, something like that. The main thing that we focus on is making much more conscious decisions and talking about how things work out, and when it's appropriate for me to tell Jason that, well, "I've been thinking about this and I didn't really like the way it worked. And this is why I didn't like the way it worked. Do you understand my view? Okay." You know, that kind of stuff. As far as with Zack, I've learned to try to catch myself when I'm feeling a bit warm for him and say, "Hey, wait a minute." I try to get him to, whatever, you know?

Jon's approach to parenting, like Tina's, follows the kind of parenting style researchers refer to as "authoritative." This includes using communication patterns that involve reasoning with children. Parents' influence is preferably rational, not coercive. This is considered by some to be the most effective style of parenting for promoting social competence in children (Baumrind 1991). Like Ann in the last section, Jon also borrows from counseling language to describe the challenges of good parenting. He is focused on parenting with "consciousness" and on sharing his feelings about events when he believes things aren't going well. He hopes that this approach will encourage greater social competence in his sons, which will help establish a positive parenting identity for himself.

SUMMING UP

A son was assaulted, a daughter molested, and a son was stood up on his first date—all examples of children's experiences that challenge parents' abilities to be good parents. Each incident serves to specify the practical meaning of good parenting, informing us that good (or bad) parenting is experienced in the details of everyday life. It is not something achieved once and for all, but is an ongoing challenge in the interactions parents have with children. While clichés such as wanting one's children to be happy, safe and healthy, and independent have an important place in narratives of parenting, it is in accounts of lived experience that the clichés' practical meaning unfolds.

While not discussed at length in this chapter, the parents' accounts suggest that background characteristics affect the meaning of good parenting. Class differences, for example, relate to particular strategies of good parenting, so that a middle-class parent's sense of doing a good job of independence training, say, can contrast with a working-class parent's sense of it. Boys and girls also seem to live in separate worlds in this regard. Gender differences also can produce different experiences for children and contrasting challenges for the parents.

The interview material also indicates that children themselves affect the meaning of good parenting. Good parenting can be located in someone else's hands, in other words. At the end of a long interview, one parent, humbled by having shared the trials and tribulations of her children's lives, made clear that raising children is not completely a top-down affair. Goals and aspirations are thwarted. Things don't turn out as planned, contrary to what the clichés about achieving good parenting would have us think.

> Having a child really diminishes your ego in some ways. I think a lot of time people think, "Oh, I'm going to have this child and this child is going to do everything, and I'm going to do all these wonderful things, and everything is going to be wonderful." And it doesn't always turn out like that and you recognize that all you've done is that you've given another person a life. And what they choose to do in their life is really their choice. You can only hope that you've given some, enough love and support to someone that they can do whatever it is that they need to do. That's all we hope for.

REFERENCES

Baumrind, Diana. 1991. "Effective Parenting During the Early Adolescent Transition." Pp. 111–63 in *Family Transitions*, edited by P. A. Cowan and M. Hetherington. Hillsdale, N.J.: Erlbaum.

Best, Joel. 1990. *Threatened Children: Rhetoric and Concern About Child-Victims*. Chicago: The University of Chicago Press.

Collins, Patricia Hill. 1994. "Shifting the Center: Race, Class, and Feminist Theorizing About Motherhood." Pp. 56–74 in *Representations of Motherhood*, edited by D. Bassin, M. Honey, and M. M. Kaplan. New Haven, Conn.: Yale University Press.

Frustenberg, Jr., Frank F., Thomas D. Cook, Jacquelynne Eccles, Glen H. Elder, Jr., and Arnold Sameroff. 1999. *Managing to Make It: Urban Families and Adolescent Success*. Chicago: The University of Chicago Press.

Garey, Anita Ilta. 1999. *Weaving Work & Motherhood*. Philadelphia: Temple University Press.

Gubrium, Jaber F., and James A. Holstein. 2002. "From the Individual Interview to the Interview Society." Pp. 3–32 in *Handbook of Interview Research: Context and Method*, edited by J. F. Gubrium and J. A. Holstein. Thousand Oaks, Calif.: Sage Publications.

Hays, Sharon. 1996. *The Cultural Contradictions of Motherhood*. New Haven, Conn.: Yale University Press.

Lareau, Annette. 2003. *Unequal Childhoods: Class, Race, and Family Life*. Berkeley: University of California Press.

Marsiglio, William. 2004. *Stepdads: Stories of Love, Hope, and Repair*. Lanham, Md.: Rowman & Littlefield Publishers.

Thorne, Barrie. 2001. "Pick-up Time at Oakdale Elementary School: Work and Family from the Vantage Points of Children." Pp. 354–76 in *Working Families: The Transformation of the American Home*, edited by R. Hertz and N. L. Marshall. Berkeley: University of California Press.

FURTHER READING

Arendell, T. 2000. "Conceiving and Investigating Motherhood." *Journal of Marriage and Family* 62:1192–1207.

Hulbert, Ann. 2003. *Raising America: Experts, Parents, and a Century of Advice About Children*. New York: Alfred A. Knopf.

Lareau, Annette. 2003. *Unequal Childhoods: Class, Race, and Family Life*. Berkeley: University of California Press.

Marsiglio, William, Paul Amato, Randal D. Day, and Michael E. Lamb. 2000. "Scholarship of Fatherhood in the 1990s and Beyond." *Journal of Marriage and Family* 62:1173–91.

Thorne, Barrie. 2001. "Pick-up Time at Oakdale Elementary School: Work and Family from the Vantage Points of Children." Pp. 354–76 in *Working Families: The Transformation of the American Home*, edited by R. Hertz and N. L. Marshall. Berkeley: University of California Press.

Discussion Questions

1. Think about difficult situations in your own family lives involving children. How does the meaning of good parenting play out in relation to the complications of those situations?

2. Children shape parenting practices in their own right. Gender, especially, plays an important role in how parents respond to and manage their children's lives. How might the scenarios described by the parents in this chapter been different if Mark had been a girl, Cindy a boy, or Zack a girl?

3. Not everything that goes on in children's lives comes to the attention of the parents. What experiences have you had, of which your parents were unaware, that might have made a significant difference for their sense of good parenting had they found out about them?

5

Keeping Tabs on Teenagers

Demie Kurz

The mass media constantly remind us that parents are failing to raise their children properly. Mothers especially are held responsible for what happens to their kids, especially for their foibles and missteps. Some argue that mothers now spend too much time at work and are too tired or distracted to supervise their children. Others believe that mothers and fathers, guilty over the lack of time they spend with their children, are afraid to discipline them. The media are especially inclined to target poor and minority women as inadequate mothers who, because of overwork or deficient parenting skills, neglect their children. These views of mothers build on the long-standing and widespread belief in our culture that mothers are solely responsible for what happens to their children. When children encounter trouble, one of the first questions asked is: What did the parents—particularly the mother—do wrong?

Unfortunately, these popular views obscure what mothers and fathers actually do in raising their children. They do not show parents' urgent concerns and constant worry about the welfare of their children or the work they do to educate their children and keep them safe. Nor do the views take into account the conditions under which parents do the work of parenting—the neighborhoods in which they live, the schools to which they send their children. Popular views falsely assume that the family is a contained, protected space, with relatively few outside influences. They oversimplify by assuming that if parents just cared enough and tried hard, their children would do well. These views are based on one-dimensional images of the family where mothers and fathers are in charge and children obey. In fact,

I would like to acknowledge the support of the Philadelphia Education Longitudinal Study and the MacArthur Family Study, Department of Sociology, University of Pennsylvania, in carrying out the research on which this article is based.

children play an active role in growing up and are in constant negotiation with their parents.

In this chapter, I present a more nuanced picture of parents and parenting that moves beyond the oversimplifications and tendencies to cast blame. Parenting in today's society is challenging. Parents worry a great deal about their children's future job and career possibilities as the path to stable, secure work becomes uncertain in the global economy. Parents also worry about instilling good values in their children. Consumer culture surrounds youth through media and advertising in public places and in homes on television, radio, and the Internet, sending messages about violence and sex that many parents find disturbing. In addition, parents are very concerned about their children's safety. We live in a "culture of fear" (Glassner 1999) where stories of danger and violence are reported daily. Parents worry about how to protect their children.

My purpose is to show what parenting is like from the point of view of parents. Rarely do we hear from them. Because it is women—mothers— who have done most of the parenting, it is assumed to be "natural" to them; the efforts they put forth to care for their children remains invisible in the popular media and is not taken seriously. By contrast, I view parenting as a kind of work—caring work. "Caring" and "work" can initially seem contradictory. The word "work" is typically associated with paid labor, is traditionally done by men, and only recently is done by large numbers of women. The common understanding of "to care" is to "care about," to have feelings of love or affection for another person. However, researchers have recently focused on the "caring for" aspect of carework (Cancian et al. 2002) —which includes feeding, bringing together, tending to the sick, raising children—that can be seen as work. As we are coming to understand it, caring can involve multiple activities, practices, and strategies. Certainly parenting children involves a great deal of *caring for*, as well as *caring about*.

In my research, I have focused on the work of parenting teenagers in the contemporary United States. This is an especially challenging time for parents and teens. Teenagers want more autonomy; the older they become, the more teenagers believe they have the right to make their own decisions about where they will go and with whom they will associate. Although parents understand that their children must have more freedom to make their own decisions, they still want to maintain a significant amount of control over their children. As a result, parents and teenagers can sometimes be at odds. My specific focus in this chapter is on the work parents do to keep their children safe. While "keeping children safe" sounds like a natural and obvious part of a parent's responsibility, it involves many challenges and a lot of effort and time to meet those challenges. As I will show, parents don't have sufficient control over many factors that affect their children's safety, including schools, neighborhoods, and social and cultural activities.

Parenting work involves extensive negotiations between parents and teenage children in which each party tries to get the other to do things their way. This is true of all child-parent interactions, but teenage children typically make more forceful demands and are harder for parents to control than younger children. My analysis focuses on one particular area of activity around which parents and teenagers interact and negotiate: control over teenagers' freedom of movement. Parents see control over their children's whereabouts as essential for keeping children safe. I focus primarily on mothers, as they do most of the work of parenting and maintaining families, including families with teenagers. According to Reed Larson and Maryse Richards (1994), mothers are likely to be in better communication with their teenagers and have more emotional connection with them than fathers.

In the first part of the chapter, I describe mothers' fears about their children's safety. I then examine the strategies they use to control their children's mobility and the difficulties they face in keeping children safe. In the second part of the chapter, I describe how mothers negotiate with their teenagers over issues of freedom and autonomy. While my focus is primarily on the work of adults, I also consider teenagers' perspectives to understand better the complex dynamics of parenting.

My study is based on interviews with parents—primarily mothers—and teenage children. I have interviewed mothers from four samples, three of them random samples. Two are from the city of Philadelphia—one of mothers of high school students, one of mothers of twenty-two-year-olds. A third random sample is from a suburban white middle-class community and includes interviews with mothers of junior high and high school students. The fourth is from a sample of upper-middle-class mothers who are professionals and came from different urban and suburban neighborhoods. While these samples are not representative of the state they are in or of the nation as a whole, they do provide data on families with a range of class, race, and urban-suburban backgrounds.

I have interviewed eighty mothers, 61 percent white, 34 percent black, and 5 percent Hispanic. Sixty percent are from the city of Philadelphia and 40 percent are from middle- and upper-middle-class suburbs of Philadelphia. Thirty percent of the sample is single mothers. I have also interviewed twenty teenagers, analyzed data from twenty-five more teenagers, and done focus groups with three groups of high school students and three groups of college students.

Finally, to gain some understanding of the role fathers play in parenting adolescents, I have interviewed fifteen fathers. It is beyond the scope of this chapter to present an in-depth analysis of fathers' roles in raising teenagers. Briefly, my study confirms Larson and Richards's (1994) findings that fathers are not as close to their teenage children as mothers are. In addition, most fathers do less of the work of parenting teenagers. Many fathers do help mothers with the work of parenting teens, however, and many participate in major decisions affecting their teenagers' lives. Some fathers express a wish to become closer to their children, especially as these children approach high school graduation and are likely to be leaving home.

MOTHERS' FEARS FOR THEIR CHILDREN'S SAFETY

At younger ages of adolescence (twelve to fourteen), mothers want direct knowledge of the whereabouts of their children. They often insist that their kids be directly supervised. At older ages, through high school, many still want to know the general whereabouts of their children. Mothers want this knowledge and the control it can bring because they fear for their children's safety. Countless things make parents fearful. For example, violence in the streets and schools make even everyday settings seem fraught with peril. Drugs and alcohol compound the problems.

One woman I interviewed, from a relatively safe urban neighborhood, worried because her daughter didn't take the threat of danger seriously enough.

> A lot of times she doesn't believe that anything can happen to her in this neighborhood. She feels it's the safest neighborhood anywhere. That scares me because I tell her no, it's everywhere. It's in this neighborhood too. You might not hear about it as often, but it's here. And that scares me because she doesn't seem to think anything can happen to her.

Another interviewee, like many mothers, had special concerns about her daughter. (In this and subsequent conversational extracts, R is the interview "respondent" and I is the "interviewer.")

R: I protect her [R's daughter] more.

I: Why is that?

R: She's more vulnerable, more could happen to her. And she has to consider her reputation.

I: You worry about her more than about your son?

R: Yes, although I worry about him too. He's six foot four though.

I: Oh, so you don't have to worry as much.

R: Well, sometimes I worry about what would happen to him if somebody did attack him. They would have to do a lot to him [*groaning*]. But women really have to put up their guard more. They have more restrictions. They have their reputation.

Mothers also fear that their daughters are sexually vulnerable. Not only can they be mugged and robbed—like sons—but daughters can also fall victim to predatory boys or men. They are more likely to be raped or have other unwanted sexual experience. And they can get pregnant.

Mothers who live in unsafe neighborhoods are especially fearful for their children, as the following quote indicates.

> When he's out and my phone rings my heart goes, dear Lord Jesus, don't let it be bad news. That's how afraid I am for him. Now just last year my cousin's son got killed, seventeen years old, over there in [a neighborhood] around the corner from the house. She always tell him, "Stay away from that corner, stay away from that corner."
>
> Now see this is what I tell my grandson. I say, "They don't have to be after you, it could be someone else." He just says, "Oh, Grandmom, ain't nobody gonna bother me. You always think something be happening to people. You shouldn't think like that." He just don't believe me. He just do not believe that he can get in harm's way out there. But I pray all the time when he's out in that street. When my sons are out in that street, I pray too.

Mothers' fears are reinforced through personal experience. Some mothers in my study had extremely serious things happen to their own families or to their friends' children. One inner-city mother's son died of AIDS, which he got from being a drug user. Several young men had been imprisoned. In my sample, poor mothers—who are disproportionately mothers of color— reported more assaults, encounters with the police, and imprisonment of their teenage children, particularly boys, than did other mothers, as well as several deaths. However, although they reported fewer troubles, middle-class mothers also reported serious incidents. Several deaths due to drug overdoses occurred in the middle-class suburb where I interviewed. The niece of a suburban woman in the sample, who lived in a different town, died of a drug overdose. Suburban mothers also reported incidents where police stopped and questioned their children.

Mothers' fears for their daughters and sons are reinforced by their overwhelming sense of responsibility for what happens to their children. Mothers share the widespread belief that children are the individual responsibility of their parents, primarily their mothers (Hays 1996). Parents also have some legal responsibility for their children's behavior. For example, if a child drives a car in a negligent or reckless manner, unless the child drives against the wishes of the parents or purchased his or her own car, the parents incur legal liability for any damages (Arnest 1998). Laws in some jurisdictions hold parents criminally liable for the truancy or delinquency of their teenage children, and certain jurisdictions have statutes that mandate that parents be imprisoned if their children are repeatedly truant (Cahn 1996).

Mothers' fears are augmented by the media, which present news about teenagers in a sensationalized manner, often portraying teenagers as out of control. Despite the fact that the actual level of serious delinquent behaviors among teenagers is fairly low (Furstenberg et al. 1999:50), news coverage leads parents to believe that all teens are at risk of injury. Barry Glassner (1999) has written about the "culture of fear" in U.S. society—the sense of danger that is created by the constant barrage of negative news in the media, greatly exaggerated by those who stand to benefit from an overblown depiction of a social problem. Mothers remember "horror stories" about bad things that happened, or almost happened, to teenagers whom they've heard about in the media.

In this culture of fear, it is very difficult for mothers to assess accurately the dangers their children face. Experts express uncertainty as well. On the one hand, some report that overall rates of serious delinquent behavior among American youth are fairly low. Other reports, however, show that of today's youth between the ages of ten and seventeen, over half have engaged in two or more risk behaviors, including drug or alcohol abuse, school failure, delinquency, and crime, as well as unsafe sex and intercourse leading to teenage pregnancy; 10 percent of these youth engage in all of these behaviors (Lerner et al. 1994; Zill and Nord 1994). Tragically, mortality rates among adolescents have been increasing (Carnegie Corporation 1995), with particularly high rates of injury and death occurring in poor communities.

ASSESSING DANGER

Assessing danger in order to monitor their children isn't easy for mothers. When teenage children "hang out" with each other after school or in the evening, go to each other's houses, or go to malls and parks, mothers don't typically know all or even most of what their children are doing. Mothers worry that because their teenage children haven't had a lot of experience, they aren't necessarily in a good position to assess danger. Further, teenage children also do not often tell mothers what they are doing. As part of becoming older, teens typically want to keep more aspects of their lives private.

Mothers believe the biggest danger to their children comes from their association with the wrong peers—those who do dangerous or illegal things. Mothers fear that taking a wrong direction through associating with a "bad" crowd can lead to serious consequences in which, once a certain chain of events gets set into motion, children go down a slippery slope toward danger. When I asked one mother why her daughter wasn't allowed on the corner, she replied: "Too much happens on the corners. There are all kinds of kids on the corner, you know. Then they start getting involved in drugs and then the next thing you know they're having sex and you know, they're getting locked up because they're drinking on the corner."

In the suburbs, mothers are particularly concerned about empty houses. They fear young people will have parties with alcohol and drugs if they are left unsupervised. Mothers have particular scorn for parents who are believed to leave houses empty. Drugs are a serious concern in all neighborhoods.

Some mothers talk in terms of "peer pressure:" "The peer pressure on my son is terrible. You can tell them all you want in the house. You can talk all the time until you're blue in the face. But when they go out, the group takes over. What you said isn't there."

Other mothers are concerned about particular teenagers that their children are associating with, such as the following mother, who believes that her daughter's friend is a "bad influence." Even though the mother speaking in the following extract doesn't have much evidence against her daughter's friend, she believes this friend has done many dangerous things that she fears her own daughter could be drawn into:

I: Have you ever disliked any of your daughter's friends?

R: Yes and I did tell her about it. I like the kid, but I don't trust her. And I feel that she has a lot influence on her. Like my daughter will come to like me or another friend and ask advice and it's like she's wasting our time. She really doesn't want to hear what we have to say. It's like a courtesy type thing. But she'll go to this girl and her word is gospel.

As is the case with the mother just quoted, many parents fear that, under pressure from their peers, their children will stop thinking for themselves and adopt the peer group perspective. Mothers feel caught in a difficult place. They don't want to worry unnecessarily about their children's friends. On the other hand, as noted, many teenagers engage in what adults believe is risky behavior and there are delinquent peer groups that engage in antisocial, dangerous, and criminal activities, particularly in dangerous neighborhoods (Anderson 1999).

STRATEGIES OF CONTROL

Mothers develop multiple strategies for monitoring and controlling their teenage children, too many to describe comprehensively in this chapter. First, they try to keep their children around home as much as possible, where they can keep track of them. One way they do this is by making spaces in their houses for their teenagers to use—typically basements. Mothers without such rooms or spaces are happy when their children go to the homes of people who do have them. Mothers sometimes monitor their children's activities inside the house, screening incoming phone calls and limiting the number of calls, the hours that children can receive them, and who can call.

Mothers also monitor their children's use of the Internet. They fear the Internet has too much violence and pornography and potentially violent people who prey on children through the Internet. However, mothers have difficulty controlling their children's Internet use. Children are often on their computers, which they need to do schoolwork, and can therefore easily access the Internet and keep in active touch with friends through email, instant messaging, and Internet chat rooms.

Second, mothers try to monitor their children's whereabouts outside the house. All mothers try to educate their children about signs of danger in their neighborhoods. They frequently create rules about where children can go. In the early stages of adolescence, boundaries include only nearby streets and blocks. As children get older, they are allowed to go farther, to other neighborhoods. Mothers also make curfews and typically allow their children to stay out a little later each year. Other things mothers do include watching carefully for signs of alcohol and drugs in their children. One mother laughed and talked about how after her teenage children come back from parties, without their knowing she manages to smell for alcohol on their breath. Some mothers buy cell phones and pagers for their children to communicate with them frequently. Others tell their children they won't fall asleep at night until their children return home, thus increasing the pressure on them to come home on time.

Danger is a ubiquitous concern. Middle-class and professional mothers worry most about alcohol, drugs, and auto accidents. As noted earlier, in the middle-class suburb where I interviewed, several children had died from drug overdoses in the last few years. Poor mothers' accounts feature many more examples of school truancy, violence, crime, and dropping out of school than those of other mothers.

Because of the greater immediate dangers they face, mothers in poor neighborhoods have to have particularly well-developed monitoring strategies. They teach their children to stay away from certain corners, to avoid groups of kids, and to know when "you can just feel that something's going on." One mother spoke of how she and her husband would instruct their children in what to do when they heard the shots of drug dealers. Two African-American mothers who live in the inner city memorize the color of their children's clothing before they leave the house. That way, if they hear of an accident or shooting involving teenage children on the radio or television, they may be able to identify their children.

Unfortunately, many African-American mothers do not feel they can turn to the police to help them if their children are in trouble. They don't trust the police and feel they will treat their children much more harshly than white children. This is in contrast to some of the white middle-class mothers in my sample who, if their children are engaging in risky or illegal behavior (using drugs, stealing things), are sometimes happy when their children have a police encounter. They feel this will "knock some sense" into their children.

Third, mothers try to monitor their children's associates. They make rules about who their kids can spend time with, they try to get their children's friends to come to their house, and they try to get to know their children's friends and the mothers of their children's friends. There is a heavily gendered component to these interactions. As previously noted, mothers worry about their daughters' vulnerability. Consequently, they closely monitor their daughters' relationships with boys. They want to meet the boys, and some make rules that their daughters can't date boys who are more than a year or so older than they are.

In addition to the strategies I have just discussed, there are many more that mothers use to try to control where their children go and with whom. Mothers are in constant monitoring mode with their children, giving them advice on how to be safe, often by trying to be subtle and frame things in such a way that it doesn't look like they are giving advice, because they are afraid their children will "tune them out." When talking doesn't work, mothers turn to lecturing, yelling, or making rules. When rules are broken, some mothers resort to punishments such as taking away something that their children value, suspending their phone privileges, or "grounding" their children, who are then prevented from going out on evenings or weekends. Attempts to influence their children permeate their interactions with them.

Mothers also use more indirect strategies to keep their children safe, such as getting them involved in sports activities and clubs in and out of school. They also try to get their children into private schools. This requires resources, however. A number of poorer mothers in my sample contemplated putting their children into private school, particularly Catholic or Christian schools, but couldn't afford it. A few did and had to withdraw their children because it became too expensive. Similarly, poorer people, particularly single mothers, usually lack the resources to move to better neighborhoods. Housing policies in the United States create shortages of low- and moderate-income housing, a problem that is exacerbated by discrimination against minorities.

NEGOTIATING CHILDREN'S AUTONOMY

Initially, mothers may be able to keep track of their children and help keep them safe most of the time, but as time goes on, their children demand to go out more and more, without their parents. As a result, parents are constantly negotiating how much freedom their children will have. Mothers often compromise. While many have bargained with their children for many years, they must now negotiate more issues, more frequently, and they find themselves ceding more decision-making responsibility to their children. Finally, mothers must decide when to back away from their monitoring and rules and let their children make their own decisions.

Mothers typically believe that children must have some freedom and are somewhat sympathetic with their teenage children concerning rules and curfews. But mothers struggle with how much to compromise and how hard to negotiate and bargain with their children. They agonize over when to make changes and when to allow children more freedom. In the follow-ing quotation, a mother speaks for many:

R: We're willing to compromise. It's not just this is what I want and I don't want to hear nothing. You know, we're willing to compromise and com-municate. Like, you know, if we sit down and talk to her it's not like what I say is rule and that's it. You know, we're willing to hear your side of it. And then we'll take it from there.

I: Okay, so it's taking what she says into consideration.

R: Right. And then either working with it or not but at least we hear her out.

Some mothers compromise on restrictions like curfew hours. This mother, while interested in striking a reasonable agreement with her daughter, frames the compromise as a contest, which she still wants to win:

What you have to do is compromise. So if my daughter's curfew is 10:30, but she really wants to stay out until 11:30, I say all right, you can stay out to 11:00, and then you can be out on the porch until 11:30. So we both win. Except it's me, I've really won. Because I got her here on the porch. She's not down on the corner.

Some of the time, mothers experience a positive give-and-take with their children and are able to come to agreement with them. They make bargains with their children and trust that their children will do as they promise. As one mother said, "We have a lot of trust. I don't know what we would do if we lost that trust with any of the kids . . . if we found them smoking marijuana in their room or something." Many mothers, however, are chal-lenged by at least one of their teenage children. Challenges come at all ages, but particularly when children become teenagers and no longer auto-matically accept everything their mothers say and are eager to go places outside the home, especially to be with friends (Larson and Richards 1994).

Mothers have a difficult time with these negotiations. As one mother said, "It's like they've taken psychology classes and they come back and play mind games with you. And they say, 'If you'll do this, I'll do that for you.'" Sometime mothers question themselves. One mother noted, "My daughter would say to me, 'You're too hard on me, you're not giving me enough space.' I really thought about that, I had to think, 'Is this my fault?' And then after a while, I realized [with feeling], 'It ain't my fault. I am doing the best that I can. It's her.'" Another woman changed her style of discipline and became more flexible to get her children to observe their curfew and follow her rules. Mothers constantly adjust their childrearing strategies as they learn what works with their different children. Based on their experiences, some become stricter while some become more lenient.

When to let children change and do new things can be a parent's dilemma. Mothers are uncertain about what standards to use in monitoring, guiding, and disciplining their children. In making parenting decisions, mothers often consider their own experience. Unfortunately, mothers cannot always rely on standards used in their childhood because they are outdated. Puberty occurs earlier and young people are exposed to the facts of adult life, including sex and sexuality, at younger ages than was common during the adolescence of most mothers (Modell 1989). Further, older authoritarian standards have gone out of fashion and there is no consensus about what should replace them. Mothers worry about being both too harsh and too indulgent.

Finally, while parents gain considerable experience from parenting each child, all children are different in temperament, personality, and abilities. Mothers can't necessarily rely on the knowledge and experience gained from one child to parent another. This is why many mothers don't read childrearing books at this stage of parenting. They feel that their teenage children have become distinct individuals and that most of what childrearing books have to say doesn't apply to them.

Sometimes mothers allow their children more freedom in response to new activities and events that arise as children move through the teenage years: participating in school trips or club activities, going to proms, or getting drivers' licenses (see Best, this volume, on kids, cars, and family life). Sometimes teenagers use these activities to bargain for more freedom. The following discussion illustrates the kinds of negotiations that can take place, in this case around a school play. The mother interviewed here was initially reluctant to give her child more freedom. Her daughter then took the steps to change her mother's mind about attending the cast party. The mother decided to follow her daughter's lead and the outcome of their negotiations was mutually satisfying.

> They [children] are always a little ahead of us and they make us come along. My daughter would sometimes tell me I was inappropriate. But I had to know about things. Like my daughter was involved in theater in high school. She started going to cast parties. She was fifteen years old. I realized there was beer at these parties, and older people, in their twenties. I said to her, "This isn't right." She said, "Yes it is, you don't understand, yes it is, it's fine." Finally, I said, "I'm coming to one of these parties." My daughter

said, "You can't do that. You're intruding on me. These are my friends. I can't have my mother coming to the party. You don't trust me." I said, "Well, I'm coming."

So I first went to the play. It was a terrible production; I had to put up with that. Then I went to the cast party. Well, it was a great group. I could see that the younger people and the older people had a lot in common. They really shared this interest in the theater. And there was no question that the younger people would not drink the beer at all. It was like at our house, when I have people over and the older people drink alcohol and it's just understood that the younger people don't.

So I said to my daughter, "This is great." Then she said, "Why didn't you trust me?" I said "Look, I could have done two different things that would have been a lot easier than going to a play I wouldn't have otherwise seen and going to a party where I didn't know anyone." But this is the way I did it.

Other mothers find themselves in similarly difficult situations. Some live in neighborhoods where teenagers are engaged in unsafe activities. Mothers also know that their children may be doing things they promised not to do, or things they are simply not telling them, but mothers have no way of assessing the safety of these activities. Teenagers may bargain to go to places that are unfamiliar to their mothers. Some parents engage in power struggles with their children, which can generate strong emotions all around, with each party angry that the other will not cooperate. In these conflicts, mothers may lose influence over their children, who simply "tune them out." Part of the skill of bargaining is knowing how to respond to teenage children while still retaining some degree of control and influence.

Teenagers' accounts similarly demonstrate that they play an active role in negotiating with their mothers. As time passes, teenagers not only begin to take the initiative and negotiate for more and more freedom to be out in the places they want to be, but they also become more skilled at negotiating. In seeking more autonomy, some teenagers act much like their mothers, strategizing about how to get what they want, sometimes quite intentionally. For example, many speak of positioning themselves so that they earn their parents' trust and get to do what they want. As one teenage boy indicated in an interview:

You have to compromise. They have to trust me and I have to show that they can trust me, like if I get in a bad situation. It takes time. You have to prove that you are learning things. And another thing is you take into account what they say, that you're not just writing them off because they are your mothers.

The following young woman reported a strategy that involved adroitly framing information and manipulating the timing of its presentation to gain maximum advantage in dealing with her parents:

I: So did you sort of figure this out, that if you did OK on things that mattered to your mother, that then you'd get to do more?

R: Yes, I figured out that with good behavior, I'd get in her graces. If I asked for baby steps, I would get her blessings. If I asked for too much, I would get the silent treatment.

I: So did you like even set things up so she would see it as a baby step?

R: Yes, I did. One time I went over to a friend's house. We watched videos and we smoked cigars. So my mom asked me the next day, how was it? And I said [*very casual voice*] "Oh nothing big, we watched videos, ate pizza, smoked cigars." She said, "Oh fine." Now if I had told her the night before, "I'm going to so and so's house and we're going to watch videos and smoke cigars," she would have said, "I don't think that's a good idea." My strategy was to tell her after the fact. If I told her before, she would say, "Oh, that's stupid."

Some teenagers also mention using humor to get what they want from their mothers, while others speak of trying to charm them into giving them what they want.

In addition to compromising and strategizing, teenagers sometimes just *do things*, without consultation, warning, or regard for future consequences. They simply don't let their mothers know what they are doing and they conceal things from them after the fact. Of course, this doesn't always have the anticipated or desired outcome, as we hear in the account offered by a teenage daughter in response to an interviewer's question about how she got what she wanted in dealing with her mother.

I lied. But that kind of backfired. Like I had this group of friends a couple of towns away. My parents didn't like them and didn't want me being with them. But I had a friend who lived near where these friends lived. So I told my parents I was going to her house. But then we would just walk to these guys' houses.

Then my parents found out. I don't know how they found out. How do parents find these things out? I guess someone saw us. Anyway, they were angry. They said, "You lied, and we're punishing you more because you lied. We would still punish you if you hadn't lied, but it would be less." So I said to myself, "I guess I better tell the truth."

So let's see, after I stopped lying, well, I guess I used my grades for leverage. Like if I wanted to go to a concert and it was on a weeknight and they
said no, I could always say, look I get straight As. So they would let me go.

As teenagers act with increasing autonomy, their power increases and their
parents' decreases. From the point of view of some teenagers, their parents'
control becomes quite limited. As one teenage boy said, "Punishments are
not very effective. You can still do what you want. Like if you have to
come in at 11 instead of 12, you can still have sex before 11. You can still
go out at recess in school and smoke a joint."

LETTING GO

As they compromise their positions and change their views, mothers allow
their children to make more of their own decisions about where they will
go and with whom they will associate. Mothers sometimes refer to this
as "letting go" and hoping that their children will do the right things.
However, mothers often find it difficult to know *when* to let go. In the
following extract, a mother indicates that she lets go when her children
"prove themselves," but she is not clear on when this is.

I: So how do kids become more responsible and take more on?

R: High school is a big transition. And getting a license. One of my
   younger ones is fifteen and he is already studying for his license. They
   have to prove themselves, prove that they are responsible.

I: So how does that happen?

R: I have to be ready to "let go."

I: What does that mean?

R: Giving them more liberty, allowing them to do more things. Like go to
   the movies with friends. Like let their curfew hour be later. You have to
   learn who their friends are. I have to be able to trust them.

Another mother also spoke of "letting go" and the role her husband played
in this process.

It can be painful. Like when you first start letting them go to the store. You
think, "Oh my god, I just sent my ten-year-old to the store with a ten-dollar
bill." But then he came back with the milk or whatever, he came back right
away. He didn't buy a Slurpee [a type of drink] and then stop by and see a

friend. He came back. He is trustworthy. I trust my children. A lot of my control was based on fear. My husband would say, "Let them go." We were a good balance. I was more afraid.

Several other mothers in families where fathers were involved in raising the children spoke of relying on the father's advice about when to let go. On the other hand, several mothers reported that fathers also worried about aspects of "letting go," particularly about letting their daughters go out with boys. Further research is needed to understand the gendered aspects of raising teenage children—when do fathers become involved in worrying about, monitoring, and disciplining their children?

As mothers attempt to let go, children strive for more decision-making power:

Now they are teenagers. Now I have to let go. I thought I needed to protect my daughter more than my son. Well, my daughter started to tell me it wasn't fair. She was being too restricted. I told her I understood. It's because of society. But then she sat me down and she told me that I was being too strict. That I had to let her do more things. Then I changed. I always viewed them as my babies—that I was supposed to protect them. I decided that they weren't my babies anymore. She said, "You can't hold me back." She helped me. I thought I was helping her. The kids see things differently.

The accounts of teenagers confirm that, at a certain point, they stop negotiating and start doing what they want, whether or not their mothers approve. When an interviewer asked a teenager, "So you're telling me that when you're the child, you accept more of what your mother says, but especially when you become a teenager, you do more negotiating?" the teenager said, "Well, what it's really like is that you reach a certain age and you say [*with feeling*], 'I'm gonna do this.' And then my mother says, 'OK, you're going to do what you're going to do. But be careful, watch out for this and that.'" An interviewer asked another teenager the following: "What about how you got more privileges as time went on, how did that work?" The girl replied:

Well, in junior high and the first part of high school, my mother just struggled to control me. Then the summer after junior year of high school, I went to a summer program at a college. When I came back from that summer, they said, "Well, you should be in at such and such a time." And I said, "Curfew, what's a curfew?" I think that when they saw college coming, it was like she's going to be on her own so soon, we won't be as strict. So they weren't, so I'd say around eighteen.

As the previous quotation indicates, age eighteen can be a turning point for parents and teenagers. This is when many young people finish school, take steady jobs, marry, and vote (Arnest 1998). Others go to college, join the Armed Forces, or start their own families. Most mothers discuss these career and life options at length with their children, give them advice, and urge their children to make good decisions. Most are pleased with the way things turn out for their kids.

CHILDREN IN TROUBLE

A smaller group of mothers—many of whom are economically disadvantaged—are unhappy with the way things turn out for their children. Some have daughters who get pregnant during high school, children who drop out of high school, and boys who get arrested and go to prison. Some have children killed before they become adults. The following respondent regrets deeply that her son began to get in trouble even before he finished high school.

R: After my husband's death, one son kept it all in and one didn't. One strayed away and one didn't. It's just the way life is. You all keep on going. He just got with the wrong crowd and got in trouble. Got to stay in jail for it. He only was two credits away from graduating high school. He was only two credits behind. He was the best, he was the brains. He was the one that had all the knowledge and didn't use it right. He had two points, that's all he had . . . and all he had to do was finish school. But he didn't do that.

I: Wow. So what did he get in trouble for?

R: Cars—stealing, sellin', he was in with all the crowds. And he took the rap for 'em. And I mean he didn't do it but he took the rap on himself. So he had to pay the price then. He didn't want to give them up and he had to do it, so that's what he did, he learned the hard way, that's all. He had to learn the hard way.

I: Right. So whenever he gets out, do you think he'll be able to stay away from that crowd?

R: We hope so. Most of them are grown up and a lot of them are married and moved on with their life so there ain't too many of them out here now. Most all of them is growed up. While he was in there serving time they was growin' up. Stuff that they did—but he's the one that was caught with most of the stuff. So he'll come around I guess.

I: Right. So . . . and that took a lot of your time and . . .

R: It took all our time. Family . . . friends . . . and all.

Another mother reports that her child was failing in school because he wouldn't attend classes or do his homework. In addition, he had just had his first encounter with the police. Another woman, whose child was in prison for five years for theft, felt hopeful that maybe her son would get on the right path when he was released because he completed a high school equivalency course in prison. A woman who lost her son to AIDS—which was brought on by drug use—reflects on the homelessness the family endured while her son was growing up and the impact this had on her son.

While middle-class and professional parents report that their children experience school problems and police encounters, the majority of mothers whose children confront serious problems with the law and with school are from poor neighborhoods. Some are single mothers. These mothers talk as if they did everything they could to prevent these things from happening: getting their children into extra classes, finding them mentors, signing them up for summer programs, taking them to school counselors. What, then, accounts for higher rates of injury and death of young people from economically disadvantaged families? Some would argue that poor mothers have inadequate parenting skills—that they failed to learn these skills, aren't motivated to use them, or, overwhelmed by long work hours, don't have enough time with their teenagers. However, based on a systematic study of working-class and poor neighborhoods with a wide range of income levels, Frank Furstenberg and associates (1999) have concluded that there are no significant differences across class groups in mothers' competencies at parenting.

What then accounts for these higher rates of difficulty if it's not competencies in parenting? It is beyond the scope of this chapter to debate this issue, but many social factors disadvantage poorer families. These include many of the things described here: a lack of constructive activities and resources for teenagers, delinquent peer groups that actively compete for children's allegiances, schools that fail to provide students with adequate educations, and minimum wage jobs or no jobs at all. Mothers and fathers, who must let teenage children have much more freedom, face great challenges in counteracting these influences. Poorer mothers may also work longer hours than other mothers and consequently have less time to monitor their teenage children or to involve them in constructive activities. And finally, research has shown that institutions like schools and the criminal justice system are not as responsive to poor parents. They, too, stereotype them as "bad mothers."

SUMMING UP

This chapter has described one aspect of the work of parenting—carework —and the concerns and compromises that go along with keeping teenage children safe. There are a number of skills involved in this type of carework, including assessing danger, monitoring children's activities, managing children's environments, and learning when to "let go." I have highlighted the ways in which this type of carework is interactive, with children playing an important role in negotiating their own autonomy. I have also shown the ways that the environments in which families live influence caring work.

Unfortunately, the carework parents do to prepare their children for successful adult lives is insufficiently acknowledged and appreciated. Parenting is commonly viewed as an individualistic endeavor, dependent on parents' personalities and moral character. This assumption makes it easy to blame mothers—particularly single mothers and mothers of color—for children's problems. It also leads to social policies that fail to address structural problems that plague families. While personality is certainly important, successful parenting work critically depends on safe environment and adequate resources. Without these, parents face serious challenges in ensuring the well-being of their children.

REFERENCES

Anderson, Elijah. 1999. *Code of the Street: Decency, Violence, and the Moral Life of the Inner City.* New York: W.W. Norton and Co.

Arnest, L. K. 1998. *Children, Young Adults, and the Law: A Dictionary.* Santa Barbara, Calif.: ABC-CLIO.

Cahn, Naomi. 1996. "Pragmatic Questions About Parental Liability Statutes." *Wisconsin Law Review* 3:399–445.

Cancian, Francesca, Demie Kurz, Andrew London, Rebecca Reviere, and Mary Tuominen, eds. 2002. *Child Care and Inequality: Re-thinking Carework for Children and Youth.* New York: Routledge.

Carnegie Corporation. 1995. *Great Transformations: Preparing Youth for a New Century.* New York: Carnegie Corporation.

Furstenberg, Frank F., Jr., Thomas D. Cook, Jacquelynne Eccles, Glen H. Elder, Jr., and Arnold Sameroff. 1999. *Managing to Make It: Urban Families and Adolescent Success.* Chicago: University of Chicago Press.

Glassner, Barry. 1999. *The Culture of Fear.* New York: Basic Books.

Hays, Sharon. 1996. *The Cultural Contradictions of Motherhood.* New Haven, Conn.: Yale University Press.

Larson, Reed, and Maryse H. Richards. 1994. *Divergent Realities: The Emotional Lives of Mothers, Fathers, and Adolescents.* New York: Basic Books.

Lerner, Richard M., Doris R. Entwisle, and Stuart T. Hauser. 1994. "The Crisis Among Contemporary American Adolescents: A Call for the Integration of Research, Policies, and Programs." *Journal of Early Adolescence* 4:14.

Modell, John. 1989. *Into One's Own: From Youth to Adulthood in the United States, 1920–1975.* Berkeley: University of California Press.

Zill, Nicholas, and Christine W. Nord. 1994. *Running in Place: How American Families Are Faring in a Changing Economy and an Individualistic Society.* Washington, DC: Child Trends.

FURTHER READING

Cancian, Francesca, Demie Kurz, Andrew London, Rebecca Reviere, and Mary Tuominen (eds). 2002. *Child Care and Inequality: Re-thinking Carework for Children and Youth.* New York: Routledge.

Furstenberg, Frank F., Jr., Thomas D. Cook, Jacquelynne Eccles, Glen H. Elder, Jr., and Arnold Sameroff. 1999. *Managing to Make It: Urban Families and Adolescent Success.* Chicago: University of Chicago Press.

Hays, Sharon. 1996. *The Cultural Contradictions of Motherhood.* New Haven, Conn.: Yale University Press.

Larson, Reed, and Maryse H. Richards. 1994. *Divergent Realities: The Emotional Lives of Mothers, Fathers, and Adolescents.* New York: Basic Books.

Discussion Questions

1. How restrictive do you think parents should be with their teenage children? How much freedom and autonomy should teenage children have? What factors influence how we answer these questions? Would your answers be different if you were a parent?

2. When do teenagers feel unfairly restricted by their parents?

3. What dangers do teenagers face today that might not concern parents of prior generations?

4. Who is responsible for how teenagers "turn out"—that is, whether they succeed or fail? What factors play important roles?

6

Kids, Cars, and Family Life

Amy L. Best

> My mom is glad that I have my license because then she doesn't have to come and pick me up at 12 o'clock and she's not too thrilled about doing that. So, she was counting the days of when I would get my license, I would always say.
>
> Ken, age seventeen

> There's this power that I have to be that I'm able to be wherever I want to be and not having to compromise and accommodate other people's schedules and it's just a really free feeling.
>
> Richard, age twenty

For most young adults, obtaining a driver's license results in more time spent away from family. At the same time, "the license" may also be accompanied by increasing responsibility to family. Parents often expect their teenagers to share some of the work that maintains modern family life once they are able to drive. How young adults encounter the "push and pull" of freedom from, and responsibility to, family is the focus of this chapter.

Concerned with safety, parents can be reluctant to grant greater freedoms to their children (Kurz 2002b). Parents exercise considerable authority especially over their young adult children, placing limits on how they may drive, when they may drive, and where they may go (Gecas and Seff 1991). Yet, the conventional depiction of parent-youth relationships as embattled, while at times fitting, in the end is unable to capture the complexities and contradictions that arise as parents and kids struggle to make sense out of the related transformations in family responsibilities and family roles in contemporary American life. The following discussion considers the negotiations between parents and their adolescent children around driving and having a car within the context of broader economic and social shifts arising from a changing world economy that results in longer hours at work, greater economic burden, and a decline in leisure time (Hertz 1986; Hochschild 1997; Schor 1992). I will pay particular attention to gender and class as forces shaping these negotiations.

I draw from material gathered in focus groups and through in-depth interviews with one hundred young men and young women ages fifteen to twenty-four. All were from a northern California city and its surrounding suburbs. Interviewees were recruited with the purpose of capturing diverse ethnic, economic, and gender perspectives. Participants in both focus groups and in-depth interviews were Filipino American, Southeast Asian American, Chicana/o, Latino/a, black American, and European American. A significant number of participants were second-generation Americans.

NEGOTIATING FOR THE FAMILY CAR

A driver's license carries the promise of freedom and independence for many teens since parents are no longer able to monitor their exact whereabouts. This, of course, is central to its appeal, as Allison, one of my interviewees, explains.

> When I got my driver's license, I looked at it as freedom, getting out from my parents, going places you couldn't get to before because you had to have your parent's permission . . . not having to be worried about being dropped off and being picked up. Going to the library even or a dance club or a party and not having to worry about, I don't know, your parents having to come pick you up. Not necessarily, it wasn't embarrassment for me, it was more, just like OK, I make my own choices I can leave when I want to you know, I made this decision to come here you know I'll drop you off. I felt more like an adult but um, I don't know, I went to the beach, to people's houses, friend's houses, the movies.

Yet for many of these young adults freedom is hard won. One young woman's father expected her to postpone getting her license until she was seventeen (one year older than is required by California law). Once seventeen, she was allowed to drive only when directly supervised by her mother for an additional year. As she explained, "I was just like, basically that one year, it's just like I was driving with my mom like to errands and stuff." Another young man was required by his mother to wait two years beyond the legal age requirement before obtaining his license. In most instances, freedom is realized only after a series of negotiations with parents. Hortencia, a high school student, commented:

My parents, I don't think they were strict, but then again they weren't maybe because I challenged them on it, I mean, it wasn't, when they would say no to something I would say, but why? Here are my reasons why I can do this, what are your reasons? So I kind of engaged them in a conversation and because like I was always totally involved in school when I was, it was just like by chance if I went somewhere, like I didn't, I didn't, for me like, I was never into drinking, I was never into, so I knew what I was doing was fine. After I talked to them they would let me go.

Like Hortencia, most young adults defined these as negotiations where parent(s) were at least willing to listen. Sarah and Christina, both white and female, were two notable exceptions.

AB: Do you have a car?

SARAH: I'm gonna get a car when I have money. Yeah my parents don't like me and they don't like the fact that I would ever get a car because I'm a B-I, B with an itch and I would probably run people off the road, trust me PMS straight out. . . . I'll get my driver's license but no car.

AB: Will your parents let you drive their car?

SARAH: I don't think they trust me.

CHRISTINA: I got my permit when I was fifteen and I had kept wanting to go get my license. I took all the driving lessons and everything. My mom finally decided you know "we'll just put this off, put this off." So when I was eighteen I got my license on my own. Since they [parents] don't have to sign anything. She'd used it as a punishment because I wanted to drive myself to school and work and everything else . . . umm . . . she would say "no, no, no you have to do things my way" and if they weren't done the right way "you can't get your license."

Christina's situation was especially tenuous. Her mother forbade here from using the bus and prohibited her from riding with her friends in their cars, while also not allowing her to drive. Christina was literally forced to rely on her mother to drive her or otherwise be left at home.

Young adults actively negotiate with parents. Yet most see themselves as relatively powerless in these interactions since the car ultimately belongs to the parent. Unlike parents, young adults are expected to justify their reasons for using the car. Usually, they must explain where they are going, with whom, and for how long. After all is said and done, the parent sometimes still says no. When asking to borrow her mother's car, Lucena explains that sometimes, "They would be like; 'No you can't take the car,' but it wouldn't be like for punishment; it's just that they didn't want me to. They didn't feel like it [*laughs*]."

Sometimes parents were unwilling to let them use their car and also unwilling to allow them to utilize public transit, one of the only viable alternatives for getting around for those without a car. A number of middle-class parents perceived public transit to be unsafe, though mistakenly since the city's public transportation was well known for its untarnished record of safety. This was the case for Lenny, who in the end was able to use this as means to negotiate for his own car. "My parents didn't want me to use the bus, it's not safe, but they didn't always want to give me a ride so 'well if you don't want to give me a ride I'm just gonna use the bus and . . . give me a ride if you don't want me to use the bus.'"

The largest obstacle young adults face in negotiating to borrow a parent's car is the parent's busy schedule. Consider Natasha's comments:

> I needed the car and my mom needed a car for work and it was kind of getting difficult where you know if she needed the car on her days off and I would have to revolve my schedule around her and stuff. . . . I was sharing it. It was like between me, my mom and my sister and like, the way it was set up was my sister would carpool with her friend to school and that would be the days that my mom would take it to work and then a couple of days it would be home because my mom needed to run errands or whatnot.

Demands on parents outside the home represent a significant hurdle for young adults as they struggle for autonomy and freedom. This is a fact of modern family life, since most adult family caretakers are also wage earners. Marisol explains, "I started driving because I needed a ride to go to school and they [her parents] can't take me to school, so that's why I started driving. [But] um I can only go to school and back home and they, if they wanted me to do some, like, run some errands or something, they will give me the car."

Time spent away from family, whether at work or school or involved in extracurricular and leisure pursuits, for both parents and their children is substantial and thus complicates teens' efforts to gain access to the family car (Kincheloe 1997). Jorge, who was eventually given his own car for these very reasons, points out, "All of us are so busy. Since I got my own car, we're like three units. 'Cause we have our own work. My mom works in Oakland now. I do all my stuff at school like I said, so I don't get home until 5 or 6. My dad doesn't get home until 6 or 7. We all arrive home at different times we do our own things on the weekend." Jorge's scenario is increasingly common. His parents both work full-time, each commuting well over an eighty-mile stretch each day, and Jorge's life is swamped by the demands of school and extracurricular activities. For middle- and upper-middle-class children struggling to gain an edge in what could only be described as the ever-increasing competitive marketplace of high-stakes education, all of this is a matter of course (Lareau 2003; Proweller 1998).

A RIDE OF ONE'S OWN

Given this situation, it is hardly surprising that many young adults initiate an entirely new set of negotiations that revolve around getting their own car. Mena, the same young woman who had to wait an additional year before getting her license, was eventually given a Honda Civic during her junior year in college. She remarked, "I remember I started telling my parents I want a new car, I want a new car, I totally initiated it." But again, these young adults exercise very little power in these negotiations. Allison explains:

> My parents bought me a car. I used my dad's car for a good year and a half and then my parents bought me a car and um, we went and looked at cars together and I was trying to pick the right color and the right style because I wanted to look good. And then um, then they just decided to get a car and show up with it one morning and um they just showed up with it . . . they ended up getting me a Mazda Protégé, four-door sedan, you know, beige, nice and neutral. . . . I was all excited and just the idea that I had my own car. . . . But um, after a while of driving it I was kind of bummed out, I would see my friends get cars and they got cars they wanted and cars that were cooler. . . . I didn't get what I wanted.

While aware that being given a car by her parents is a privilege, Allison had little say in the process since her parents' preferences won out over her own. Pam, a junior in high school, describes a similar scenario during one of the focus groups:

PAM: My mom's buying me my own [car] right now.
AB: What's she buying you?

PAM: I don't know.

AB: Do you have a say in it, like what you get?

PAM: No. Whatever she picks that's what I get. I don't care if both of the bumpers is falling off she's gonna get it for me.

In another focus group, Lenore, a sophomore, noted:

AB: He's gonna give a car for your birthday?

LENORE: No [not for my birthday but], just because I asked him to.

JEANIE: Can I borrow your dad?

PATTI: Spoiled.

LENORE: I am not 'cause I have to beg him before he lets me get one.

AB: Anyone else, get a car?

PATTI: I wish . . .

Patti and Jeannie look upon Lenore's position with envy. She is, after all, getting a car while they must continue to wait, experiencing life without their own wheels. Yet, Lenore quickly points out that the car was promised only after considerable work on her part. "Begging," a word teens routinely use to describe their negotiations with parents, suggests making appeals in the context of unequal power. In the end, it's a parents' prerogative to give a car to a child as a gift.

LESSONS OF CAR OWNERSHIP

Cars are usually given in celebration of significant milestones, like high school or college graduation. The ability to bestow such an expensive gift is far more common in middle- and upper-middle-class households since these parents are more likely to have the economic resources to do so. Natalie's words are revealing.

AB: Oh, so you didn't get it [a car] when you were sixteen?

NATALIE: No.

AB: How come?

NATALIE: I didn't get it because I was very lazy and the classes that you had to take for that were tedious to me and I was not into that. I was very,

I was the type of high school student that enjoyed the weather a little too much. Didn't really enjoy going to ten-hour classes on a Saturday to learn driving skills so my parents offered to buy me a car and that's when I was getting the motivation to be like, OK I'll do it, if I pay for the insurance and the gas and the tune up.

Natalie's parents used a car to motivate Natalie to change her lethargic ways. Another young woman was given a new Pontiac Firebird for her sixteenth birthday because her parents wanted her to maintain her focus on valued goals.

> They paid [for the car and related expenses] because I was in high school and I didn't have a job, you know my parents wanted me to focus on school and sports and I didn't have time to do a job after that. So that was my job, basically . . . my parents just never like, you know, said don't worry about it.

In either case, parents used cars to cultivate desired behaviors in their kids.

In a sense, getting a car also teaches kids about the economic realities of their families. Decisions over whether to buy a car, what kind of car, and its intended uses reveal to kids how their parents think about spending money, what sort of disposable income they have, and their willingness to assume additional debt. These negotiations are also occasions for young adults to form their own ideas about spending and consumption.

This was also evident in talking with a number of kids about having an expensive car. In talking about other kids they knew who were given what were seen as unreasonably expensive automobiles, some teenagers morally objected. One young man who drove a used Ford Taurus station wagon, which he almost entirely financed himself, remarked, "They're not going to appreciate their car because they didn't work for it, they just kind of got it." A young woman who drove her father's four-year-old Camry offered a similar story: "One of my Dad's friends, he's a doctor and he got his daughter a Mercedes convertible and so I was like, I was a little bit jealous, I was like jeez . . . but then again I don't know, that sounds like you're spoiling your kids a little bit." Almost everyone seemed to have a story to tell about the overindulged child.

> I have a neighbor and she just got her license and she's a junior and her dad bought her a BMW. And I was like "whaaaaat" and I wasn't hating on her like hey, if that's what you're going to get for your first car, go for it. But I don't know knowing that it's your first car most likely, hopefully not, but most likely if you're not an experienced driver you know what I mean. Something can happen.

Another young man, who was given his grandfather's relatively new Jeep Grand Cherokee, made the following observation:

> I find it kind of funny when you know someone who like got a brand new car and totaled it. Then, like, her mom gets her a brand new car, I mean you know, it's fine because, that's what her mom chose to do and everything but I, I don't, maybe she'll get the impression that cars can be, you know just tossed away and you'll get a new one for free.

Conflicting social ideals are enmeshed as this young man and the others struggle to resolve the contradictions inherent in buying a teenage child a high-priced luxury car.

My interviews also reveal taken-for-granted ideas about who in American culture deserves to consume expensive objects. Since teens are generally regarded as economically nonproductive, despite the fact that nearly 70 percent of teenagers work full- or part-time according to the *2000 U.S. Census Report on the Youth Labor Force*, they are often seen as undeserving.

Although some parents were willing to buy cars for their young adult children, other parents expect their kids to shoulder some of the financial burden. "They were paying the payments under their name and I was paying them cash every month for my car. I would pay like $200 and it was like $350 so they would like pay [the remaining amount], you know what I mean," one young woman explained. This was the case for Tony, who learned that the luxury and freedom of car ownership came at a price.

> I was working um, I had got this job through my mother's, one of my mother's coworkers. It was a bad job that's why I'm always thankful that I have a good job now. It was like janitorial work and yeah, so I had to commute all the way from the south side of San Jose all the way to like Fair Oaks, which is in Sunnyvale and it was it was a horrible job but I did that for three months and I just saved and saved and saved and saved until I had like $3,000 and I went put a, got my Probe.

When a young adult helped pay for a car, this sometimes convinced his or her parents that the teenager had learned responsibility and maturity.

> I was like, I think I have enough money where if you guys put the down payment maybe I could make the monthly payments, you know. And then they were just like, hmmm, we'll see, we'll see, don't worry about it . . . coming around. So I used that as an excuse. I was like, come on you know and then I think either my brother got a raise or something, something happened where he, I asked him to help me out. So then we came up with a plan, okay if my dad put the down payment then we would both pay half of the monthly.

And so but they were still kind of like, yeah we'll see, we'll see and then my dad got a new car so I kind of laid a guilt trip on him. So they ended up getting me a car and now I have to pay half the monthly installments.

While some parents are willing to buy a car for their child, they expect the child to cover the cost of car-related expenses. If this serves as lessons in financial responsibility for young adults, it also enables parents to monitor their child's whereabouts and how they spend their own money, since kids typically must have a part-time job to cover these expenses. These jobs consume considerable time outside of school and the money earned often goes directly to cover car costs instead of being spent elsewhere.

A PRIVILEGE NOT A RIGHT: PARENTAL CONTROL

Because parents often play such a sizable financial role in buying and maintaining their young adult child's car, the car can be a means of parental control. Parents frequently revoke car "privileges," sometimes, ironically, for transgressions unrelated to driving. "My dad's actually gonna give me a car this summer but I can't drive it until next year 'cause I kind of got in trouble," one young woman explained in a focus group interview. Andrea had similar experiences:

ANDREA: It was basically kind of like held over my head a lot, you clean your room or you don't get the car this weekend. Always, you know, the car was always taken away if I didn't do what they wanted.

AB: Did you lose your car a lot?

ANDREA: Yeah. I was pretty good but my dad was big on keeping the car clean, keeping your room clean, it was mostly household chores, it was a way to get me to do things and I didn't do them all the time so I would get my car taken away a lot.

Importantly, those kids whose parents did not buy them cars rarely mentioned the use of the car as a resource of parental control.

Issues of control range from mundane everyday matters like doing household chores to high-stakes confrontations. Many parents use the car as leverage in arguments over performance in school and decisions over future career and educational plans. For Augusto, high school graduation was the issue: "Okay my first car I uhhh . . . I got uhhh . . . it was a present to me. If I graduated high school with good credits and high grades . . . so I did. High grades uhhh . . . got a couple of awards and stuff and I got the car." Mike's parents offered to buy him a very expensive car if he agreed to commit himself to his college studies.

> They'll probably buy the next car, half of it or most of it. They're talking about getting me a new car, and getting me the one I want if I do well in college. There's the ultimatum. But I'm totally ready for that and I hella want to. Six years of suffering for an Audi S4. It's like a $41,000 car, that's really nice.

One family even used the promise of a car to draw an alienated son back into the family fold: "I want to get a sports utility . . . my parents said they would help me buy a new car if I move back in so that's another reason I want to move back into my parents' house."

Only parents with the resources to buy a car in the first place are able to use such strategies of control. They use cars to educate their kids about spending and saving within the context of the family economic and social class position. The fact that parents are able, or are unable, to buy a $40,000 car for their child reveals something about the economic context of their lives to their children and the values they carry with regard to status displays and the accumulation of material objects. It is also through these decisions that teens come to think of themselves and their families in terms of class membership and status, since cars are meaningful status-conferring objects.

GENDERED STANDARDS AND PARENTAL CONTROL

Parents often exercise control over their kids "for their own good," but the dynamics and standards for control often play out differently for daughters and sons (Kurz 2002a). Many of the young adults I interviewed acknowledged specific safety-related rules about the number of passengers they were allowed to have in their car and about playing loud music while driving. While kids didn't always observe these rules, they typically viewed them as reasonable because they understood that they were motivated by their parents' love for them and concern for their well-being. Amanda and Mena, two young women, explain:

AMANDA: My parents had like rules.

AB: What were the rules?

AMANDA: The rules were that I couldn't have very many people in the car or the music, always music. Yeah, because there's so much distraction going on. But I did it anyway. It's just one of those things . . . they didn't want me driving, like my sister's friends, they didn't want me want me driving my sister's friends home because they didn't have an OK from their parents in case anything happens and they're in the car then I'm responsible.

MENA: I never got to drive it to school; my dad would not let me drive it to school.

AB: How come?

MENA: Just because he's like, no it's too risky and then your friends probably want, you have to probably pick up your friends 'cause that was a big deal, like, oh pick me up I don't have to go take the bus or something. And he's like I don't want, you just started driving and then they get in the car it's you know, it could be dangerous and all that. And I remember one time, I almost got my mom to let me take the car and not tell him but she got kind of nervous too she's like no, 'cause what if somebody, something happens and then I'm going to be the one to blame, so I could never take the car to school as much as I wanted to.

But these rules and restrictions were not always evenly applied. For example, boys and girls—even brothers and sisters—sometimes faced different restrictions in terms of car use rules, driving curfews, and punishments for traffic violations. Boys typically enjoyed far greater freedom than girls did. Their activities and whereabouts were far less closely monitored. Second-generation South Asian and Latino teens more often cited a gender double standard than did Anglo- and African-American teens. For Mena, a South Asian young woman, gender was especially relevant insofar as she and her sister experienced a set of restrictions that was different from that of her brother.

MENA: My dad didn't want to give us the responsibility of driving. . . . I got it [the driver's license] at seventeen because he knew I would be going to college, I would have to commute so I would be better if I got it then and be able to you know drive and practice before I started going to college by myself. So, he gave me my license.

AB: So, how did you learn how to drive?

MENA: My dad had, he, 'cause I think at, oh maybe that's after a certain age, 'cause you're suppose to take twelve hours or six hours of driving lessons? There's a certain number that has to be but then I went through a school and he had us take at least twenty-four hours of driving school. 'Cause he's so paranoid and so he's just like put us through that . . . me and my sister went through it kind of similarly. . . . But my brother was like, not so much of a training.

Nearly all the young women identified rules their parents had invoked around driving, while only a few young men identified having to obey parental driving rules or getting in trouble when such rules were violated. Jorge was one exception:

> Yeah, I stayed out too late one night. I was out with a girl, stayed out too late and they took my keys away for about a week. I was supposed to be home at midnight. I walked in the door very scared, scared shitless at about 2:30. So, my Pops came out and ooooh, Bronx Puerto Rican at his best, cursing me out in Spanish and English. Took my keys.

Today, parents evidently still need to watch over their daughters more than their sons (McRobbie 1991; Tolman 1994). This has significant consequences for girls' ability to move around public settings and engage in public life. As feminist scholars noted long ago, core adolescent experiences involving risk, adventure, and experimentation remain open to young men but closed to young women since they are often at odds with prevailing codes of feminine conduct (Brown 1999). This may mean that girls remain safer than boys, as statistics on seatbelt use, traffic accidents, and speeding seem to indicate (Williams 2001). Yet this also means that some types of healthy "boundary pushing" are denied to girls. Boys who participate in risky activities face the paradox inherent in socially becoming a man. They face legal sanctions for risk-taking behaviors and often put themselves in dangerous situations. Yet it is through those risky activities that they receive the rewards that accrue to masculine identity.

BENDING THE RULES

Kids openly and actively negotiate with their parents about driving rules, but they also try to circumvent those rules, sometimes ignoring them outright. Many rules are difficult to enforce since parents are rarely with their kids when the kids are driving. Parents are forced to trust their children, and, as one might expect, kids sometimes betray that trust. As one young woman shared, "They told me not to take my friends around but I did; I was the first one to have a car so I took everyone around and it was about fun and enjoyment." Another young woman offered the following account:

NATALIE: There was like written out rules, my dad had typed out these rules, it must be cleaned once a week. . . . He writes them down and he thinks that you know, it's going to work and it never works.

AB: So he like wrote it out as kind of a contract and did you sign it?

NATALIE: Yeah, we both signed it.

Sometimes this involves creative story-telling in order to avoid having to tell the truth. "I wouldn't sneak out. My parents are way too strict. I was just like, you know, tell them I was like going to her [pointing to Adrianna] house and we would cruise; I would never sneak out of the house," Marisol explains. Sandy recounts a similar experience when she crashed her father's car:

SANDY: I wrapped my dad's Toyota around a light post.

AB: Did you get in trouble?

SANDY: Well, yeah but no. I blamed it on my cousin 'cause she was in the car with me and she kind a took the blame cause she is older than me, and so she knew that she wouldn't get in that much trouble anyways.

Efforts to conceal the truth can be elaborate, as the quote from Mena, another young woman, reveals:

I had one accident which my dad knew about and the second accident. . . . I rear ended somebody while going to school and it was because I was putting on makeup so that was my mistake and I totally had to lie and change the story. . . . Then I got in an accident in my new car, it was two days after I had gotten it and I, what happened was I thought this guy was going to go, he was yielding and there was enough space and I thought he left but he didn't so I sped up and I rear ended him. And I was so nervous like oh, my God, what am I going to do, what am I going to do, so luckily he was just like, don't worry, he didn't say anything, he just came out of his car and looked to see if anything was wrong and he just like left, he didn't even speak to me and I remember I was just like crying and I was like, oh my God, oh my God you know. . . . And after the accident I had pulled into a gas station and I thought everything was fine but afterwards I noticed there was a dent in my bumper and so what I went home and told my dad was that somebody hit me in the parking lot. . . . I still remember when I came home I was bawling my eyes out trying to make it seem like oh my new car got hit and stuff . . . maybe, you know, a few years down the line it'll be something to laugh at with my dad. . . . I don't really mind because it's not very visible you know so at least I got away with it you know, so I was happy about that.

When later asked if she had ever been pulled over, Mena comments on another incident: "Yeah, we did get pulled over one time for not wearing our seat belts. Yeah, and my dad doesn't know about that 'cause we sent the ticket 'cause it doesn't go on your record, it's not a moving violation. So we just, I had it sent to like my friend's work and then I just paid it off." Lying or postponing telling the truth until a later date are ways for young adults to manage the contradictory demands placed upon them by parents and peer group while keeping conflicts at bay (Olsen 1997).

It is striking that young women are much more likely than young men to admit to telling these tales. Young men are remarkably silent in this regard. Given this apparent difference, it seems likely that lies and partial truths emerge when parents attempt to restrict girls' access to spaces beyond the home. Like parental rules themselves, these tall tales reveal the role gender continues to play in family life. Boy children and girl children seem to live in separate and in some respects unequal social worlds, where boys and girls are subject to different rules and saddled with different expectations for behavior. Girls must craft elaborate—and sometimes deceitful—plans to preserve the freedom that boys enjoy simply because they are boys.

THE COST OF FREEDOM

Getting a driver's license and a car generally leads to spending more time away from the family as young adult children exercise their freedom. But for many teenagers, getting a driver's license also brings greater responsibility. Mothers and fathers can expect kids to assume more adult responsibilities as they learn to drive. Driving other family members around and running errands were regularly expected of kids. "I have to do the laundry and pick up groceries and stuff," Crystal offered during an interview. Maria had a similar experience:

MARIA: My dad wanted me to take my mom out shopping and take the responsibilities that he didn't want to do anymore.

AB: Did your mom not drive?

MARIA: She never learned.

AB: So when you had that responsibility what were some of the things that you did?

MARIA: Oh, just take her to the store, grocery shopping mostly, yeah, doctor's appointments and all that.

Nan also picked up new responsibilities:

AB: Your parents let you drive to school?

NAN: Yeah. I dropped my sister, my sister didn't go to the same school as me at that time, she was in junior high, so I would drop her off.

Richard, whose mother resides in Taiwan but hopes to visit soon, was encouraged to get a car with the expectation that this would benefit both of them. "I'll be able to drive her around and that seems like something that she really looks forward to," he noted. Hortencia, whose mother was collecting disability payments for a work-related injury and whose father was getting "too old" to drive, conceptualized her responsibilities in terms of her duties as a daughter. She explains:

> Well, the thing is in my situation I kinda had to learn how to drive. My parents are older, my mom is like fifty something, fifty-five and my dad's sixty-six, so they're older and my dad's sick too, and huh, in case of an emergency, I need to know how to drive cause my sisters are way older than me. I'm like ten years younger than my younger sister. So, I'm like really young so I kinda had to learn just in case of an emergency if something happens, you need to learn to get yourself out of a situation or take somebody somewhere.

Hortencia had yet to get her license. The driving she did, mostly local driving helping her parents out "in case of an emergency," was illegal and posed a considerable risk.

Often parents are willing to cover car expenses in exchange for their children providing family carework. This was explicitly the case for Mike: "They paid for everything. They still pay for my insurance. They're covering all that stuff. I just have pick up my sister here and there. I really don't mind because my sister's like totally cool." Lenny had a similar explanation for how he came to have a new car:

LENNY: All I had to do was drive my sister around, like from here to there. So like if she wants to go to dinner, I take her out to dinner and I like pay for it . . . or if she like wants to go to the mall, I'll drive her and her friends to the mall or to the movies. . . .

AB: So, how about the insurance and all that?

LENNY: Oh, yeah! They take care of that too.

Family and childhood researchers have documented the varied and routine ways children contribute to family life (Corsaro 1997). Yet, childhood continues to be defined in terms of dependence on adult family members. While children are primarily seen in terms of the economic demands they place on families, sometimes they are also essential contributors. Along with cars, teenagers can acquire significant caretaking commitments. Responsibility is the family payback for freedom.

CARS AND PARENTAL FREEDOM

For many parents, their own freedom increases when their kids get driver's licenses and cars. Parents may gain considerable time if their young adult children no longer need them to drive them to and from school, work, and other activities. To impose restrictions on kids would result in more restrictions placed on the parents. Mike illustrates this point:

> They really couldn't take their car away from me for awhile because of like the fact that my sister needed a ride to school and I was her ride to and from school. It was a necessity for me to be driving so I always pretty much have my car. Maybe if I were do something really bad they'd take it away for like a week. No big deal.

The parental freedom that comes when their children start to drive is clearly not without its own costs and limitations. Parent often have to be more flexible about driving rules than they would like because they can't afford to restrict their kid's driving. Mena elaborates:

> In high school, my parents were very strict so we didn't really get to go out much, so that was another thing about me taking out the car or anything. . . . I never had the car when I was in high school, so he never restricted us and then he, I don't think he had much of a choice to restrict because when we use [the car] to go to college. We had to commute so if he took the car away from us then [we couldn't get to college].

CHANGING TIMES AND THE CAR

Kids, cars, and family life need to be understood within the context of historical shifts in family roles for parents and teens. Movement toward a global economy and eroding public services for families over the last three decades have created a situation where more family members must work to make ends meet (Ehrenreich 2001; Fine and Weis 1998; Heath 1999; Rank 2001; Schor 1992). Times are increasingly tough for a larger number of families, particularly those with lower incomes: immigrant laborers, single mothers, workers of color, and the downwardly mobile white working class. Making ends meet is increasingly difficult. These families, as they struggle to adapt to changing economic and social circumstances, turn to their teenage children to provide family carework and often wagework that will enable them to survive as families. In these circumstances, driving is a practical necessity, not a teenage pastime or a privilege.

Middle- and upper-middle-class parents also rely on their teen children to run errands and drive younger siblings around. Recall for a moment the scenario Jorge described early in this chapter, involving his family's busy schedule. Like Jorge's parents, many middle-class parents come to see the benefits of getting their children their own cars once they are able to drive legally. Driving a child to and from various organized activities while trying to fulfill myriad professional and personal obligations of their own is increasingly difficult.

To be sure, this is the changing reality parents and children confront as the economy demands longer working longer hours from family members at all income and occupational levels (Sassen 1998; Schor 1992). However, the services young adults provide for those families concentrated on the lower end of the economic ladder are not optional. This work is necessary for parents to generate income. These families are the least likely to be able to pay for childcare, eldercare, or other family services upon which middle- and upper-middle-class families increasingly rely (Sassen 1998). When their kids get cars, they are likely to put these cars to work helping the family.

For upper-middle-class families, buying a car for their teen often means something quite different. These families depend less on their teenage children for family carework because they can afford to pay for such services. Their kids will therefore enjoy greater freedom to pursue their own interests. For many upper-middle-class kids, this will mean greater investments in their futures—investments made possible only by disposable time. Since these kids are often given cars as gifts by parents, they are less likely to have to work to cover the expense of a car. In this way, the car reproduces the very class inequities it reflects, revealing and amplifying the fault lines between "the haves" and "the have nots." For teens living in families "on the fault line" life is harder than it should be.

SUMMING UP

What can we learn about the dynamics of contemporary domestic life from young adults' talk about cars and driving? The preceding discussion illustrates how young men and young women negotiate freedom and responsibility in relation to car use. Their talk reveals their location in the complex web of people and places within which family life is located. Two themes emerge. The first relates to the importance of gender in organizing family rules and roles. The second theme highlights the importance of social class in contemporary transformations of family life.

Gender organizes teenage children's lives in family contexts, even at a time when gender differences are ostensibly diminishing. Teenage children play an active and meaningful role in family decision-making. Still, one cannot help but notice that girls' voices concerning cars and driving were often more muted than boys'. Girls are frequently subject to tighter control and experience more and greater sanctions for normative violations, including those involving cars and driving. Recall the young women who saw themselves as having little negotiating power with their parents or the number of young women who constructed elaborate stories to avoid getting in trouble at home. Recall also that girls were subject to a more rigid set of rules around driving than were boys. The point here is that gender often influences the way family decisions are made. In this sense, gender plays a subtle, sometimes hidden role in family "democracy" that deserves sustained attention if we are to understand the ways in which our lives inside and outside family are constructed.

Social class is also relevant to our discussion of kids, cars, and family life. A family's economic context is a major influence on how much freedom and responsibility go along with cars and driving. The decisions parents and their teen children make together reflect a set of class arrangements that play out in how teenagers are asked to use their driving "privileges" (DeVault 1991; Hertz 1986; Lareau 2003). Lower-income families depend heavily on their teenage children to cope with the economic and time demands of living in a changing America where "getting by" for millions of families often requires holding two jobs, working long hours, and spending less time with families. For upper-middle-class families, a car may be given to a teen child as a luxury or a sign of independence. For families that are less well off, a car may represent more responsibility than freedom.

REFERENCES

Brown, Lyn Mikel. 1999. *Raising Their Voices: The Politics of Girls' Anger.* Cambridge, Mass.: Harvard University Press.

Corsaro, William. 1997. *The Sociology of Childhood.* Thousand Oaks, Calif.: Pine Forge Press.

DeVault, Marjorie. 1991. *Feeding the Family: The Social Organization of Caring as Gendered Work.* Chicago: The University of Chicago Press.

Ehrenreich, Barbara. 2001. *Nickel and Dimed: On (Not) Getting By in America.* New York: Henry Holt and Co.

Fine, Michelle, and Lois Weis. 1998. *The Unknown City: The Lives of Poor and Working Class Young Adults.* Boston: Beacon.

Gecas, Viktor, and Monica Seff. 1991. "Families and Adolescents: A Review of the 1980s." Pp. 208–23 in *Contemporary Families: Looking Forward, Looking Back*, edited by Alan Booth. Minneapolis, MN National Council on Family Relations.

Heath, Terri. 1999. "Single Mother, Single Fathers: The Intersection of Gender, Work and Family." *Journal of Family Issues* 20 (4):429–31.

Hertz, Rosanna. 1986. *More Equal Than Other: Women and Men in Dual-Career Marriages.* Chicago: The University of Chicago Press.

Hochschild, Arlie R. 1997. *The Time Bind: When Work Becomes Home and Home Becomes Work.* New York: Metropolitan Books.

Kincheloe, Joe. 1997. "'Home Alone' and 'Bad to the Bone'": The Advent of Postmodern Childhood." Pp. 31–52 in *Kinderculture: The Corporate Construction of Childhood*, edited by Shirley Steinberg and Joe Kincheloe. Boulder, Colo.: Westview Press.

Kurz, Demie. 2002a. "Caring for Teenage Children." *Journal of Family Issues* 23 (6):748–67.

——. 2002b. "Adding 'Generation' to Family Studies: Studying Families with Teenagers." Paper presented at the 97th annual meeting of the American Sociological Association, Chicago.

Lareau, Annette. 2003. *Unequal Childhoods: Race, Class and Family Life.* Berkeley: University of California Press.

McRobbie, Angela. 1991. *Feminism and Youth Culture: From Jackie to Just Seventeen.* Boston: Unwin Hyman.

Olsen, Laurie. 1997. *Made in America: Immigrant Students in Our Public Schools.* New York: The New Press.

Proweller, Amira. 1998. *Constructing Female Identities: Meaning Making in an Upper Middle Class Youth Culture*. Albany: State University of New York Press.

Rank, Mark. 2001. "The Effect of Poverty on America's Families: Assessing Our Research Knowledge." *Journal of Family Issues* 22 (7):882–903.

Sassen, Saskia. 1998. *Globalization and Its Discontents*. New York: The New Press.

Schor, Juliet. 1992. *The Overworked American: The Unexpected Decline of Leisure*. New York: Basic Books.

Tolman, Deborah. 1994. "Doing Desire: Adolescent Girls' Struggle for/with Sexuality." *Gender and Society* 8 (3):324–42.

Williams, Alan. F. 2001. "Teenage Passengers in Motor Vehicle Crashes: A Summary of Current Research." Insurance Institute for Highway Safety. [Online]. Available: http://www/highwaysafety.org.

FURTHER READING

Best, Amy L. 2000. *Prom Night: Youth Schools and Popular Culture*. New York: Routledge.

Brown, Lyn Mikel. 1999. *Raising Their Voices: The Politics of Girls' Anger*. Cambridge, Mass.: Harvard University Press.

Lareau, Annette. 2003. *Unequal Childhoods: Race, Class and Family Life*. Berkeley: University of California Press.

Lesko, Nancy. 2001. *Act Your Age: A Cultural Construction of Adolescence*. New York: Routledge Falmer.

Gaines, Donna. 1990. *Teenage Wasteland: Suburbia's Dead-End Kids*. Chicago: University of Chicago Press.

Weis, Lois. 1990. *Working Class Without Work: High School Students in a De-industrializing Economy*. New York: Routledge.

Discussion Questions

1. Sometimes we don't really think much about how cars affect family life. How does driving and car ownership affect teens' roles in family life and their relationships with adult family members?

2. In what ways do we see gender roles formed in relation to cars and driving? How do sons' and daughters' lives differently play out in relation to cars?

3. In what ways do changes in the social and economic life of families shape how teens and their parents handle driving privileges and responsibilities? How does social class shape car privileges and car responsibilities for teens?

7

Sissy Boy, Progressive Parents

Daniel Farr

Gender is part of our lives from the very beginning. From early on, children begin to conceptualize and integrate an understanding of gender into their identities and actions (Jordan and Cowan 1995; Rogers 1999; Thorne 1986). Families, the media, and other children continually re-create, develop, and perpetuate regulating behaviors both within and between individuals that work to legitimize and maintain the dichotomous nature of gender. One is either a boy or a girl, a man or a woman. When gender is not evident in this conventional way, there can be disapproval, concern, and even loathing. These responses may torment both girls (tomboys) and boys (sissy boys) who do not conform to dichotomous gender characteristics. Some research suggests that tomboys may be less stigmatized than sissy boys (Martin 1995), but the experience of growing up as a "too masculine" girl does have lifetime implications (Carr 1998).

In adulthood, many of the gendering events that shape one's life have been forgotten or minimized. For most, the act of fitting into one's socially approved gender feels natural—seamless and simple. The social rules about how to behave in the spheres of work, education, and recreation or in the private sphere of the family are so deeply imbedded into our persona we can be unaware of their existence. Not only does one learn how to behave, but how *not* to behave. These rules and norms unwittingly limit us in our daily lives in how and to whom we should speak, how we should dress, perhaps even how we should think if we wish to adhere to our "natural" gender.

Our induction into a gendered world is so deeply ingrained that individuals who do not seem to support the gendered norms of appropriate masculinity and femininity stand out in stark relief. We can be ill at ease if we are unable to neatly allocate individuals the appropriate slots of man or woman (see Lucal 1999). Without being able to categorize individuals, we don't know how to interact or interpret the behaviors, situations, and interactions we are encountering.

LOOKING BACK AT CHILDHOOD

Applying an autoethnographic analysis of my experience growing up as a gender nonconforming boy—yes, a "sissy boy"—offers insight into the social construction of gender and the manner in which gender is incorporated into the various social organizations and structures that guide our lives. As a sissy boy, I seldom interacted with tomboys so I cannot offer insight into their experience, but I will explore facets of my own early experience as an effeminate male to describe the way gender dichotomy affects those who don't readily fit into one gender category or the other.

Critically evaluating and looking back at one's experience offers a rich tapestry of information about the social world. Informed in part by Arlie Hochschild's concept of the "magnified moment" (1994:4), I explore several of the key moments and events of my life that have reverberated through my memories. These are happenings which, at the time they occur, seem to tell it all, so to speak. In the process, I point to the many threads of gender socialization and related power dynamics at play in our society, which, oddly enough, work themselves out in the smallest ways, such as through toy selection and favored books. Setting out to examine my own social history in terms of magnified moments has been both challenging and insightful. These memories, while sometimes painful or embarrassing, offer a glimpse into the times that experience can telescope our understanding of our selves and society. Clearly, my perception and interpretation of these moments are not representative of the experience of all sissy boys, but they do offer insight into the experience of growing up as an effeminate boy in a culture where the two words—"effeminate" and "boy"—are considered anomalous terms of reference.

Looking back to being children, we all can probably recall being called a cruel name or feeling out of place. Fortunately, most of us do find a place or group in which to fit and we learn to cope with those with whom we don't fit. Sometimes we cope by setting ourselves apart from the groups that treat us poorly. Sometimes we cope by demeaning the group from which we are apart. Sometimes we pretend the others are unimportant and don't matter. Sometimes we cope by reaffirming the importance of our own group. Regardless of how we deal with this, we've all experienced these varying social mechanisms at play as we grew up. The scary reality is that we can experience these mechanisms our entire lives if we aren't careful, perhaps without even noticing it.

Looking to childhood, one is likely to recall a quiet boy who never quite fit in. Maybe he was shy. Maybe he was socially awkward with boys but comfortable with girls. Maybe he liked music and art too much. Maybe he was too smart. Maybe he was too fat or too skinny, or not athletic. Perhaps he was a bit too effeminate (girly acting)—who knows what specifically marked him as different, but surely you knew this boy. This boy was probably picked on and teased, perhaps even physically assaulted in some manner, but he was clearly marked as the outsider, the one you knew you didn't want to be—even if he was you. This chapter will examine some of the experiences of one such boy, the trials and tribulations that he experienced, the pains felt, and the victories that can be won. Examining the various moments that have shaped my early life will allow us to explore the numerous manners in which the notions of gender and sexuality are taught, learned, lived, and challenged.

Growing up I was what many might call a precocious child. I was intelligent, creative, imaginative, and "too" sensitive to fit into the social conception of boyhood. I was the boy who was constantly picked on by my peers for being unmanly, for being a sissy, and later for supposedly being a faggot. I don't know that I can pinpoint when I first realized I was unique and different, but I certainly recognized I was not just unlike other boys, but other children in general, at an early age (at least by first or second grade). The path of my unique childhood is not the same as that of all other effeminate boys or even other outsider boys in general, but the various experiences I will examine are ones to which we can all relate in one way or another.

BOY VERSUS GIRL TOYS

As children of the late twentieth century, many of us have a collection of toys and other recreational and educational objects. Coming from a middle-class background, I was fortunate to have a respectable assortment of toys and tools at my disposal, to help ward off childhood boredom. Looking back to my childhood, I don't think my parents took too strongly to the idea that there were specific toys for boys and specific toys for girls. I know my sister got dolls and I got teddy bears, but at the time I only saw this as their giving us what we each liked.

Is this a matter of what we instinctively prefer, or is it what we are taught to prefer? Had I been more like other "normal" boys of my age group, maybe I would have received more action figures and appropriately masculine toys. For example, Transformers were all the rage at the time. I don't recall ever expressing desire for, or interest in, them. My one friend had a large collection of these types of toys, but I never found them especially interesting. The time I spent playing with this friend and his toys was more the result of neighborhood proximity than strong feelings of camaraderie. Fortunately, my parents were able to step away from some, though of course not all, of the categorization of toys by gender. Despite the frequent gender stereotyping of toys by parents (see Campenni 1999), my own parents were more open about the types of toys with which my siblings and I could play. I was thus able to enjoy "masculine" toys, such as Legos and Construx, as well as "feminine" toys like looms and cooking kits. My parents were exceptional in this way. As far as I knew, they never stereotyped my interests. They never discouraged what my peers viewed with disdain as sissy boy inclinations. To my progressive parents, I was simply their son—the one who was good at so many things and who loved his family— not the boy child in their lives.

One of the favorite toys I received as a child was a Fisher-Price loom. It's used to weave yarn into fabric, to make scarves, for example. I didn't view it as a girly type of gift; I saw it as a cool new crafty toy. I still recall the circumstances of receiving the loom; it was an unexpected gift, unassociated with a holiday or birthday. It was new and exciting. As I look back, I can still vaguely see the box. It seems that there was a boy on the box cover. I have unsuccessfully searched online trying to locate a picture of this box. I believe it was a boy on the cover, but it may have been a girl with a "masculine" haircut. This led me to assume that this was a gender-appropriate gift. If there was a boy on the cover, it must have been OK for me also to play with the loom.

The freedom of toy selection I experienced at home was not something I would experience in school. One winter, in second grade, my class had a holiday party and a gift exchange. On the day of the big party, we each drew numbers for the gifts that were sorted as being either a masculine toy or a feminine toy. I was lucky in that I drew the number for the biggest box! After all the boxes were distributed, the tension grew as we all opened our gifts at the same time. My initial excitement of receiving the biggest box was squelched when I opened it to find a Nerf football. I was disappointed; I had no clue about what to do with it. I had grown up in a household where sports were rarely, if ever, watched on TV. I promptly made a trade for a cool dinosaur kit where you could put the bones together to build a T-Rex. I loved building that T-Rex and kept it for many years, but the boys of my class branded me a "wuss" because I didn't want the football. One would think that bones and dinosaurs would be adequately masculine, but a football superceded this in the toy-related hierarchy of masculinity in the classroom.

HOBBIES AND BOOKS

Through much of my childhood I had an interest in artistic endeavors. Despite my parents' lack of concern for gender-appropriate toys and interests, I soon became aware of the gendered division of hobbies and how to regulate and manage the public (school) and private (home) side of this. I had grown up with parents who both enjoyed arts and crafts. From as back as I can remember, my mother had sewn, quilted, crocheted, and cross-stitched. My father also had interest in crafts, particularly working with wood and stained glass. Given the dangers innate to a wood shop, I was primarily exposed to the fiber arts with which my mother was working. From an early age, I found her hobbies intriguing and was eager to learn. I was six or seven when my mother showed me how to cross-stitch. Her efforts to teach me didn't work out very well. I had a hard time emulating what she was doing. I ultimately did learn to cross-stitch from a book. I can still remember the first piece I stitched of a little brown bear.

Looking back, I now know that my interest in cross-stitch must have been challenging for my parents. Sewing is culturally regarded in our society as a craft for women. I feel it was quite progressive of my parents not to have told me "cross-stitch is for girls" and push me toward stereotypical masculine pastimes. I even recall my father's positive support for my first little project. My parents never instilled shame or embarrassment in me because of my "feminine" hobbies.

Early in my school years, I found great joy in the world of books. I became a hungry little reader, taking out as many as three books a week from the library—a heavy stack for such a little person. At the pace I worked through the library books, it was inevitable that I would hit upon books that boys "shouldn't" read. I recall one series of books where a doll traveled to different places around the world. I don't recall ever having an interest in dolls as a child, but I enjoyed those books because of the travel aspect and the exposure to different cultures and places.

The other children in my class did take notice. Since boys aren't supposed to read books about dolls, I used to hide them from my classmates. I don't recall if they teased me about this, but I knew, even at that age, that these were books for girls. Further reflection upon these books makes me wonder about my parents' response. I don't remember any. As far as I can recall, my parents never made any negative or derogatory comment about it; they simply supported my interest in reading, even if my books weren't really boy books.

Later, in this same library, I discovered a children's series of biographies where I was exposed to individuals such as Abraham Lincoln, Martin Luther King, Jr., and Thomas Jefferson. These books were most certainly appropriate for a boy. I checked out a new one every week. One week, I got one about a woman, for which I received a great deal of harassment from my male classmates. Over and over, I heard, "Why would you want to read about a girl?" I was embarrassed and dejected. Helen Keller remains the only woman from the series about whom I ever read. It's odd how a simple act of reading about a woman can put one's masculinity at risk.

A growing interest in arts and crafts, combined with my love of books, led me to borrow various arts books. Initially, I was vaguely familiar with the craft of crocheting, having seen my mother working with the funny hooked needle. I was curious, so this was the topic of the first of these books I borrowed. I took the book home and taught myself how to crochet, making a white washcloth.

I was proud of that little project, so I took it to school for show-and-tell. This led to another magnified moment, in which I learned one of the harshest lessons of my gender socialization. My classmates picked me on endlessly. I was beginning to see that there were certain hobbies and activities that I might be interested in and had talent in doing, but which could never be shared with the kids at school. The teacher was supportive and said what a nice job I had done, but the kids were cruel. I was confused. After all, we all took the same art classes. How was this different? I had no idea that this wasn't stuff I was supposed to be doing. I had two options: give up this hobby entirely or continue it at home and keep it secret from my peers. I chose the latter.

At first blush, the library would seem to be gender-neutral territory, a place of knowledge and entertainment. But this is gendered too. A boy must be careful not to overstep the boundaries that define appropriate masculinity. One is constricted by the gendered information we are taught by peers, teachers, and families. While adults certainly have a profound influence upon youth, it also seems that much of the gender policing of boys is accomplished by their male peers. Girls, who may participate in taunting and harassment in conjunction with other boys, are unlikely to police and taunt boys for feminine behaviors or interests on their own (Zucker et al. 1995). In my experience this was true. Girls were much more willing to accept my interest in art and the books that they may have also read, and they enjoyed discussing them with me. This probably helped lay the groundwork for my ability to establish friendships more readily with girls than with boys.

MOVING ALONG IN SCHOOL

The lesson learned about what constitutes an appropriate book extended beyond the library to schooling. There is an expectation that both girls and boys in our culture will attend schools, but the types of involvement and the interest demonstrated by the differing genders is regulated differently. Subjects and information taught and presented to children help to reinforce conceptions of masculinity and femininity, as well as power, in our culture. Subjects that have the connotation of being of "lesser" importance, such as handwriting, tend to be associated with the feminine. Thus, it may be socially expected that girls will earn higher grades than boys in such subjects. People notice the "girly" writing of a man who writes nicely. The social construction of gender also reaches out from the books of the classroom to suggest that there are subjects, topics, and careers that are for girls and others that are for boys.

By the fourth grade, I was selected to join my school district's Academically Gifted Program (AGP). This became another nail in the coffin of my popularity. It's strange how as children we tease and insult both the overachievers and the underachievers. I yearned through those years to merely be "average." Alas, I was not, as I was in a special program where I was permitted to leave my regular school one whole day a week and ride a bus to another school to interact with other "gifted" students in a special class. We had access to various academic and activity-experience opportunities. It was a good experience while I was at AGP, at least initially. This was the first time that I had a chance to mingle with peers who seemed to be at my own intellectual level. I also was no longer the main target of harassment in my class. I was grouped with those who I can only assume were also targets in their own schools. In a funny kind of way, it was a rewarding to be grouped up with the other nerds, geeks, sissies, and weirdos, one of the first times I didn't really feel alone.

Children can be incredibly cruel and I was an easy target, being in a gifted program, being a bit pudgy, being too effeminate, and wearing glasses.

It was in fourth grade when I first tried to go on a diet in hopes of fitting in better with my classmates. I knew to hide this from my peers because, as with so many other things in my world, being on a diet was something girls did, not boys. So even in my aim to fit in better, I was trying to get there by way of nonmasculine approved routes (though as adults we know that both men and women go on diets).

During those years of fourth through sixth grade, I found myself becoming increasingly isolated and distant. I was a sad child in many ways. I spent a lot of time reading and doing artistic projects by myself. I struggled with the emotional limitations of schooling, with my inability to fit in with my peers. I spent many nights hiding under my quilt in bed crying about it. I simply could not understand why my peers held such a negative view of me. I tried to reason the circumstances away as being the result of superior intellect, but this didn't work. I'm sure it was not an easy thing for my parents to see me so sad, so I also tried to keep it hidden from them. (Isn't that what boys are supposed to do?) I sought to reconcile some of the emotional strain of the situation by withdrawing and convincing myself that I was fine alone.

Having relocated to a new town toward the end of sixth grade, I merged into the life of junior high school much like my peers. We were all new to the school, with an equally low status in the grade hierarchy, all seeking to establish our standing in the local scheme of things. I was placed in all the advanced classes that were offered. While this was great in that I was with a group of intellectual peers, I also was separated from the majority of my classmates, who I only met in gym, chorus, and maybe in the cafeteria.

During the seventh grade, all students were required to take a home economics class. For the first time, I was able to flaunt my domestic abilities with a needle and thread as well as in the kitchen. From a young age I had learned to cook, in part because of personal interest, but also in part because I was a Cub Scout. I no longer had to hide the fact that I could cook and sew from my peers, but I did have to be careful in showing how much I knew and how much I enjoyed these activities. I ended up being at the head of my class for home economics and even started helping other students with some of the sewing and embroidery assignments. It was the first time that the feedback I was receiving from peers was not reinforcing the negative associations of my gender identity in connection with stereotypically feminine activities.

Because the course was required and I was part of a class of high-achieving students, I wasn't seen as a boy participating in feminine activities.

Instead, I was just a student who was doing well in class. But as soon as the semester in home economics ended and I entered the wood shop class, I had to send my domestic abilities and interests into the gender closet. This produced another magnified moment, this time highlighting how quickly valued abilities in one context can became a source of embarrassment and taunting in another.

Heading into wood shop, many of my peers expected that I would be uncomfortable and fall flat on my face. I surprised them when they learned that I actually knew as much or more about the tools and equipment as they did. All the time I had spent with my father in the garage had paid off. I was a competent woodworker and did just fine in making the semester's big lamp project. One might think that the ability to fulfill both the roles and tasks traditionally classified as feminine and those classified as masculine would have been regarded positively by my peers. Unfortunately, this was not the case; the dichotomous nature of gender reared its head once again. While both my feminine and masculine skills required similar abilities— precise measurement, the operation of machines (be it a sewing machine and mixer or a table saw and drill press), envisioning how differing parts or different ingredients work together to create a final product—the incongruity across situations of being a boy who was successful in the feminine tasks was unacceptable. We seem more likely to recognize difference while remaining blind to the similarity that is demonstrated by differently gendered youth (Messner 2000). This is especially true for boys who demonstrate "feminine" skills.

I was never blessed as a child with good hand-eye coordination or balance; I was a "big 'ole klutz." Early on, I learned to dread gym class, in part because of a disinterest in athletics and in part because of my peers' responses to my lack of athletic prowess. There were, of course, some things I loved about gym class, such as the little wheelie carts for scooting around, dodge-ball, playing with the big parachute, and square-dancing, which I adored. Another magnified moment unfolded at this time. It was a Wednesday and we had gym in late morning, right before lunch. My second tooth was loose. It had gotten to that cool stage where you could spin the tooth round and round, but it held tight by a single thread. It was climb-the-rope day. To me, the rope was the very worst part of the gym classes. I did not have the upper body strength to climb the rope; I even had problems with the interval knots. I was waiting in line, spinning that tooth with all my might, and it finally came out when there was just one person remaining between me and the dreaded rope. I felt tremendous relief in being able to avoid the rope and go to the nurse's office. But I also knew this could have been a gender-defining moment.

In those early years, in addition to scouting, my parents also offered me the opportunity to join various local youth sports teams, like baseball. My one sister and I had both taken swim lessons when we were young and enjoyed that greatly, but the thought of an organized team sport didn't appeal to me. As it was, I was already spending enough time figuring ways to get out of gym class. But my parents never forced these opportunities on me. They surely knew that I was not the most masculine boy, but they never demeaned me for lacking an interest in sports. Actually, in contrast to many of my classmates' parents, my own parents weren't very interested in sports. Organized sports were rarely, if ever, seen on television in my house. One could argue that this could have "caused" me not be interested in sports, but this is unlikely considering that both my siblings participated in various sports in their youth.

When I was about six years old, I had another of those eye-opening experiences (another magnified moment) during which I began to under-stand some of the "real-world" differences between males and females. I had mastered riding my bike with training wheels and was finally ready to move on to riding without them. At the time, I was only allowed to bike back and forth on the sidewalks on either side of my house. Two sisters, Ann and Stella, lived in the house on the left and had a driveway that was perfect for turning around. In the transition to riding without training wheels, one of the hardest parts is learning to turn, continue to stay upright, and keep going where you want to go. At the side of Ann and Stella's drive-way was a large bush. During one of my first efforts to turn around, I turned abruptly, crashed into their bush, and simultaneously learned what happens when a hard object—like handle bars—hits a boy in the groin. I was stuck, entangled in both the bush and bike, and in tremendous pain. I cried and was very upset, of course. Who knew that such an occurrence could hurt so badly? As I was a modest child, I was embarrassed by the entire incident. I knocked on Ann and Stella's door to apologize for breaking branches on their bush. They took me very seriously, inspected the bush, and actually thanked me for having broken out the branch that had some rot on it. (At least, that was their story). I was so relieved. I eventually mastered the act of turning on my bike with not too many scars to my ego or body, but my neighbors' support and understanding stayed with me.

Third grade brought my first regular visits to the playground. Of course, we had gone outside to play in the past, but it had been intermittent, as the big kids in higher grades were "too wild" and might hurt us. While it is common for children to create single-sex play groups (Martin and Fabes 2001), I found I was more comfortable playing with the girls. They were less violent and didn't always talk about the stereotypically masculine toys about which I had little knowledge or interest. I didn't fit in well and was picked on and posited to the lowest boy status. However, with the group of girls, I was able to be one of the leaders and had a lot of social support from them. I learned how to play cat's cradle at lunch, got to just relax and sit and talk in the sun at play time, and competed on the swings for who could go highest and jump off.

The dread of gym class persisted throughout my junior and high school years. My gym class loathing was reinforced one year when I was placed with students two years my senior because of my academic and choral schedule. That was a very rough year of gym class for me. As one might suspect, my classmates (who seemingly comprised the majority of the football team) were not pleased to have to count me among them. Making matters worse, the gym teacher "inadvertently" mentioned that I was in a class of seniors "because of chorus." Involvement of any male in choir was regarded with disgust by most the boys of my school.

I had learned to deal with the psychological harm accompanying this masculine departure, but that year I understood that gender violations could also result in physical pain. That fall, one of the games of flag football, which was supposed to be noncontact, resulted in my first cast. This was the first concrete example of my life in which the disapproval of my gender portrayal by my peers, together with the bolstering disapproval of adults (my gym teacher), caused me real harm. I had always wanted to believe that each of my classmates felt different and out of place to at least some degree, but from that point on I became increasingly critical and distant from my peers and even wary of the adults in my school. I was disappointed that adults would not present a better example for students, but I now recognize that deeply imbedded categories of masculinity are part not only of youth culture but of adult culture as well.

Athletic interest and involvement has long been held a bastion of masculinity. Being a successful athlete enables men/boys to affirm and define who and what they are, especially in opposition to femininity (Connell 1995; Messner 1992). Having had little athletic interest or skill as a child (and I still don't today), my experience of masculinity was problematized in this regard by my peers as well as the adults of my world. I had become a large-bodied, strongly built youth, with the quintessential football figure.

The idea that I was disinterested in the football and wrestling teams seemed utterly foreign to my athletics teachers.

CUB SCOUTS AND MASCULINITY

While I didn't participate in organized sports in my youth, I did become involved an organization that is commonly regarded as a cornerstone of masculine childhood socialization, the Cub Scouts. I do not recall if I joined of my own volition or if I had been encouraged to do so by my parents. Looking back, I can see how I might initially have perceived Cub Scouts as the "in thing" to do, but I can also see how my parents, like many other parents, may have been encouraged to involve their sons in activities such as this. My scout troop was small because of the area where I lived. It was just me, Gus (a boy who was even more of an outsider than myself), and Brian (whose dad was our pack leader). Such a small pack was limited in the activities it could undertake. I remember the occasional craft projects and the emergence of my competitive nature as I sought various beads and patches that marked one's ranking and skill as a scout. As the years passed, I obtained quite a few badges, but I did not find the overall experience fulfilling.

While "character development" is the first purpose of scouting, I do not know if I experienced much of this within the scouts or if, instead, I was encouraged to regard certain behaviors, activities, and characteristics as masculine and thus appropriate, or feminine and thus inappropriate. There were many conflicting messages in this regard. While we primarily participated in "masculine" activities such as woodworking, nature and environmental appreciation, and various competitions such as the building and racing of small wooden cars, we also had an annual cake-baking contest. Fathers and sons were to bake cakes without the help of a mother to raise funds for the troop. At the time, I did not understand why my mother wasn't allowed to help with the cake. I felt that since my mother did most of the cooking and baking at home, she would be the appropriate parent for the task. In other scouting tasks, such as seeking patches, my mother was able to help, so why couldn't she here? The annual cake-baking contest was in many respects a magnified moment, an affirmation for me that men and women were in opposition in our society. To be a real man meant to be separate and independent of girls. Any task a woman could do, a man could do better—if he wanted to.

I eventually left the Cub Scouts, just before advancing to Boy Scouts. My parents encouraged continued participation, but I asserted that I was not

enjoying the activities, especially given the shortcomings that resulted from
my troop's small size. My parents sympathized and allowed me to make the
final decision; I always appreciated the choices they allowed me to make.

COOKING AND CLOTHING

While there were conflicting messages conveyed in the cake baking of
Cub Scouts, it didn't reduce my interest in cooking. I found I loved mixing
and making things in the kitchen. It amazed me that you could put various
ingredients together, add heat, and presto! I first learned the miracles of
kitchen chemistry through the use of Bisquick. I would get up early on the
weekend, not only for the cartoons, but also to make pancakes for the
family. I became quite skilled at it, even though it took many bad pancakes
to master the timing. My parents were always encouraging, and around the
age of seven or eight I received my first cookbook. I still recall the gleam-
ing red plaid cover of my little *Better Homes & Gardens* kids' cookbook. I
loved that book and have kept it. The first real thing I ever made from it was
potato salad, which was a hit with the family. Despite all the comfort and
praise I received from my family for my cooking, and despite my cookbook
having pictures of both boys and girls, I somehow knew that this was not
something I should mention at school. I was already labeled an outsider; no
need to add fodder to my peers' ammunition.

It is odd how, as children, we receive such mixed messages about what
establishes various tasks as masculine or feminine. We often see our parents completing similar tasks, at least on occasion. If raised in the home
of a single parent, with all the adult tasks needing to be accomplished by
that one parent, how is it that certain tasks and skills are then demarcated
masculine or feminine? I recall most cooking and kitchen tasks being
done by my mother, but I can also vividly recall occasions when my father
cooked and worked in the kitchen. We probably all experience childhood
in this way, but at the same time we create a cultural understanding of
gender through the subtle messages surrounding us, such as that while
both men and women cook, kitchen and cooking are gendered feminine.

During my early adolescence, like most of my peers, I became fashion
conscious. I aspired to dress in style and to fit in. I was never quite able to
pull it off. When I was in junior high, I had a pair of jeans that caused me
problems and sparked a new wave of taunting. When I sat, the jeans would
bunch up in front, causing the zippered area to visibly bulge. At the time,
we were having our first big sex education sections in health class. All the

sex talk combined with my bulging jeans and led one of my male classmates to ask me loudly whether I was gay because I was allegedly looking
in his direction while sexually aroused. I was completely embarrassed and
angered, prompting another magnified moment.

Regardless of my response, I was branded. No longer was I just a nerd,
geek, and sissy boy, but I was to become the gay boy of the class. The
months that followed were horrendous. Despite assertions to the contrary,
no one listened. Being regarded as gay was the worst thing anyone could
be branded.

DATING, SEX, AND COLLEGE

In time, I became increasingly aware of dating and sex. However, unlike
many of my peers, I did not date. I had crushes on some girls, but given my
outsider and stigmatized status, it did not seem likely that I could get a
date. The combination of rumors that I was gay; my participation in music,
art, and theater; and my academic achievements put me in a tough spot.
Socially, I did spend some time with a small group of my classmates, much
of it during lunch. It was reassuring to have some bonds with a group of
other nerds, sissies, and outsiders of both genders. Few members of this
group dated or were sexually active as far as I knew, and we were all dis-
paraged to varying degrees by the "populars."

High school is not an easy journey. It is particularly difficult if you
do not adhere to established gender norms. Even though those norms are
sometimes unclear, and the ability to cross the borders of gendered behavior is occasionally warranted, there is privilege associated with adhering to
normative gender behaviors. In our society, we privilege those who clearly
demark their heterosexual status by having a romantic partner of the
opposite sex. This affirms one's gender identity as appropriate. An appropriately masculine male should be emotionally and erotically oriented to
appropriately feminine females. Sexuality especially seems to supercede
the other gendered markers that we take into account when viewing another
person. Had I been more inclined to date or establish a heterosexual relationship in my teen years, perhaps my journey would have been less painful.

College offered me a clean slate on which I hoped to write a new story.
After years of being labeled and taunted for not being masculine enough,
I found college to be a liberating experience. I had visions of being a new
person, a man who would be masculine and free of taunts and labels, someone who would leave behind gender-bending attributes. But I found I could

not be anyone other than who I was—a man who enjoyed sewing and quilting, a man who loved to cook, a man who enjoyed art and music, and a man who became immersed in the soap operas the girls would watch at lunch time. College was a world away from the one I had known. Not only was I no longer picked on, teased, or taunted, but I was fully accepted by my floormates, classmates, instructors, and coworkers. With this new freedom, I became more confident and outgoing. Those unique "nonmasculine" activities and interests that had confined me as a youth now worked to my benefit, making me special. I reveled in newfound popularity with my peers and found the obstacles that had impeded dating in the past were now all but gone.

THEN AND NOW

As the years have passed, I have often reflected on my past and contrasted my own experience with that of other men with whom I've spoken. I have realized my parents were far more progressive than I had imagined, providing me with a regular refuge at home to be myself. In our culture, the acceptable expressions of masculinity are quite restrictive, but my parents somehow managed to establish an environment that offered flexibility. My parents are not psychiatrists; they had not even acquired college degrees when I was growing up. But they supported my own, as well as my siblings', choices to live our lives as we chose, to be the individuals we preferred. I believe it is their acceptance and support that made my childhood successful despite the odds.

Today, I am proud to admit that I still partake in many feminine stereotyped activities. I no longer feel shame for the ways that I challenge the stereotypes of gender. Yes, I am clearly a man. I dress in appropriately masculine clothes. I wear my hair in a masculine style. I am "masculine" in many ways. Yet I suspect my sexual orientation is often in question. Many may wonder—am I gay or am I straight? Were all those taunts and teases of my youth correct? I actually find this to be humorous, something reflecting the need for clear dichotomies. Perhaps some readers did not question my sexuality as they read this chapter, but I suspect that most did, given the "demasculinizing" title of the chapter and the various masculinity-challenging behaviors exhibited throughout my life. I know that I challenge the conceptions of masculinity in numerous ways, but nearly every man challenges our stereotypical beliefs of masculinity in some manner. In practice, gender for many is an endless range of grays.

Yes, many gay men do express recollections of a childhood in which they experienced masculinity in problematic and stigmatizing manners (Savin-Williams 1998). There also are many gay men who experienced a fairly nonproblematic masculine gender identity as they grew up. We see little problem in questioning the experiences of gay men, presuming that somehow their gender inclinations are clear, but we rarely question the gender of heterosexual men whose gender depictions challenge our conceptions of masculinity.

Does it matter? Why do we tie together gender and sexual orientation—are they really the same thing? Don't you, yourself, know individuals whose gendered behavior and depiction do not align with our stereotypical beliefs about homosexuality and heterosexuality? Why do we stigmatize and label the sissy boys of our culture as gay but are more accepting of tomboys? There are tomboys who grow up to be heterosexual women and there are tomboys who grow up to be homosexual women. The same is true for sissy boys. Is masculinity so much more valuable than femininity? This sissy boy has grown up, and I have been fortunate to find a wonderful person to share my life—a progressive individual like my parents who supports my interests and abilities and loves me for the sissy boy I am.

SUMMING UP

Based on my own social history, I have examined the experience of growing up as a boy/man who embraces stereotypically feminine activities. Through this autoethnography, some of the complexities of socialization have been examined for those who are different. Looking at the education system, one of the primary socialization environments for youth, we can readily recognize the mechanisms of peer policing and gender regulation, which are further linked with society at large. Individuals who do not adhere to dichotomous definitions of masculinity or femininity are often stigmatized, considered polluted and suspect. Negative responses often conflate sexuality and gender, whose magnified moments showcase difference.

REFERENCES

Campenni, C. Estelle. 1999. "Gender Stereotyping of Children's Toys: A Comparison of Parents and Nonparents." *Sex Roles* 40:121–38.

Carr, C. Lynn. 1998. "Tomboy Resistance and Conformity: Agency in Social Psychological Gender Theory." *Gender & Society* 12:528–53.

Connell, Robert W. 1995. *Masculinities*. Berkeley: University of California Press.

Hochschild, Arlie Russell. 1994. "The Commercial Spirit of Intimate Life and the Abduction of Feminism: Signs from Women's Advice Books." *Theory, Culture & Society* 11:1–24.

Jordan, Ellen, and Angela Cowan. 1995. "Warrior Narratives in the Kindergarten Classroom: Renegotiating the Social Contract?" *Gender & Society* 9:727–43.

Lucal, Betsy. 1999. "What It Means to Be Gendered Me: Life on the Boundaries of a Dichotomous Gender System." *Gender & Society* 13:781–97.

Martin, Carol Lynn. 1995. "Stereotypes About Children with Traditional and Nontraditional Gender Roles." *Sex Roles* 33:727–51.

Martin, Carol Lynn, and Richard A. Fabes. 2001. "Research Cited in Marianne Szegedy-Maszak's 'The Power of Gender.'" *U.S. News & World Report* 130 (22):52.

Messner, Michael. 1992. *Power at Play: Sports and the Problem of Masculinity*. Boston: Beacon.

——. 2000. "Barbie Girls Versus Sea Monsters: Children Constructing Gender." *Gender & Society* 14:765–84.

Rogers, Mary F. 1999. *Barbie Culture*. Thousand Oaks, Calif.: Sage.

Savin-Williams, Ritch C. 1998. *. . . And Then I Became Gay: Young Men's Stories*. New York: Routledge.

Thorne, Barrie. 1986. "Girls and Boys Together . . . but Mostly Apart: Gender Arrangements in Elementary Schools." Pp. 167–221 in *Relationships and Development*, edited by W. W. Hartup and Z. Rubin. Hillsdale, N.J.: Lawrence Erlbaum.

Zucker, K. J., D. N. Wilson-Smith, J. A. Kurita, and A. Stern. 1995. "Children's Appraisals for Sex-Typed Behavior in Their Peers." *Sex Roles* 33:703–25.

FURTHER READING

Carr, C. Lynn. 1998. "Tomboy Resistance and Conformity: Agency in Social Psychological Gender Theory." *Gender & Society* 12:528–53.

Martin, Carol Lynn. 1995. "Stereotypes About Children with Traditional and Nontraditional Gender Roles." *Sex Roles* 33:727–51.

Messner, Michael. 2000. "Barbie Girls Versus Sea Monsters: Children Constructing Gender." *Gender & Society* 14:765–84.

Pollack, William. 1999. *Real Boys*. New York: Henry Holt and Co.

Rottnek, Matthew, ed. 1999. *Sissies and Tomboys: Gender Nonconformity and Homosexual Childhood*. New York and London: New York University Press.

Discussion Questions

1. Think about a situation you've come across in which an individual's gender was unclear. How did you come to a conclusion about the individual's gender? If you can still see this person in your mind's eye, what features stand out to you as gender markers? What other aspects of the situation influenced your interpretation?

2. Recall the toys you played with as a child. Did any of the toys you wanted to play with relate to the opposite gender? In what ways? How did the adults and other children in your life influence your choices and preferences?

3. "Magnified moments" is a key concept of this chapter. Describe moments of this kind in your own life that seemed to make everything in question fall into place. What was it about these occasions that caused this to happen? How did this apply in your schooling, leisure activities, and dating experience?

4. What is the difference between gender and sexuality? Can one be truly masculine, yet be gay? Can a lesbian be fully feminine?

Part 3

Rearrangements

8

Couples Facing Divorce

Derek Ball and Peter Kivisto

People talk about divorce—their own, their friend's, their neighbor's, those of the rich and famous, whoever they find interesting. Catherine Kohler Riessman (1990) called this "divorce talk." In her work, Riessman was concerned especially with how such talk differs for men and women as they look back and take account of what led to their final separation. This chapter focuses on an earlier point in time that has received relatively little attention by researchers. This occurs when one or both marital partners are still contemplating divorce, have given voice to the prospect, and are considering the possibility of saving their marriage. In contrast to Riessman's focus on retrospective accounts after divorce, here we consider the kinds of divorce talk that take place before partners know what the outcome will be.

Specifically, we explore the divorce talk provided by couples in marriage counseling sessions. The couples have recently entered counseling and the counselor is attempting to learn who they are, what their marriage looks like, and what their future prospects as a couple might be. Four case studies are used to illustrate a typology of talk that one of the authors (DB) has constructed from his experience as a marriage counselor. The case studies are representative of the approximately four hundred couples counseled during the past eight years. These couples provide the information from which the typology was constructed. The typology provides an overview of the kinds of divorce talk engaged in by couples who come into the office for help. It also serves as a way of understanding how the children of particular couple types respond to the prospect of divorce.

THE DIVORCE OPTION

Divorce is an option for individuals who deem their marriages unsatisfactory. The option increasingly is chosen in all of the advanced industrial nations (Goode 1993). While divorce has been possible for Americans from the colonial era to the present, it was not until the past century that sizeable numbers of couples availed themselves of this choice. It was only during the last three decades that a large surge in divorces occurred. Although the rate of divorce has declined slightly in recent years from its peak in the late 1970s, it still remains high. Indeed, the rate of divorce in the United States is among the highest in the world, along with Britain and the Scandinavian countries. The United States resembles all modern industrial nations insofar as all have experienced increased divorce rates over the past century.

The Census Bureau estimates that about half of the current marriages will at some future date end in divorce. About 50 percent of first marriages for men under the age of forty-five will likely end in divorce, while for women in the same age group the figure is between 44 percent and 52 percent (Kreider and Fields 2001:18). The nation is more or less evenly divided between those contemporary couples whose marriages end "when death do us part" and those whose marriages end in divorce court. Social conservatives view this situation negatively; they would like to turn the tide, in part by encouraging the government to play a more assertive role in preserving marriage and in making divorces more difficult to obtain. The experiment with so-called covenant marriages in Louisiana is an example. Nonetheless, there is general agreement among marriage and family scholars and counselors that the divorce rate will continue to be high in the foreseeable future.

A number of factors contributes to this. First, the liberalization of divorce laws, especially with the advent of no-fault divorce beginning in California in 1970 and expanding to include about half the states, made it less legally difficult to exit an unhappy relationship. However, it is not entirely clear whether no-fault divorce laws are a cause of increased divorces or a response to changing attitudes about divorce (Cherlin 1992:48). Still, changes in the law did reduce the barriers to marital dissolution.

Second, there have been changes in the way religious institutions deal with divorce. The more liberal religious institutions, such as mainline Protestant denominations and Reform Judaism, have not only come to accept the reality of divorce, but also see it as a viable and reasonable choice on the part of the faithful. Those institutions that have historically been the most negative about divorce, such as the Roman Catholic Church and conservative Protestants, have had to accept the fact that many in the pews already have and others in the future will opt to end their marriages, and these churches have been adapting to this reality.

Third, the stigma attached to divorce has eroded. While a particular divorce may be seen as a failure on the part of one or both partners, divorce in general is viewed a second chance for people to find happiness. Overall, a sea change has occurred regarding perceptions about divorce. Ordinary Americans see marriage less in terms of the responsibilities associated with the socialization of children and more in terms of life satisfaction. Marital partners place a premium on self-fulfillment and nurturance within the bonds of marriage. If one or both of the partners in a marriage no longer find the relationship to be deeply satisfying, there is relatively little social ostracism if the decision is made to terminate it.

Fourth, the high rate of female labor force participation has meant that women today hold the prospect of financial independence, which they did not possess in earlier periods when their lives were confined to the private sphere and they were financially dependent on their husbands. In an earlier era, divorce often spelled financial ruin for women and many divorced women were forced to return to their parents' homes. Andrew Cherlin (1992) contends that this change is the single most important factor leading to the increase in the number of divorces.

A related factor is the emergence of dual careers for husbands and wives. Family life is subject to additional stress because of what sociologist Arlie Hochschild (1997) calls "the time bind." As couples attempt to juggle the demands of work and family life, they find that they do not have enough time to genuinely invest in their marital relationships. In part, this is because dual careers demand a renegotiation of the traditional division of household labor and emotion work, which were once seen as solely the purview of the woman whose role was defined as "homemaker." This renegotiation of traditional gender roles can be a source of marital conflict.

But Americans continue to value marriage. About 90 percent of young people not yet married regard "having a good marriage and family life" as being "extremely important" (Cherlin 1992:129). Divorced individuals generally do not give up on marriage, as the remarriage rate of those divorced is high. Indeed, individuals who have been married and divorced are more likely to remarry than never-married individuals are likely to marry for the first time (Cherlin 1992:27–30). It is within this particular sociocultural context that we consider contemporary divorce talk.

THE DIVORCE PROCESS

Willard Waller (1967 [1938]:14), in one of the earliest studies of divorce wrote, "It rarely happens that people wake up one morning, find that they want to get divorced, and proceed to consult a lawyer the same day. Such a decision usually is reached after long deliberation, if not lengthy debate, in which one or the other of the mates takes the aggressive role." In other words, divorce is a process; it takes time for couples to move from intimacy to separation, and ultimately to marital dissolution.

Several models of the divorce process have been formulated. Robert S. Wiseman (1975) views divorce as similar to mourning and applies Elisabeth Kübler-Ross's stages of dying to marital dissolution. In this model, the first stage of the process is denial, followed by loss and depression, anger and ambivalence, a reorientation of lifestyle and identity, and finally acceptance and a new level of functioning. Sheila Kessler (1975) conceives of the divorce process as having seven stages: disillusionment, erosion, detachment, physical separation, mourning, second adolescence, and exploration and hard work. Joseph Guttman (1993) proposes a psychosocial model entailing four stages: deciding, separating, struggling, and winning. Guttman's model is preferable for two reasons. First, rather than viewing the divorce process as unilinear, the model allows progression from one stage to the next as well as regression from a stage achieved to an earlier one. Second, Guttman does not assume that divorce is always or only about a painful sense of loss; it also can involve feelings of exhilaration and liberation.

Joseph Hopper (1993) has questioned whether the divorce process actually unfolds sequentially. In interviews with individuals who were either recently divorced or late in the divorce process, he found that what was perceived as a complex, ambiguous, and indeterminate situation in the early phase of divorce was later presented in coherent retrospective narratives, replete with clear-cut motives for how they arrived at their situations. He also found that, depending on whether a partner was the initiator or the noninitiator of the divorce, different motives were conveyed, parts of distinctive narratives of marital dissolution. An initiator is likely to contend that she left the marriage because her spouse neglected her. The noninitiator, in contrast, is in a position to cast blame on the partner, accusing that person, for example, of giving up on the marriage (Hopper 2001:129).

Regardless of how the overall process is conceived, it begins when one of the partners starts to think about the prospect of divorce. Just how many people contemplate divorce without articulating the thought is unknown. We can assume that a large number of married people merely *think* about divorce—whether it is for one brief and nonrecurring moment, sporadically, frequently, or persistently. For some, such thoughts remain private, and the divorce process is stalled in silent ruminations. For others, these thoughts are verbalized. A person might confront a spouse, alerting the partner that divorce is on his or her radar screen. Or a person might use the statement as a threat, a warning, a challenge, a confession, an apology, or a sad realization.

A person might also initiate divorce talk with someone other than the spouse. For example, someone engaged in an extramarital affair might first express an intention or desire to divorce to a lover. Or an individual might broach the topic to a close friend, a relative, a coworker, a pastor, a counselor, or someone else the person trusts and is willing to confide in. Some prefer to raise the topic to a stranger, such as someone met in a bar, in a beauty salon, or on a commuter train.

The motives for translating private thoughts into public discourse vary. An individual might simply be trying to get his or her thoughts "out in the open." She might be seeking advice. Or he might be looking for encouragement and support. Or perhaps the individual is hoping that a confidant might attempt to talk her out of it. Likewise, the nature of the account that the person provides to the confidant can vary. Some offer excuses or apologies for contemplating divorce, while others offer justifications (Scott and Lyman 1968).

For those who take the next steps, after initially thinking and talking about divorce, the road leading to legal termination of a marriage typically is long and winding (Guttman 1993:31). Likewise, couples who contemplate divorce and, in the end, decide to stay married take varied routes. Ideas about the sanctity of marriage may play a role in the final outcome. Anxieties about finances, fears about living alone, and the impact on children of staying together or separating can also play into a couple's considerations.

WITH THE MARRIAGE COUNSELOR

Here, we describe the divorce talk of couples who take a route that includes marriage counseling. The counselor might be a marriage and family therapist, a psychologist, a social worker, or even a clergyman. The percentage of couples contemplating divorce who enter into marriage counseling is unknown. For those who do take this route, the decision to seek counseling not only requires the recognition that there are problems in the marriage, but also an acceptance of the idea that treatment is worth trying. Entering counseling is colored by many factors, including the couple's financial means, religious restrictions, and attitudes toward counseling (Doss, Atkins, and Christensen 2003; Briggle and Byers 1997).

Consider four different types of couples contemplating divorce that share in common the decision to seek help. Each is concerned with the need for change in their troubled marriage, but each talks about change differently. Their shared assumption is that the problems in their marriages have resulted in a situation where a crossroads has been reached requiring a change in the status quo. However, the ways in which they describe the need for change relates to how they view their relationship and how hard they work at changing their marriage in the therapy setting. The four types consist of (1) couples who see their relationship as beyond change, (2) those who are unclear about what needs to change, (3) those who place the responsibility for change on their spouse, and (4) those who share the responsibility for change.

We have adapted David Olsen's (1993) "circumplex model" in putting the types together into a single framework. Olsen's model has two dimensions that form a four-cell grid into which any couple or family can be placed. The first dimension is organizational and refers to how the various roles in the marriage or family are structured. On this dimension, a relationship can be overly structured, such that the roles played are rigid, or it can lack adequate structure with few clearly designated roles and thus can be viewed as chaotic. The second dimension refers to the emotional

CONNECTION

	Enmeshed	Disengaged
Rigid	He/she needs to change	It's too late to change
STRUCTURE	We need to change	
Chaotic	Something needs to change (aggressive)	Something needs to change (passive)

Types of Couples Facing Divorce

contours of the relationship, on how much emotional closeness or distance there is in the marriage. A relationship can be so emotionally flooded that there are no personal boundaries and the partners are emotionally "enmeshed," or it can be so distant that they are emotionally "disengaged." The accompanying figure combines these dimensions with a slightly altered version of the four types of couples identified earlier.

We discuss the divorce talk of these couple types under the following headings: (1) It's Too Late to Change; (2) Something Needs to Change (passive); (3) He/She Needs to Change; and (4) We Need to Change. Note that the figure indicates that there are two varieties of the "something needs to change" type, one passive and the other aggressive. We will not present an example of the latter, as such chaotically enmeshed couples consider and often threaten change during crisis situations, but are not motivated to pursue change once the crisis subsides. This couple type is less likely than any of the others to seek counseling.

IT'S TOO LATE TO CHANGE

The first couple type is involved in a relationship in which at least one member sees the marriage as being beyond hope of change. In such a situation, the other partner is usually the one to initiate therapy, but on occasion the hopeless partner does so as a means of finding validation for his or her assessment. These marriages typically have a long history of emotional, physical, and/or sexual abuse. Addiction, serial affairs, and neglect can also bring a couple to this point. Because of a history of hurt, enough emotional scar tissue builds up so that the relationship becomes rigid and inflexible. The wounds become too deep and intractable and one of the marital partners loses any sense of a possible future for the relationship.

Take Chris and Miriam, for example, who appeared for counseling after twenty-three years of marriage. They have two children who are twenty-two and seventeen years of age. The younger of the two, Tracy, is graduating from high school in a month. Miriam, a housewife, reports that she feels very alone and constantly put down by Chris, a very successful realtor. Here is a snippet of their divorce talk.

COUNSELOR: Chris, how do you see things?

CHRIS: I don't understand what her problem is. This is stupid that we have to be here.

MIRIAM: This is what I'm talking about.

CHRIS: I've always provided for the family AND for you. What more do you want?

MIRIAM: I don't want this anymore. That's the point. I'm done.

COUNSELOR: What do you mean by "done"?

MIRIAM: I want a divorce. He can't change. He won't change. He'll always run me down. He's always seen himself as superior. He bashes me in front of the kids so they don't respect me either. I've done nothing but cry alone for over twenty years. It's time for me to stand up for myself. I want a divorce.

Although the counselor worked with this couple to redefine the problem and look for new ways to relate, Miriam was resolute in her desire for a divorce. Her account riveted attention on Chris's history of verbal abuse and emotional withdrawal, serving as justification for insisting on a divorce. For his part, Chris showed little interest in sharing hurt or any other vulnerable feelings, which only seemed to confirm Miriam's decision to leave. Throughout counseling, Chris described the proper role of a husband to be an economic provider, and nothing more. By his reckoning, he had performed the duties expected of him, and thus it struck him as absurd that Miriam would want a divorce.

The couple was divorced seven months later. For these two individuals, divorce was the only option, even while counseling was sought. Talk about their relationship was filled with hopelessness and negativity. They denied anything but their own hurt and disappointment. Their positions were extremely inflexible and there was very little if any closeness or intimacy reported by either partner. In general, such rigid disengagement bodes ill for a couple's prospects of changing in therapy. Typically, therapy for them is either a place to "drop off" a spouse one is leaving with a supportive counselor or a safe place to make the final pronouncement of divorce. Typical talk indicates that therapy is not viewed as a place to heal, either by both partners or at least by one partner who repeatedly describes the situation as too late to change.

For children in families with this couple type, life seems hopeless. Given that at least one parent is intractable, the children are cut out of the process. They have very little, if any, emotional leverage in the negotiation of the decision to divorce. Because the problems may have been going on for several years, there are two common responses on the part of children.

First, they talk of feeling relieved. Adult children, especially, see the decision to divorce as an end to the negative cycle they have observed in their parents' marriage, a cycle of which they have been forced to be a part. Divorce may actually be described by the children as a healthy step for the departing spouse. Second, children may feel powerless. Younger children tend to describe the decision to divorce in this couple type as a sudden move, even though it may have been a very long process for the parent. This is in part because, while the children have been witness to the strains and problems in the marriage, they have not been privy to discussions about the prospect of separation and divorce.

SOMETHING NEEDS TO CHANGE

A second couple type consists of two people who communicate being distressed but who provide no clear explanation of why. This type of couple tends to be very passive regarding their marriage. In their accounts, problems are described as something that happens *to* them rather than something created together *by* them and the ways they choose to interact. Typically, there is not a crisis or clear issue of immediate concern said to confront them like there is for the first couple type. Instead, these couples talk about their relationship as withering before their eyes and say that they cannot find a way of articulating why this is happening.

This is well illustrated by our next example. Mark and Jennifer were college sweethearts. They met in their junior year, dated each other exclusively, became engaged, and got married following their graduation because it was "the next obvious step." They have been married for seven years and have a two-year-old son, Cody. Neither of them reports any clear issue of distress, but they have mutually consented to counseling because Mark has told Jennifer that he is considering divorce.

COUNSELOR: Why have you been thinking about divorce?

MARK: I don't know. I mean, I love her but I'm not "in love" with her, you know?

JENNIFER: What is that supposed to mean? Do you love me or not?

MARK: It's tough to explain. It's just a feeling.

COUNSELOR: Can you put a name to that feeling?

MARK: I guess I'd say it's boredom. I'm not sure I know her anymore and I know she doesn't know me.

JENNIFER: What are you talking about? I know you! We have a son together.

COUNSELOR: How did things change when Cody was born?

JENNIFER: They haven't changed! Everything is like it's been since we started going out!

MARK: Yeah, they are the same. Only, I don't feel the same. That's why I wonder about whether or not we should be married.

In his own work, Hopper (1993) has stressed that the motives employed by people in the process of divorce take shape over time and that, at the beginning, divorce talk is full of expressions of ambiguity and confusion. This is clearly evident in this case. Mark is beginning to develop an account of the marriage that stresses his lack of fulfillment, but he is not quite prepared to place the blame on his spouse.

For this couple, given that the problems were so vague and undefined, Mark saw divorce as the easiest option. Their relationship story is filled with expressions of helplessness and confusion over their roles and responsibilities. The only thing Mark states that he understands is that he feels unhappy. Therefore, he concludes at a different point that he should look elsewhere for a partner who would be able to keep him constantly engaged and invigorated. Jennifer is baffled, hurt, and angered by the very fact that Mark talks about leaving her. She has a difficult time contemplating the idea that she needs to change in any way. She likewise sees their relationship as something that should not need to change as time goes on. That they are experiencing problems is confusing to husband and wife alike.

The counselor worked with this couple for three sessions. Although they showed initial improvement in their ability to articulate feelings and understand patterns that characterized their married life, they were only starting to address change when they dropped out of therapy. When contacted by the counselor, they reported that things were "fine" and that they wouldn't need therapy anymore.

This couple type can be described as "chaotically disengaged." The marriage lacks internal organization and hierarchy and is also very disconnected. The couple's relationship is a feather in the wind, blown to and fro by influences beyond their control, like unwanted or unexpected thoughts or feelings. This couple type tends to be more reactive than the other types because there is little or no solid structure that gives their relationship regularity. Although more open to therapy than the previous type, they have little staying power and tend to drop out of therapy, as Mark and Jennifer did when their feelings improved.

The children of such marriages tend to be as confused as their parents are. The decision to divorce is seen as a random event, and it can create a difficult transition and adjustment to the divorce. Typically, the parents make the decision to stay together "for the sake of the kids."

HE/SHE NEEDS TO CHANGE

A third couple type involves partners who place the responsibility for change on the spouse. This is the most combative type seen in therapy. Their relationship is marked by severe and frequent conflict. In this type, one spouse regularly mentions divorce as a means of persuading and even threatening the other spouse into a change of behavior. Emotionally, this couple type manifests a high level of dependency, especially regarding each partner's identity. Each partner constantly seeks approval from the other. In addition, they cannot tolerate it when the partner thinks differently from them. Because of this dependence on the other's agreement and approval, differing opinions become frightening and threatening. Differences are a threat that must be eliminated at all costs. The crisis is obvious and so is the solution: the spouse needs to change. The counselor is hired to change the spouse, the assumption being that if the spouse changes all will be right with the world.

Jeff and Michelle are typical of this type of couple. They have three children, ages thirteen, ten, and six. They have been married for eighteen years and are both well established in their jobs. Nevertheless, the family has financial problems. The role of bookkeeper has fallen to Jeff, who tends to avoid conflict whenever possible by not mentioning finances. When creditors call, Jeff keeps the information from Michelle to avoid "yet another blow-up." Michelle feels locked out of the process and becomes enraged when she finds the telephone disconnected or the electricity stopped because of unpaid bills. A passage of divorce talk from a therapy session is telling.

JEFF: You have to understand, she's impossible to live with.

MICHELLE: I wouldn't do half the things I do if you'd just be honest!

COUNSELOR: Michelle, what are you asking for, specifically?

MICHELLE: For my spouse to stop lying to me! Is that an unfair request?

JEFF: Unfair? You want to talk about unfair? How about having the finances shoved onto you and then getting grilled about it every month?

MICHELLE: I wouldn't have to grill you if you'd stop hiding things!

JEFF: Why would I tell you things just to get my head ripped off?

COUNSELOR: This doesn't seem to be working . . .

MICHELLE: No kidding. Maybe filing for divorce is the only way to get him to change and see that what he's doing is dishonest and killing our marriage!

This couple had been engaged in divorce talk for some time. Jeff and Michelle blame each other for their marital problems. Jeff's account focuses on Michelle's argumentative challenges as the reason for withholding information from her, while Michelle blames her aggressiveness on Jeff's secretiveness. In her account, his behavior offers ample justification for her to interject the possibility that divorce is the best route.

The counselor worked with this couple for ten sessions. Once they were able to achieve common ground, with the counselor's guidance they were able to work toward a concrete and pragmatic solution. They renegotiated their roles regarding the finances and established a routine in which they held a weekly meeting where they discussed together the prioritization and organization of bill payment. This made a significant change that they were able to apply to other areas of their lives together.

Both partners described the problem as having its root causes in the other spouse's behavior. Neither of them seemed willing to look at their own contribution to the problem, and Michelle resorted to threatening divorce when what she really wanted was openness. Her persistent threats of divorce actually resulted in the opposite of her desire for openness because Jeff would distance himself from her following her threats. This couple was locked in its positions. It was only when they were able to understand the other's position that they were able to achieve change.

This couple would be categorized as "rigidly enmeshed." Their identities are so fused that any differences are threats to personal well-being. These couples practice a relationship style that is fraught with talk of guilt trips, manipulation, and resentment. Their prognosis for therapy is mixed. If they are able to relinquish the blaming position and collaborate together to be less rigid in their roles and responsibilities, they can achieve constructive change. If, however, one or both parties maintain a blaming stance and insist on being "right" rather than "understanding" the other person, they are likely to divorce.

The children of this couple type get swept up in the parents' problems. Depending on their age, children either blame themselves (younger children) for their parent's divorce or blame one of the parents (older children and adolescents) because they get manipulated by the other parent. Children in these families are the most likely of all four types to be involved in the negotiation of divorce, themselves engaging in extensive divorce talk, often at the unwitting behest of one or both parents. Although unhealthy for the children, they are simply following the family rule of enmeshment set forth and reinforced by the parents. When involved in their parents' negotiations, children suffer because of the loss of relationship with one parent, the feelings of resentment that follow from being manipulated, or the loss of innocence resulting from too much information regarding the parents' marriage.

WE NEED TO CHANGE

A fourth couple type is composed of partners who are distressed, but who are willing to take responsibility for their part in the troubled marriage. This is the type of couple that tends to have high self-esteem and to be very active regarding their marriage. In divorce talk, problems are defined as something to which both parties have contributed and, therefore, something to which both parties can and must participate in changing. Problems are still very distressing, and divorce may be mentioned as an option, but it is frequently mentioned as a "last straw" rather than the first option. As the following example illustrates, the prospect of divorce is not raised as a threat or a bargaining chip.

Mike and Cheryl have been married for seven years. They have one child, age two, and were considering having another child before Mike changed jobs. His new job has resulted in greater stress, in part because he has to work longer hours and has taken on new responsibilities. This has contributed to an increased level of conflict in their marriage. Cheryl also is concerned that Mike may be having an affair with a coworker, Heather. The following exchange exemplifies their relationship.

COUNSELOR: Why do you suspect that he is having an affair?

CHERYL: I saw how they talked so easily at the Christmas party and we haven't talked like that in months. I don't want to get a divorce but if he's considering or having an affair, maybe it's the right thing to do.

MIKE: I'm not having an affair. We were talking about the Holdorff account.

COUNSELOR: I wonder if you could look at it from Cheryl's perspective?

MIKE: OK, I understand that we've been out of touch lately. If I were in your shoes, Cheryl, I guess I'd feel pretty bent out of shape, too.

CHERYL: It's just that you've been working so hard, it seems like you've got nothing left for me and Lucy.

MIKE: I know what you mean, I feel really detached from you guys, too.

CHERYL: But what can we do? I mean, I've kind of given up lately, too, and that's not good. [*To counselor*] Do you have any suggestions?

COUNSELOR: It sounds like you're both feeling a need for more nurturance in your marriage.

Mike and Cheryl's accounts parallel each other insofar as both parties in this marriage express unhappiness with the current state of affairs, with a resulting convergence of motives. While the prospect of an affair is raised, talk converges on a more benign understanding for why things turned out as they did. In this couple, Cheryl is prepared to see divorce as an option, especially if the problem cannot be resolved. Their divorce talk is filled with hurt but also with a willingness to accept responsibility and to exhibit caring for the partner. They are able to see the other's perspective with some prompting and, as a result, are able to express empathy. This eventually creates the precondition for working toward a solution that is satisfying to them.

This couple type's relationship can described as balanced. The healthiest place to be located on the grid presented in the figure is in the middle of each dimension rather than at the extremes. On the structural dimension, the healthy relationship is one that balances clear relational responsibilities with unhampered personal freedom. On the connection dimension, the healthy relationship is one that balances emotional closeness with separateness. In this couple type, there is independent thinking and at the same time a connection between partners that motivates them to deal with conflict constructively. Their relationship is stable and balanced, while also having the capacity to change and adapt as life requires. This couple type is likely to experience the greatest benefit from counseling. They are able to take the challenges presented in therapy and have enough strength to practice newly learned skills outside of the counselor's office.

The counselor worked with this couple for seven sessions, looking not only at the current situation but also at how both of them came from "work first" families. Mike realized he needed to reevaluate his priorities and set appropriate boundaries at work. Cheryl realized that she hadn't articulated her needs clearly, writing off her complaints as frivolous compared to Mike's job pressures. When they both made changes in their respective roles in this regard, they saw a significant improvement in their level of marital satisfaction.

Children of this couple type tend to be the healthiest of the four. The decision to divorce, should it occur, is seen as a loss, as with the other couple types. The difference is that parents who decide to divorce with these skills will often apply them to their postdivorce parenting relationship. They are the most likely to minimize conflict regarding the children and to realize that each parent continues to have a unique relationship with the child after the divorce. The children are rarely involved the divorce. This is not to say that they are kept in the dark about it, but rather that they do not become vocal participants in the process. Typically, the parents are motivated to work things out "for the sake of the kids" as opposed to staying together and sacrificing their happiness, as with the "something needs to change" couple type.

SUMMING UP

These cases capture a particular moment in the divorce process, when uncoupling is being contemplated but has not yet occurred. Most narrative accounts of marital dissolution begin after a separation has occurred, such as in Waller's (1967 [1938]) classic exploration of divorce and in Riessman's (1990) interpretive analysis of individuals who are attempting to make sense of divorce after the fact. Our contribution has been to discern types of divorce talk at a point when both partners do not yet know the outcome.

Counseling is a distinctive setting for divorce talk, one in which the partners, for a variety of reasons and operating with varying degrees of good or bad faith, have opted to share their accounts and motives with a trained professional they do not know. Sometimes they enter therapy because one or both partners want to find ways to salvage a troubled marriage. Sometimes they do so because one or both partners are looking for a neutral third party to provide a rationale for either staying together or separating permanently. Sometimes they appear intent on using the counselor as a referee.

In this chapter, we have described the divorce talk of four problematic types of marriage, referenced in terms of "he/she needs to change," "it's too late to change," "something needs to change (passive)," and "something needs to change (aggressive)." The last type seldom seeks therapy. Couples not found at the extremes of these dichotomies are identified as "we need to change." This type is the most likely to find a positive resolution to marital difficulties.

REFERENCES

Briggle, Robert G., and Diane Byers. 1997. "Intentions to Seek Marriage Counseling." *Family Relations* 46:299–304.

Cherlin, Andrew. 1992. *Marriage, Divorce, Remarriage.* Cambridge, Mass.: Harvard University Press.

Doss, Brian D., David C. Atkins, and Andrew Christensen. 2003. "Who's Dragging Their Feet? Husbands and Wives Seeking Marital Therapy." *Journal of Marital and Family Therapy* 29:165–77.

Goode, William J. 1993. *World Changes in Divorce Patterns.* New Haven, Conn.: Yale University Press.

Guttman, Joseph. 1993. *Divorce in Psychosocial Perspective: Theory and Research.* Hillsdale, N.J.: Lawrence Erlbaum Associates.

Hochschild, Arlie. 1997. *The Time Bind: When Work Becomes Home and Home Becomes Work.* New York: Henry Holt and Company.

Hopper, Joseph. 1993. "The Rhetoric of Motives in Divorce." *Journal of Marriage and the Family* 55:801–13.

——. 2001. "Contested Selves in Divorce Proceedings." Pp. 127–41 in *Institutional Selves: Troubled Identities in a Postmodern World,* edited by Jaber F. Gubrium and James A. Holstein. New York: Oxford University Press.

Kessler, Sheila. 1975. *The American Way of Divorce: Prescription for Change.* Chicago: Nelson-Hall.

Kreider, Rose M., and Jason M. Fields. 2001. *Number, Timing, and Duration of Marriages and Divorces: Fall 1996.* Current Population Reports, P70–80. Washington, DC: U.S. Census Bureau.

Olsen, David. 1993. "Circumplex Model of Marital and Family Systems." Pp. 104–37 in *Normal Family Process,* edited by F. Walsh. New York: The Guilford Press.

Riessman, Catherine Kohler. 1990. *Divorce Talk: Women and Men Make Sense of Personal Relationships.* New Brunswick, N.J.: Rutgers University Press.

Scott, Marvin B., and Stanford M. Lyman. 1968. "Accounts." *American Sociological Review* 33:46–62.

Waller, Willard. 1967 [1938]. *The Old Love and the New: Divorce and Readjustment.* Carbondale: Southern Illinois University Press.

Wiseman, Robert S. 1975. "Crisis Theory and the Process of Divorce." *Social Casework* 56:205–12.

FURTHER READING

Cherlin, Andrew. 1992. *Marriage, Divorce, Remarriage*. Cambridge, Mass.:
    Harvard University Press.
Guttman, Joseph. 1993. *Divorce in Psychosocial Perspective: Theory and
    Research*. Hillsdale, N.J.: Lawrence Erlbaum Associates.
Mills, C. Wright. 1940. "Situated Action and the Vocabulary of Motives."
    American Sociological Review 6:904–13.
Riessman, Catherine Kohler. 1990. *Divorce Talk: Women and Men Make Sense
    of Personal Relationships*. New Brunswick, N.J.: Rutgers University Press.
Vaughan, Diane. 1986. *Uncoupling: Turning Points in Intimate Relationships*. New
    York: Oxford University Press.

Discussion Questions

1. Scholars and counselors agree that the divorce rate in the United States
   will continue to be high in the foreseeable future. In your view, what
   would have to happen to lower the divorce rate significantly? Should
   this be a goal, or is the current rate acceptable?

2. Think about a couple you know whose marital relationship is troubled.
   Describe them in terms of being rigid, chaotic, enmeshed, and disengaged. Now locate them in one of the cells of our typology. Do they fit
   well? Explain why or why not. Or, conversely, explain why the typology does not apply well to troubled marriages.

3. Marriage counseling—which is a form of talk therapy—assumes that
   altering divorce talk can lead to changes in troubled marriages. Discuss
   other situations in which a change in communication patterns, or in the
   way relationships are framed, alters our sense of the situations.

9

Children's Stories of Divorce

Susan Walzer

When my daughter, Leah, was in first grade, she came home one day and told me that the parents of a friend of hers were getting divorced. Leah knew this was serious business. She told me that when her friend shrugged and said that she didn't care, she took the child by the shoulders, looked into her eyes, and said, "You don't understand. This is important!" Leah then predicted that her friend might feel sad or scared if her parents kept fighting; but if they didn't, things would eventually be OK.

My daughter was engaging in what sociologist William Corsaro (1997:18) calls "interpretive reproduction." Corsaro offers this concept to capture "the idea that children are not simply internalizing society and culture, but are actively contributing to cultural production and change. The term also implies that children are, by their very participation in society, constrained by the existing social structure and by societal reproduction." When Leah said that parental divorce is important, she was both producing and reproducing a social experience. She was describing the already existing divorce into which she had been thrust in her own family; she also was constructing the experience and meaning of divorce for her friend. It is the latter part of this equation we focus on in this chapter—not only the ways in which divorce happens to children but also how they actively make sense of and respond to it on their own. Divorce is a story that children themselves tell, sometimes with the same words that they hear from others and sometimes in ways that alter the story line.

CHILDREN AND DIVORCE RESEARCH

Exploring how children actively interpret divorce turns upside down one of the primary questions that drive research: How are children affected when parents end their marriages? Judith Wallerstein and colleagues (2000) generated headlines when she stated that the legacy of divorce is bleak for children, arguing that it is an experience in which the needs of adults take precedence over those of children. She concluded that divorce has a long-lasting negative impact on children's lives. Reviewing a multitude of studies on the consequences of divorce, Paul Amato (2000:1278) summarizes the findings less dramatically: "Divorce probably helps fewer children than it hurts." He reaches this conclusion based on an analysis of research comparing the adjustments of children of divorce to those with married parents, and he characterizes gaps in well-being between these two groups as "small but consistent."

Some researchers emphasize children's resiliency in the face of divorce, differentiating between the psychological pain they experience and their overall adjustments (Thompson and Wyatt 1999). Among the factors that appear to make a difference in how children fare are their use of coping skills, support from family and friends, and access to therapeutic interventions (Amato 2000). In other words, children are not just passive recipients of divorce experiences. The actively interact, interpret, and cope with their situations. Yet children are not necessarily "given credit" for thinking about what they see and hear around them during the divorce process (Pruett and Pruett 1999), even though very young children are able to communicate what happened from their perspective and how they feel about it (Stewart et al. 1997).

It turns out that the stories adults tell about their divorces make a difference in how they adjust to them.[1] When ex-spouses explain their marital difficulties in terms of troubles *between* spouses rather than *because* of one of them, they tend to perceive each other more positively following divorce (Grych and Fincham 1992). People who address their own responsibility in negative marital interactions may have less conflict with their former spouses (Walzer and Oles 2003). But even though researchers suggest that adult stories have implications for couples after divorce, there are few studies that focus on how children—especially those who are not yet adolescents —come to terms with their parents' relationships in their own lives. This may have something to do with the tendency for adult perspectives on children to view children as passive learners of adult culture (Thorne 1987). In this chapter, however, we view children as active interpreters of their cultures.

---

[1] If you are interested in reading more about the storytelling processes that adults use to make sense of their divorces, see the work of Hopper 1993, 2001; Riessman 1990; and Vaughan 1986, as well as Ball and Kivisto, this volume.

In emphasizing children's agency, I don't want to suggest that their needs are not often subordinated to those of grown-ups in divorce processes, or that divorce does not influence their long-term approaches to relationships and marriage (Staal 2000). Nor is my intention to subvert the clear themes of loss that emerge in studies of children's responses to divorce. As Robert Emery (1999:4,18) points out, there are subtle costs to coping with divorce even for well-adjusted children. Most children are "resilient," he notes, but they "experience and express much subclinical distress." The psychological consequences of divorce for children, Emery notes, defy "the simplistic characterization . . . of 'devastated' versus 'invulnerable.' " Divorce generates pain and loss *and* hope and resilience, and its impact changes over time (Harvey and Fine 2004). My goal in this chapter is to use children's own words to explain some of this complexity.

Even though it seems that adults' divorce narratives have implications for adults' well-being, I will not argue here for any particular relationship between the stories children tell and their levels of adjustment. The focus is not on outcomes, but on how children sound as they attempt to make the adjustments that other divorce research measures. Clearly, children do not sign up for divorce. But once divorce is unfolding in their lives, how do they deal with it?

To answer this question, I draw on interviews from a sample of children from 136 families as well as a couple of stories from my own children (with their permission). I did not actually set out to study how children make sense of divorce. Most of my own research has focused on adult accounts. I began reading interviews of children simply because they were part of a data archive I was using—the Family Transformations 1981–1982 data set, which was made accessible in 2000.[2] This study was conducted in the

---

[2] These data were collected and donated by Dr. Abigail Stewart and are available through the archive of the Henry A. Murray Research Center of the Radcliffe Institute for Advanced Study at Harvard University. As noted in the title of the data set, this study was conducted in the early 1980s, a time that, as Stewart et al. (1997) point out, divorce was relatively frequent and perhaps at its peak in terms of social acceptability. The year 1981 was, in fact, a peak year for divorce rates nationally (Clarke 1995). So while these data are historically interesting, I wondered if they could be considered relevant more than twenty years later. I concluded that they can, based in part on an analysis conducted by Amato and Keith and cited by Stewart et al. (1997) of the degree to which studies of children's outcomes differ depending on the year of a divorce study (1950–1969, 1970–1979, 1980–1989).

greater Boston area and included families that had at least one child between the ages of six and twelve. The researchers interviewed any children in the family who were willing to participate. They first studied the families within six months of physical separation and followed up a year later, using several methods of data collection including questionnaires, interviews, observations of structured play, and legal records.

When I began, my aim was to use the Family Transformations archive to analyze the interview transcripts of the parents' divorce narratives. But when I turned to the children's narratives, I found myself moved by their frankness and by their attempts to make sense of their situations. I noticed that sometimes their interpretations fit with those of their parents and sometimes they did not. This caught my attention because I was once surprised to hear my son Alex set a different timeframe for my own marital separation than I had remembered. I was struck by the relatively young children in the Family Transformations sample who saw things differently than their parents and identified disagreements they had with them.

I began to more systematically read the interview data from children, noting how they described their families, their wishes, and their explanations for their parents' divorces. As I read the children's words, it generated thoughts about the broader meanings that I consider in this chapter. To put this more technically, the ideas in this chapter were generated through an inductive process of moving from interview data to a theoretical argument. In other words, I did not set out with certain ideas about what I would find and test hypotheses with data, and I make no claims that what I say here has been proven or represents all children of divorce or even all of the children in this sample. Rather, my goal has been to argue for the potential in children to engage in the active interpretation of family processes, grounded in the accounts of specific case material.

The rest of this chapter illustrates some of the ways in which the children in the Family Transformations sample told stories that interpretively reproduced divorce, reinforcing and revising dominant cultural images

---

Amato and Keith found that, in some areas, there were weaker effects of divorce in later years while in other areas there was no variation within different historical moments. In other words, it appears that historical factors have relatively limited influence on the results researchers identify from measures of children's psychosocial responses to divorce.

associated with family, parenthood, marriage, and love. At the same time, these children's stories illustrate specific variations. When you hear one child of divorce, you have *not* heard them all! Even siblings in the same family might not necessarily experience the "same" divorce.

DIFFERENCES IN VIEWPOINT

The parents in the Family Transformations sample tended to describe their families as "breaking up" in some way, and some children expressed an awareness that their family's change was perceived by other people as a transforming event for them, or, as one girl put it, "the end of the world." Their narratives illustrate active decision-making about whether and how to interact with other people about divorce. Explaining why he doesn't talk to anyone about his parents' divorce, a five-year-old boy said, "Cause they go telling one person, then another, then another, and it goes all around the neighborhood. That's what I hate . . . cause kids keep saying it back to me . . . going 'are you moving?' or something like that." A nine-year-old girl advised: "You can cry at home, but don't go out and go, 'Hey, my mother and father are getting a divorce' and all that junk. Because there's a girl on my street and I told her and every time I see her she goes, 'Oh, I feel so bad for you.' It's like she thinks it's the end of the world for me."

Although children were aware that others thought of divorce as an ending of sorts, when they were asked in the second year of the data collection to name the people in their family (this question was not asked the first year), many of them responded with a list that included both of their parents. One six-year-old girl said, "My father, my mother, my sister. Only my father don't live with us." Another six-year-old girl first described her family as "my mother and my father," but she later qualified that her family was "mostly" her father since she didn't see her mother except on weekends. For other children, the absence of a parent did not seem new: "It'll just be the same like when you never see your father anyway."

A significant difference in the viewpoints of children and parents is reflected in children's responses to a question they were asked about what they would choose if they were offered three wishes. In the first year of the study, over three-quarters of the 136 children expressed some form of a wish that their parents would reunite. One five-year-old boy offered an explanation for his parents being divorced—"They don't love each other, that's why. Except they like each other. And if Dad lived with Mom . . .

they would fight." But when he was asked how he feels about his parents being divorced, he replied, "Awful . . . I want my dad back." Another seven-year-old boy, when asked what divorce means, responded: "It means no father comes home from work. It means no more onion rings. It means no more kisses good night. No more hearing Dad say 'ouch' when his razor blade cuts him. No more hearing the shower run twice. And that's all." An eleven-year-old boy said that he wished the divorce could be stopped, "get it back the way it was." "But," he went on to say, "I don't think they could. Well, they could, but they won't. Neither of them are willing to put enough effort into it." This boy clearly differentiated between his desires and those of his parents; he corrected himself when he began to suggest that his parents had no choice about what they were doing.

Beyond the differences in parents' and children's viewpoints, however, there was ambivalence in some children's own reactions as well as an attempt to merge their accounts with others they heard. One nine-year-old boy stated, "I wish that my parents were back together." When he was asked what advice he would give to other children, however, he said, "I'd tell them that it isn't so bad. It's good . . . cause if they stayed together for a few years and they were arguing, it'd be a real bad influence on you." It was common in this sample of children for them to recognize both good and bad aspects to their situations (they were directly asked by interviewers what was better and worse). One five-year-old boy described it being better that "we don't hear all this blah blah blah," but "I want to see my daddy every day 'cause I miss him." Another boy remembered having said in his first interview that he wished his parents were back together. Reflecting a year later, he went on to say, "I don't wish that no more, but I wish that I could live with my father and my mother both at the same time."

Even in the cases of overt conflict for which there is a consensus among researchers that divorce is the best possible course, the experiences of children may not be simple. For example, a six-year-old girl who reported her parents had separated because her father hit her mother, said that "sometimes if your mother lets you see your father, like, you feel happy." Another child advised, "If you dislike your father, don't, unless there's a very, very good reason for it. Still, you should like your father even if he's killed somebody. You shouldn't dislike your father. And the same thing goes for the mother." These children struggled with how they were supposed to feel about their parents, especially parents who did bad things and felt badly about each other.

DISCERNING RESPONSIBILITY

Children in the Family Transformations sample told divorce stories that reflected their active efforts to view their parents as still acting like parents. In some cases, there were heroic attempts to accept tension and abusive behavior. One child advised, "Try not to butt in . . . I was like, 'Why do you have to get separated?' and 'Come on, why can't you get together?' I was belted against the wall and all sorts of things." Rather than judging his parents' responses, he advised children not to get in the middle. A sixteen-year-old girl said, "Just try to understand their situation—that they're under a lot of stress and you have to be ready to understand. And don't be afraid to ask questions, 'cause you have a right to know." But a nine-year-old girl advised, "Don't ask your parents dumb questions or they might get mad or something. [*Interviewer*: What's a dumb question?] Like 'Will you help me with my homework?' or something like that."

Some comments show how children try to preserve their connections to their parents by blaming themselves or minimizing their own needs rather than blaming their parents for the divorce. A fourteen-year-old girl said:

> At first I kind of thought it was my fault or our fault or something we did, but now I just realize that it's nothing we did. It's just they don't get along. . . . [*Interviewer*: What made you think it was your fault?] It's like no real thing. It's just they say they're going to get divorced and you say, oh, I must have done something, and you're wracking your brains trying to figure out what it was that got them so mad.

A thirteen-year-old girl attributed her feelings about her parents' divorce to her own lack of confidence, while recognizing that children are not supposed to blame themselves:

> I think it helps if . . . you grow up and you learn to be independent and you have to have a lot of self-confidence. I don't have a lot, but I just feel like if I had a lot more, I'd be able to handle things like this a lot better. You just gotta feel good about yourself and that way the situation won't affect you totally, like, personally, like it's all your fault.

Although some children accepted their parents' behavior in ways that were personally costly, others advised separating oneself from parental problems. "Take it easy 'cause there ain't nothing you're gonna do about it," an eleven-year-old boy said. A teenager advised, "If you get involved in it, you'll be the loser, because you have to take sides if you get involved." Another child commented, "Don't even think about it. Just think like you never had a father. And forget about him. Or mother. Whoever. And just

live with the people you have, happily." Others were more explicit in judging their parents' behavior negatively. A ten-year-old boy said, "They just
didn't agree much. They got mad a lot. And my mom getting bombed didn't
help." A fifteen-year-old reported that her father was "immature," "Like my
mother had to tell him what was right. And she would take care of the bills.
If she didn't do it, they'd never get paid." While this girl's account appears
to be an acceptance of her mother's explanation, some children presented
interpretations that they did not necessarily really understand. One child
said, for example, that her parents had kept secrets from each other. When
the interviewer asked if she knew what that meant, she said no.

A number of children offered explanations for divorce that adults tend
not to recognize—expectations related to gender (Stewart et al. 1997).
Here, responsibility for divorce is lodged in commonplace views of gender
roles. A nine-year-old girl described her mother as not having been "right"
for her father because "the house wasn't clean and stuff like that." An older
girl talked about her mother now being able to come and go "as she
pleases." Because of her own ability to babysit her siblings, she said, her
mother "doesn't have to be held down to us." In this daughter's view, being
married had posed a constraint on her mother from which divorce had
liberated her. Another teenager also perceived gender differentiation as a
source of control embedded in marriage: "I wouldn't get married 'til I was
about forty-five . . . I go out with a guy now and I can't stay out with him
too long 'cause I feel tied down . . . I don't want to be expected to stay
home and iron shirts." One child suggested that her father's choice of his
girlfriend over her mother was linked to domestic behavior: "He feels a lot
happier 'cause he has a [girlfriend] . . . and when they're all done eating
[she] gets up and does the dishes, washes the table, all that stuff."

It is not unusual for adults to deny the role of third parties as catalysts
to divorce, since there is stigma associated with trading a spouse for someone else (Gerstel 1987). But some children in this sample nevertheless
acknowledged outside relationships, despite their parents' denials. A teenage
sister and brother, for example, agreed that the cause of their parents'
divorce was that their father had a girlfriend. One of them said, "They
didn't really decide. My father really decided. He liked this other girl
better than my mother so he just said 'bye.'" A child in another family
describes her situation: "Last night when I went out with my father I asked
him all this. He lives with another woman. He says stuff wasn't working
out. He says there was no love. And I said my mother loved him, but he
didn't love her. But he said no, that wasn't true. But it was true." This child
was clearly saying that his "truth" was different than his father's.

For some children, third parties were not just framed as causes of friction and distance between their parents, but as playing a role in their fathers' (in these particular cases) lack of availability to them. A ten-year-old girl talked about the impact of a third party on both her mother and on her: "He [father] wasn't very nice to my Mom. When he separated from my mom, he pushed us away too, and he went to his other girlfriend." An eighteen-year-old in the sample commented about her father:

> We don't visit him because he gave us a post office box, which is like more or less his cover up for where he is staying . . . He wants his privacy now . . . like if we saw what he did, like my mother's seen him already with two ladies, and if we saw one of these people, I think he'd feel ashamed, and then the guilt would really get to him.

Another ten-year-old girl simply said, "My dad's a cheater. He went out with other women." Later in the interview, she explained, "I can see now why my mother wanted the divorce . . . [Dad] always has to have his way." While this girl seemed to have taken hold of her mother's explanation for marital problems, she also said, "I've come to the point where my parents, I can't believe either of them, because one says one thing and the other says another thing. And I don't know who to believe, so I can't believe any of them." A six-year-old boy talked about how his parents would deny what he could see: "They didn't tell me that they were having fights. I always told them to stop it. I came in the middle of the fight, 'Stop it, Mommy! Stop it, Daddy! Stop fighting!' And they always said, 'We're not fighting, son.' And they were fighting." The work of sorting out discrepancies between what she was told and what she observed emerged in the commentary of this eleven-year-old-girl:

> My father told me that when my mother first got pregnant, she didn't want to, and then they got married, but they never really wanted to. And he said for ten years they wanted to get separated. But what I can't understand is how, I'm eleven, they've been separated a year. That makes me ten. Ten years and they wanted to get separated and they had me. How come they had three children—four because they had [sister] after the miscarriage? How come they had us four when they wanted to get separated?

She went on to say that her parents "still have a good relationship with each other . . . I don't know how they can still be like that? So close yet so far away."

As these comments reveal, children discern parental responsibility in a number of ways. Some excuse bad parental behavior; some recognize and disapprove of it. Some embrace their parents' explanations for their divorces, while others question their accounts. In the former cases, the accounts allow children to sustain a vision of their mothers and fathers as functioning parents. In the latter cases, the authority of parents may be undermined by the lack of congruence between what children are told and what they see for themselves, or when the accounts of their parents diverge in ways that make the children question either adult's trustworthiness. Unresolved discrepancies, holes, and outright lies in parents' accounts can turn divorce into a "never-ending" process of discernment for children (Duncombe and Marsden 2003).

MAINTAINING IDEALS OF LOVE AND MARRIAGE

Children often constructed accounts that maintained the ideals of love and marriage even as they described their parents' relationships in far less sanguine terms. As one child of a family of four siblings put it, her parents did not getting along "as husband and wife." "They get along," the fifteen-year-old said, "it's not like they have a hatred towards each other, but they didn't love each other enough to be married." While all four of the children in this family embraced the idea that there has to be a certain amount of love between a husband and wife, other children interpreted their parents' marriages as not having been loving enough. People who love each other do not end up divorced, they reasoned.

Some adolescents especially were explicit in constructing narratives that differentiated between what happened between their parents and what is supposed to happen in relationships. A fourteen-year-old girl said of her family, for example, "It was very easy for our family to split up 'cause we were all split up anyway." When asked what she thought it meant to be divorced, she responded, "Just two people who cannot live together, and for me, that's something I cannot understand. Because if I care about someone, no matter how bad something happens is, I'm not just going to walk away from them. Because there must be a problem there and they're going to need someone." Another child suggested, however, that divorce means "someone can't push you around because they're not your wife or they're not your husband." In the first case, the child reproduced a positive vision of marriage as a mutually supportive relationship. The other child provided a more negative analysis of institutionalized marital roles.

A sixteen-year-old girl explained that what was going on between her mother and her stepfather was not really love.

> At the beginning he would call her and say, "I still love you, let's get back together," and she'd say no. Which I'm glad 'cause I'd sit there and coach her and say, "No, don't you dare!" But then after a couple of weeks, he was like, "Oh, all right," which proved he probably didn't even care about her, you know. To me, if you love someone, you're going to love them for a long time and you're going to be hurt. But it was like two weeks later, "Okay, I'm fine, go get the divorce . . ." when a couple of weeks ago, he was whimpering over the phone. He's weird.

This child's account revealed not only her sense that this relationship did not fit the ideal, but also her active participation in supporting her mother's decision to break off from the "weird" man to whom her mother had been married for ten years. Her seventeen-year-old sister said more simply, "This guy's a loser. He treated my mother like dirt." These sisters proffered an idealized view of love and marriage that contrasted with their mother's circumstances. In the sisters' view, it does not make sense to remain married to someone who treats you "like dirt," or only seems loving.

The sixteen-year-old stated that she had come to this realization on her own. She described her stepfather as an alcoholic and verbally abusive to her mother. She characterized him as "messed up in the brain . . . and no one sees it but me." Her mother's account was that she and her husband had a "personality conflict," explaining that "we just seldom agreed on anything." A year later, the mother reported that she and her husband had had a long-standing inability to get along, but she still did not acknowledge the negative behaviors that her daughter identified. Interpreting the situation differently than her mother, the daughter said, "I know he is [messed up], because no man does that to his wife and says he loves her."

It was not only her mother's marriage that this daughter understood differently. She talked about her mother now having a boyfriend, "and I don't want her to get too involved with him . . . because I don't want her to get hurt like she has . . . 'cause she likes him a lot and I don't know if he feels the same." She believed that she could see something that her mother did not see. The daughter interpreted the particular events in her mother's life in ways that allowed her to hold on to a more general sense that divorce should be avoided:

> I think [divorce] is an awful thing to happen, 'cause to me, when you get married, that's the person you're with for the rest of your life. And to love

them, to be everything to you, your best friend. If there's a need for it, yeah. But a lot of people have little troubles and they won't go to a marriage counselor. And a lot of people change after you get married to them. If I was going to get married, I'd go out with them for five years first. Get to know them, 'cause my mother knew my stepfather for about four months—that's nothing! [Divorce is] sad . . . in my [mother's] case, it was needed. It was the only way out. But if you can, you should try to work things out.

Her seventeen-year-old sister also distinguished between her own idealized view of marriage and what her mother had experienced: "[Mother] enjoys not having someone tell her what to do. That's not what marriage is, but that's what she had." She made predictions about how her own experience of family life would affect her, this time portraying a future husband in terms of an idealized fatherhood.

> I haven't had the affection of a father. I know that when I get married I'm gonna marry a guy that's at least ten years older than I am. 'Cause I didn't have a father and I need a male father figure that's older. . . . I miss like in storybooks how fathers take their daughters walking through the park or buy a balloon or something like that. And I never had that. And I really missed that.

Whether or not this seventeen-year-old's image of a future relationship will actually come true, it is notable that she talked about sustained visions of what an ideal future would hold. She also spoke poignantly about trying not to generalize from her experience: "In a way, I'm afraid [to get married]. After all this, in a way, it's hard for me to trust men. But I don't think they're all like that." Eventually, she said, she guessed she would get married, but, unlike her sister, she perceived divorce as expected rather than as a last resort. This led her to say that she would not have children.

> 'Cause I don't want what happened to me to happen to them, even though when you get married you say all the vows. But it doesn't mean anything, ten or twelve years into a marriage and the kids are growing up. I don't know if I could trust anybody enough to say, "Oh yeah, I'll take the kids." Because kids need both parents, no matter what's happening today, I think they need both of them.

SUMMING UP

When he was younger, I once asked my son Alex when he knew that an imaginary friend of his wasn't real. Alex replied that he and his friend were going somewhere and he reached out for his friend's hand and it wasn't there. This struck me as sad, but I didn't say so and asked Alex how he had felt about it. He said, "It didn't matter. He could still be my friend."

I have argued in this chapter that children's stories about divorce represent a kind of interpretive reproduction, reflecting their ability to engage in active interpretation of their experiences in ways that both embrace and diverge from adult accounts. We have seen that for many of the children in the Family Transformations sample, it did not mean a parent was not part of a child's vision of his or her family just because that parent was no longer in the household. Family members can be real to children even when they are not physically present, just as Alex's imaginary friend was real to him.

Children's senses of family often extend beyond their households. Sometimes what they see within them does not fit with their idea of family at all. Some children have to work too hard to make their experiences fit with the ideal. Returning to Corsaro's (1997) notion of interpretive reproduction, children do not simply internalize society and culture, but actively interpret and change it within the context of their everyday lives. While children clearly are subordinated to at least one of their parents' choices in divorce, their agency is nevertheless reflected in their interpretations of the meaning of family, love, marriage, and parenthood.

When we examine how children talk about divorce, we can hear some of the dilemmas they encounter. The interview excerpts in this chapter illustrate children's active attempts to account for their parents' behavior, to assess their parents' explanations, and to interact with their own pre-existing ideas about what families are supposed to be. One of their big challenges is to reinterpret "moms" and "dads" as being separate from "wives" and "husbands." When children are able to disengage parenting from marriage, it enables them to sustain notion of family, even after divorce.

We know that parental functioning is considered to be one of the best predictors of children's adjustments (Amato 2000). Children's stories illustrate why. Among the most disturbing aspects of these children's accounts are their descriptions of adult behavior that is neglectful and/or abusive—behavior that is also implicated in adult narratives of marital dissolution (see Kurz 1995). Some of the children in this sample felt silenced by adults, sometimes in response to their attempts to understand their parents' relationship, and sometimes in response to other needs that they had, such as getting help with their homework. We need to pay attention not only to children's reports about this, but also to some of their reactions—their inclinations to excuse, to blame themselves, to distance themselves from other family members and their troubles.

Although I have not been able to analyze systematically the implications of children's narratives for their well-being, there is much in these accounts to suggest why the variables that have been found to influence children's adjustments do so. Employing coping skills, interacting with supportive family and friends, and making use of therapeutic intervention all involve the ability to perceive and interpret one's world as an active social agent. We are probably helpful to children when we not only identify the effects of divorce on them, but also recognize their abilities to construct and narrate their lives on their own terms.

I don't know what kind of stories about divorce my own children will tell in the future, but here is another one from the past that my ex-husband passed along to me. My daughter commented to him that it was too bad that he and I are divorced "because one of you is always missing me." I hope whatever stories our children tell, as they get older will continue to feature the notion that the divorce was indeed a loss for us, but not a loss of love for them. With the recognition that children actively discern family and love, it is possible for parental divorce to be just a subplot in the larger story of children's own lives.

REFERENCES

Amato, Paul R. 2000. "The Consequences of Divorce for Adults and Children." *Journal of Marriage and the Family* 62:1269–87.

Clarke, Sally C. 1995. "Advance Report of Final Divorce Statistics, 1989 and 1990." *Monthly Vital Statistics Report* 43:1–32. Hyattsville, Md.: National Center for Health Statistics.

Corsaro, William A. 1997. *The Sociology of Childhood.* Thousand Oaks, Calif.: Pine Forge Press.

Duncombe, Jean, and Dennis Marsden. 2003. "'The Never-ending Story': Children's Gaze and the Unresolved Narrative of Their Parents' Divorce." Pp. 49–62 in *Social Relations and the Life Course*, edited by Graham Allan and Gill Jones. New York: Palgrave Macmillan.

Emery, Robert E. 1999. "Postdivorce Family Life for Children: An Overview of Research and Some Implications for Policy." Pp. 3–27 in *The Postdivorce Family: Children, Parenting, and Society*, edited by Ross A. Thompson and Paul R. Amato. Thousand Oaks, Calif.: Sage Publications.

Gerstel, Naomi. 1987. "Divorce and Stigma." *Social Problems* 34:172–86.

Grych, John H., and Frank D. Fincham. 1992. "Marital Dissolution and Family Adjustment: An Attributional Analysis. Pp. 62–71 In *Close Relationship Loss: Theoretical Approaches*, edited by Terri L. Orbuch. New York: Springer-Verlag.

Harvey, John H., and Mark A. Fine. 2004. *Children of Divorce: Stories of Loss and Growth*. Mahwah, N.J.: Lawrence Erlbaum Associates.

Hopper, Joseph. 1993. "The Rhetoric of Motives in Divorce." *Journal of Marriage and the Family* 55:801–13.

———. 2001. "The Symbolic Origins of Conflict in Divorce." *Journal of Marriage and the Family* 63:430–45.

Kurz, Demie. 1995. *For Richer, for Poorer: Mothers Confront Divorce*. New York: Routledge.

Pruett, Kyle D., and Marsh Kline Pruett. 1999. "'Only God Decides': Young Children's Perceptions of Divorce and the Legal System." *Journal of the American Academy of Child and Adolescent Psychiatry* 38:1544–50.

Riessman, Catherine Kohler. 1990. *Divorce Talk: Women and Men Make Sense of Personal Relationships*. New Brunswick, N.J.: Rutgers University Press.

Staal, Stephanie. 2000. *The Love They Lost: Living with the Legacy of Our Parents' Divorce*. New York: Random House.

Stewart, Abigail J., Anne P. Copeland, Nia Lane Chester, Janet E. Malley, and Nicole B. Barenbaum. 1997. *Separating Together: How Divorce Transforms Families*. New York: The Guilford Press.

Thompson, Ross A., and Jennifer M. Wyatt. 1999. "Values, Policy, and Research on Divorce: Seeking Fairness for Children." Pp. 191–232 in *The Postdivorce Family: Children, Parenting, and Society*, edited by Ross A. Thompson and Paul R. Amato. Thousand Oaks, Calif.: Sage Publications.

Thorne, Barrie. 1987. "Re-visioning Women and Social Change: Where Are the Children?" *Gender & Society* 1:85–109.

Vaughan, Diane. 1986. *Uncoupling: Turning Points in Intimate Relationships*. New York: Vintage Books.

Wallerstein, Judith S., Julia M. Lewis, and Sandra Blakeslee. 2000. *The Unexpected Legacy of Divorce: A 25 Year Landmark Study*. New York: Hyperion.

Walzer, Susan, and Thomas P. Oles. 2003. "Managing Conflict After Marriages End: A Qualitative Study of Narratives of Ex-Spouses." *Families in Society* 84:1–9.

FURTHER READING

Harvey, John H., and Mark A. Fine. 2004. *Children of Divorce: Stories of Loss and Growth*. Mahwah, N.J.: Lawrence Erlbaum Associates.

Hetherington, E. Mavis, and John Kelly. 2002. *For Better or for Worse· Divorce Reconsidered*. New York: W. W. Norton & Company.

Staal, Stephanie. 2000. *The Love They Lost: Living with the Legacy of Our Parents' Divorce*. New York: Random House.

Stewart, Abigail J., Anne P. Copeland, Nia Lane Chester, Janet E. Malley, and Nicole B. Barenbaum. 1997. *Separating Together: How Divorce Transforms Families*. New York: Guilford.

Discussion Questions

1. Think about your own parents' divorce or the divorce of someone's parents you knew. At the time, what did you think led to their divorce? Did this differ from what the parents or others said? If so, in what ways? Why do you think your explanations might differ from others' accounts?

2. In addition to accounting for divorce, what are some other examples of how children interpretively reproduce society (for example, in relation to schooling, athletics, success, or failure)?

3. How do the stories that you tell about your childhood in general relate to those told by other people in your life? What implications do the commonalities and differences have for understanding the social meaning of childhood?

10

Stepfathers and the Family Dance

William Marsiglio and Ramon Hinojosa

Families come in many forms. Scholars and activists offer descriptions of all sorts of "families," from single parent households to gay marriages to traditional extended families. With divorce and remarriage on the rise, stepfamilies are more prevalent than ever, and even they take different forms. This chapter examines the most common kind of stepfamily: the *stepfather* family. It includes a man who is romantically involved and typically living with a woman and at least one of her minor children who was fathered by another man.

As in other families, domestic life for stepfamilies is built up over time through shared routines and rituals, role negotiations, and emotional exchanges. The meaning of these activities is not etched in stone, but is discerned as participants live through the experiences of being family members. But stepfamilies, much moreso than biological families, represent what sociologist Andrew Cherlin (1978) once described as "incomplete" institutions, reflecting a special ambiguity about how individuals in such families should think and feel about themselves and the family as a whole. While members negotiate the meanings of domestic life regardless of family type, these meanings tend to be murkier in stepfamilies because ideas about such families are less clearly defined than for more mainstream families.

Focusing on how stepfathers, along with the birth mother and children —and, at times, the biological father—view the contours of domestic life and their roles in it, we explore the dynamic and complex rhythms of a process we refer to as the "family dance." The metaphor calls attention to timing and the choreographic dimensions of the stepfather's relationship with other family members, who commonly dance to different tunes as each adjusts to their life together. Some stepfathers seem to have two left feet, figuratively speaking, as they join in and adapt or fail to adapt to domestic routines. Others get right into the swing of things. The family dance initially turns the stepfather's actions and other family members' responses into improvisations, the timing and paces of which may or may not settle into a mutually satisfying routine. Initially, the stepfather's dance is especially ad hoc since he is new on the scene and has to figure out how to get in step with all the others.

The best way to understand how stepfathers view their participation is to ask them about it. To do this, we conducted in-depth interviews with a sample of forty-two men whose backgrounds varied in terms of age, race, social class, marital status, and whether they had children of their own. The men were involved with infants, toddlers, young children, or adolescents in their stepfamilies. Some were involved with a specific stepchild for the child's entire life, while others had entered a child's life fairly recently. The litmus test for inclusion was that the men had to describe themselves as being actively involved in the life of their romantic partner's child who was nineteen years of age or younger and living with the mother. We also spoke with thirteen birth mothers and two stepchildren.

We make no specific claims about how comparable the experiences of men in this sample are to the larger population of stepfathers. Our intent is not to generalize in this way but to highlight key features of the family dance experienced by stepfathers because of their special circumstances. In the process, we describe stepfathers' views, actions, adaptations, and sentiments as they wrestle with who and what they and others are as partners in the dance troupe they have joined.

CHOREOGRAPHY

Becoming a stepfather involves more than signing a document or making a pledge. Even though these can carry great significance for men, men entering stepfamilies typically do not wake up one morning and say, "Hey, I'm a stepfather!" Prior to forging a stepfather identity, a man must enter into, and deal with, a preexisting family arrangement of the mother and children, who dance to tunes of their own before the stepfather joins in. It is important to emphasize that the family dance is choreographed *before* as well as after a stepfather takes part in domestic life. The family dance is under way before he steps in, and this presents a major challenge to his developing partnership.

Experiencing New Tunes and Rhythms

At whatever point a stepfather joins the family dance, the dance reflects existing members' experiences with sustaining a family unit characterized by distinct roles, routines, and a family history that encompasses shared memories specific to those members. Just as dancing entails adjusting movements to the rhythm of the music, the family dance shapes one's thoughts, feelings, and behavior in relation to the existing rhythms of domestic life. Like dancing, the stepfather's performance is influenced by others on the dance floor, including a nonresident father, teachers, neighbors, grandparents, clergy, and family physicians, among others. Other family members, in turn, must alter their actions to keep in step with the new partnership. As with any dance, participants can be awkward with each other. They may improve as partners or continue to struggle awkwardly, simply muddling along. Some may tire, and even leave the floor, which, in the case of family life, may lead to separation or divorce.

Two stepfathers, Carl and Eddie, age thirty and thirty-five, describe the uncharted territory for men joining the preexisting dance, acclimating themselves to the rhythms of new circumstances.

> *Carl*: It's odd at first, when you step into somebody's life and somebody's already been there and they've already started it for you and it's kind of like stepping in and moving into a relationship with a woman that does have a child. It's kind of strange at first. How do I say the right things or do the right thing to not alienate one or both and if I don't do the right things, will I alienate the daughter and in turn alienate the mother?

> *Eddie*: Well, it was kind of one step at a time. I just couldn't go in and rush in and try to change everything. It was kind of relax and sit back, see how things go. I had to adjust. They didn't have to adjust. It was me coming in. I was the outsider, so I had to make all the adjustments to their ways —the emotions, to eating, comings and goings, activities. I had to adjust to all that.

Each of these men is mindful of his outsider status and expresses a desire to adapt to the music of preexisting routines. The men want to be accepted into the new stepfamily and they recognize that the takes process time. The family dance has steps, wavering at first, which nonetheless need to be taken carefully on the way to becoming dance partners.

Usually, family members will have danced together for years, developing intricately choreographed routines that include particular ways of sharing emotion and styles of sleep, eating, playing, being humorous, talking, and arguing specific to their lives together. One of the birth mothers interviewed, Jennifer, age forty-four, illustrates how difficult it can be for a stepfather to become a partner in routines the rhythms of which he'd never been part. She recalls making her husband, Harry, wait as she and her daughter Kelly went through "this bedtime routine where I would have to scratch her back and sing her a couple of songs, believe it or not. I can't sing. Even when we were dating, he would have to wait out in the living room. It might take thirty minutes." Such moments of shared intimacy, in this case between Jennifer and her daughter Kelly, are quite literally tunes of family history, shared by familial insiders. Even poorly sung tunes accompany the dance that challenges a stepfather's partnership.

Some stepfamilies appear to be vibrant and healthy, while others are dysfunctional. Most fall somewhere in between. Jennifer's stepfamily is one of the latter. The domestic life she formed with Harry and Kelly is stable, but Jennifer and Harry both feel that Kelly has never fully accepted Harry as a father, even though Kelly has had no contact with her biological father. In Harry's words, "Kelly has never been very close with me and it's not at all like my two other children [with Jennifer]. She likes the idea of having a dad, but she doesn't really want the personal relationship that comes with it. It's a matter of appearance I think more than anything else for her."

Those with years of experience in a healthy family have a reservoir of shared positive memories about holidays, birthdays, vacations, other special events, and day-to-day activities that they take for granted. In times of fun or crisis, memories of past dances can be recalled at a moment's notice to strengthen family ties. Stephen, forty-three and married to the mother of identical fourteen-year-old twin girls, provides an example typical of how family histories are built up over time and how they relate to family functioning. When he was interviewed, Stephen had been a stepfather for almost ten years. His remarks point to the kinds of experience that provide family members with a sense of belonging to the dance troupe.

> We do a lot of the normal family stuff. Thanksgiving we go down to my parents' house. This summer we managed to all drive out to California with their grandmother, Paula's mom. She, her mother, Paula's grandmother, their great-grandmother spent three weeks in a minivan with five girls. It's everything it sounds like. It was sort of interesting to see how the group dynamics sort of changed after we all got sort of close in the van for extended periods of time.

Timing

Another important element in the choreography of the family dance is timing. For many participants, the hardest part is learning the steps of a complex routine that now more or less includes a new family member. Family members need time to observe each other on the dance floor, listen to the developing rhythm of the music, and adjust their dance styles to each other. In his interview, Jackson, thirty-nine and engaged to be married to the mother of four-year-old Mason, notes that such mundane events as grocery shopping and watching television can be significant steps in the family dance. Referring to the times he has taken Mason to the grocery store and home improvement centers, Jackson reports that he "thinks it took about four months or so before I started to make that transition from man-with-someone-else's-child to man-with-his-own-child." He explains that in time and with practice, they started to get into step with each other. Becoming a dance partner, it seems, is fostered and reinforced by the simplest moves.

As these men fashion their partnerships, learning unique steps and making the right moves, family members collectively begin to follow the same rhythms and the family dance becomes more evenly choreographed. This may take months, in some cases years. Not surprisingly, certain performances may not go smoothly, especially for some members of the troupe. Thomas, thirty-eight, describes how difficult becoming a dance partner can be under the circumstances.

> When I first came on . . . I believe Danny . . . he was seven or eight. And Keith was . . . I want to say he was five going on six. Danny was nonresponsive at the time. Really he wanted his [own] dad. You know, he was at that age, the dad was coming in and out of his life. He wanted to be with his dad. Me, stepping on the scene, didn't just quite get things right. Keith was so young, he just kind of blended in with it. You know? But Danny was very difficult. And there were some issues with him and his mom that they'd had before I come in, where he'd like, I guess, called the law because his mom was trying to spank him or whatever. So when I moved in, it got, it was . . . there was just some really bad . . . just really nonresponsive.

While some soon dance well together, others feel out of sync with the rest of the troupe. In their eyes, family members can seem like a mix of hip hoppers, country line enthusiasts, and ballet performers, all attempting to stay in tune with rock and roll. Those proficient in one dance style may have a difficult time finding a common rhythm that fits with the others. Asked what advice she would give to stepfamilies in situations like this, Anna, thirty-seven, recommends, "Patience. Everyone's got to have patience. Adults to kids. And everybody's got to make compromises. Everyone's got to learn to communicate."

DANCING WELL

Whether a preexisting family is dancing well or poorly, incorporating a new dance partner can still be challenging. Those who have spent time together and taken part in the dance of a particular family's domestic life have had an opportunity to establish their own rhythms and routines. For better or worse, the stepfather is the novice partner and needs a kind of script—or a score—for hopefully making the right moves.

It's evident in our interviews that stepfathers borrow from widely shared themes of good fathering as guides to partnering up. These shared themes help fathers in how to think and feel about their performances in comparison. Make the right moves and take enough steps, and one seems to a good dancer. When a man's moves are consistent with these themes, he is likely to be seen, or to see himself, as successfully fathering, or stepfathering as the case might be. At least, that's how it works in theory. But, as we'll see, practice complicates the picture as themes are applied on the particular dance floors of domestic life.

The Providing Partner Theme

A leading theme deals with provisioning. The good father provides financial and material support for the family. Of course, economic support is not exclusively the father's responsibility, but the theme of the good provider does significantly impress itself on the stepfather, who, by virtue of being new on the dance floor, is relatively untested in this regard in the local scheme of things. The theme percolated through many of the stepfathers' interviews as they commented on what it took to make the right moves on this dance floor. Jackson makes the point directly, linking the right moves to becoming part of a happy family.

> I feel like at this point I am, I want to provide the best I can for him and for my fiancée so that we can live comfortably and do the things we want to do that will help all three of us to be happy, whether it's going out for ice cream or taking a one-week vacation to see the grandparents or going camping. We want to be able to do those things and so I . . . I just do that and budget things so that we can do the things that we're going to do.

For some, the theme of the providing partner makes the prescribed dance steps difficult because of their particular circumstances. Juan, for example, finds himself struggling financially at the moment because of his low graduate student salary. He is nonetheless willing to incorporate his stepson Pedro into his financial circle of responsibility and says so in no uncertain terms. "I feel him like my son now, so for me I'm taking care of as much as I can, everything. Financially I am not being able to cover everything because of my income, but if I can I will do it. That's the way I feel about it. I have no mixed feelings about that."

The Emotionally Supportive Partner Theme

Another theme presents fathers as emotionally supportive partners. Good dancing goes beyond material provision, extending to the approachable father figure who sets the right tone. Gerald felt that one of his main responsibilities was to "provide a positive atmosphere" for his stepdaughter. He stated, "I want to be just a good role model and I want us to continue to grow as individuals." Russ conveys the same sentiment: "I just wanted to be that positive father figure." Numerous stepfathers stressed that they cared emotionally for their stepchildren a great deal, referring to them in terms signaling actual biological kinship. Herman, forty-four, sums up the feeling of many of the stepfathers in this study: "I love her. I've got to admit, I love her, man, you know. She's my daughter. When I introduce her, I don't introduce her as my stepdaughter, because I didn't step on her."

The Genuine Father Theme

The names children call a stepfather have special meanings for stepfathers; certain terms reflect genuine fatherhood. "Dad" or "Daddy" are names applied to "real" fathers, whereas "Stepdad" or "Russ," for example, might indicate that the status as a real father is being withheld. Conversely, the stepfather who comfortably refers to his stepson as "Son" or his stepdaughter as his daughter speaks like a real father. Preferred terms of reference, in other words, relate to claims of genuine family partnership (Marsiglio 2004a). For Russ, naming figures directly into fatherhood: "I'm going to be the one raising him and all. I want to be seen in his eyes as something more important than just Mr. Russ. More of a father figure type instead of just a big buddy." For Rodney, naming can signal parenthood, if not biological parentage.

I had asked Glenna, "When you call me Dad, what are you feeling?" She goes, "What do you mean, what am I feeling? I'm talking to you, that means I'm talking to you when I call you Dad." I said, "Okay. That's all I wanted to know." So, to me she was saying [that] it's a way she identifies me as her father, not biological because she knows I'm not, but as a parental role.

Actually hearing oneself being called "Dad" as opposed to by one's first name is a sign of belonging for many men. Hearing "Daddy" or "Dad" is a momentous occasion. Carl was surprised the first time his stepdaughter Vicky referred to him as "Daddy." It was thrilling and had a profound effect on defining his partnership within the family troupe.

I remember the joy and the ecstatic feeling when she did. We [Carl and his wife Lani] were unsure because we were not married. We weren't sure whether to tell her, "No, I'm not your daddy yet," to give her false impressions. So we just ended up letting her move into that transition. I think at that point, part of the decision was that we started having . . . I started, at least, having marriage-type feelings about Lani, about that too. It all came into play and came together at that point.

Carl's experience not only helped him to frame his relationship with his stepchild, but also allowed him to think about his relationship with his then girlfriend. The new name provided Carl with the sense that he wanted to be a part of the family, allowing him to construct a partnership with Lani based on marriage and partnering with Vicky as father and daughter. As it turned out, he later legally adopted Vicky as his daughter.

Emmit, twenty-nine, discussed how the ritual aspects of family choreography such as engagement and the use of kinship terms go hand-in-hand. His five-year-old stepson Jake referred to him as "Emmit" until he proposed to Robin.

After I proposed, that's when he started calling me Dad, in a sense. Before then he was calling me by my first name. It [stepson's use of "Dad"] made me feel good. It made me feel good. Because every time he calls me Dad I feel like I'm somebody important to him. Even to this day, if I have to go out to the school and talk to his teacher or something like that, he'll . . . when I come through the door he'll start smiling and he'll come grab me. Or if I have to go out there for something bad that he's done, he's happy to see me but at the same time he knows he's in trouble. It's a good feeling, a very good feeling . . . when he started calling me Dad, right there I loved him.

Public affirmation also plays a part in feeling genuine fatherhood. For example, Emmit recounts a time when he ran into an old family friend in public, and the lesson he learned about his public identity in the family context. By insisting on referring to his partnership with Emmit as father and son, Jake assigned Emmit full-fledged membership in the family troupe: "We happened to be in the store and I was seeing one of my parent's friends and so when they asked me, 'Is this your son?' I was, like, this is my stepson; this is my wife's son and he [Jake] said, 'No, I'm your son.' Ever since then I always call him my son."

But terms of reference can be contested, further distinguishing genuine fatherhood. Jackson comments at length on how his stepson Mason set the criterion for authentic members of this kind in the family troupe.

> One thing we [mother and Jackson] did do, is we read to him a book on various types of families. Some families have one daddy, some families have one mommy, some families have two mommies, some families have two daddies, some families have a grandma and a mommy, or a grandpa and a mommy. Then we went into the stepfather thing. And about a week later, Helena [mother] said, "Yeah, Jackson's like a stepdaddy to you," when he was asking about other types of families, and Mason [Helena's son] says, "No, he's not a stepdaddy yet. You have to wait until you're married." So he had already put that in order. "He's not a stepdaddy yet." I don't know what that really means in his mind.

For some stepfathers, genuine fatherhood is signaled less by the use of familial terms of reference than by particular actions coincident with the provisioning and emotionally supportive themes discussed earlier. While there is a desire to be called Dad or Daddy, for example, genuine fatherhood for them is a matter of practice, revealed in the smaller, less apparent, steps of the family dance. Keith, forty-five and married to the mother of two girls age twelve and nine, explains.

> Oh, I always kind of wished they'd call me Dad, but I don't think that's going to happen. But I don't dwell on that. I truly believe that I am that role for them. When they need to go to the doctors, I take them. They go on my medical insurance. They live in my home, so it would be nice if they called me dad instead of Keith. That'd be the biggest issue, but I don't dwell on that, because that's not important. It's how they give me a kiss every night before they go to bed and how they tell me to have a good day before I go to work. I pack their lunches every morning. Little things like that. Letting me know what I am, which is their dad. I think when they get older there may come a day when they do that, but I won't ask them to do it. I think that's something they have to do on their own.

Vern, forty-eight with two stepchildren and three biological children from a previous marriage, reverses figure and ground, preferring to think in terms of the family dance as a whole. This approach provided him with a way of conceptualizing how he related to his and his wife's children within the new family.

> Well, we are proceeding now, as I told you, when Mary Jane and I got together and then decided to marry, there were just complications abounding in life . . . so I had to lie to myself a little bit to be able to get married. One of the lies I told myself was . . . I have three children, she has two. OK? And we can kind of keep that. Well, we have five. That's the truth. We have since dropped that little fiction of I have three and she has two. We have five children and we just kind of treat it that way.

CHOREOGRAPHERS TAKE THE LEAD

Mothers play an important role in choreographing the family dance in relation to new stepfathers. They affect the men's experiences as they get involved and try to remain involved in their new families. Mothers especially control stepfathers' level and mode of access to the children. They can inhibit or promote stepfathers' involvement, as Thomas's wife Stephanie, forty-four, candidly remarks, "Like, I didn't introduce them until I felt that that he [Thomas] was worthy, basically, of being introduced to my kids." Involvement in the family dance depends significantly on how mothers lead the way.

A mother's oversight also can facilitate a man's opportunity to develop a fatherly identity. When men are encouraged by mothers to interact with the children, the ground is set for the development of a self-image as a father and, by proxy, a sense of partnership in the family troupe as a whole. In his interview, Rodney, thirty-seven, expresses frustration that this hasn't yet developed. His perceived lack of influence in relation to his wife and two stepchildren causes emotional anguish, which has led him to contemplate a divorce.

> RODNEY: Judith and I would have, you know, whenever there were . . . there was a situation, we would talk about how we thought this should be handled. Nine times out of ten our opinions were different and nine times out of ten her decision was what was final.
> INTERVIEWER: And how did that make you feel?

RODNEY: How did it and how does it and how will it continue to make me feel? Like I'm not a permanent part of the family.

But there can be lapses in exclusionary control. While Judith's oversight prevents Rodney from feeling like he is part of the family, there are occasions, especially recently, when Judith's work schedule prevents her from going to school open houses, so Rodney is able to fill in for her. These opportunities leave him happy and empowered. At times like these, he reports feeling like a father figure. Unfortunately, he explains, they occur infrequently.

Some men compare current stepfamily experiences with previous experiences in exclusive relationships. Gerald, forty-four, is currently married to the mother of his thirteen-year-old stepdaughter and comments on difficulties he had being a stepfather in a previous marriage.

> I was supposed to share the responsibilities but yet I wasn't really allowed to discipline them. I think it became pretty clear, once we were together, if I was going to take the parental role then I needed to be treated like the parent. And Joan always seemed to want to do it her way. "Don't discipline the girls. Don't do this. Don't do that." Well, I got the responsibilities. I got to feed 'em, but can't I yell at them? She would make comments like, "Well, you don't love them like I do." No kidding. They're your kids. I mean, I can't, I never will.

Gerald explained that this family fell apart because the mother did not stand aside and provide him the opportunity to play a role in disciplining the children. This led to a sense of alienation from the children and, eventually, to the dissolution of the marriage. In his current marriage, Gerald has found a more comfortable place in his new teenage stepdaughter's life; he feels that he is taking a lead in the family dance, in other words.

Some men exert choreographic control without the mother's explicit consent; they step right in on their own. When his stepchildren weren't listening to their mother, stepfather Robby felt compelled to intervene.

> For example, Jamie [his wife] would tell Tony to go to bed. Twenty minutes later, they're still out in the living room and after a couple times of that, I said "OK, I'm staying here now." I'll put my foot down and if Jamie doesn't like it, this is what I'm thinking to myself, I'll put my foot down and if Jamie doesn't like it, she'll tell me about it. Let it go about five minutes, "Tracy and Tony, your mother said go get into bed." No problem; none at all. After they leave the room, Jamie is like, "How did you do that?"

Taking the lead together with the mother's supportive stance provided Robby with the confidence to construct a family dance led as much by him as by the children's mother. Beth, forty-two, offers insight into how mothers can be silent partners in these situations as a matter of ongoing domestic policy: "He [stepfather] wanted to build a relationship with her and it was real important that I stay out of that, that I let them interact directly with each other."

Other men partner with women who expressly encourage them to take control of the children's lives. William, thirty-seven, had two resident stepsons and felt that things fell into place rather easily when he met the boys and became involved with them. His wife, Chandra, asked him directly if he was willing to be the man in their lives. She allowed him to show the boys "guidance" and encouraged him to play an active role in disciplining them. One memorable experience for William was the time Chandra asked him to spank the youngest boy. To William, this represented Chandra's acceptance of his full partnership in the stepsons' lives, serving to legitimate his leading role in the household. Chandra explains: "He didn't . . . I told him he needed to start helping me. Like he's got to start helping me discipline them. I cannot go here and do this and watch them too or I can't handle this and this at the same time. I've got to have help." In a separate interview, William elaborates:

> I have had to spank Daniel [stepson] before and I think that, along with the fact that it was with his mother's approval, has set in to his mind that, OK, this is the man. He is going to be dad. I know he's not daddy, but he will be daddy. Or, he's not my father but he will be daddy. But it was her decisions because she was, like, a . . . she talked to him and talked to him and she doesn't know what to do, and she asked me would I step in and she told me what she wanted.

Brad, thirty-eight, describes how the children's mother similarly helped ease his movement onto the family dance floor by encouraging him to take the lead.

> I've been a little more tentative in getting involved with the day-to-day things of the kids because I wasn't sure to what extent she wanted me to get involved or to make my presence known, and she's actually drawn me out and said no, it's OK, you can. If Sherry does something that bothers you, you can say, "Sherry, please don't do that. That bothers me." Or if you want to give input, please do. Like I said, she draws me out a lot more. I've been more tentative and kind of hung back. Well, you know, it's not my house. Or maybe it's not my place to interject something here, or whatever. She's been

very good about actually drawing me out to do that, to participate like that. So I don't have any complaints about that. If anything, she wants me to be more—to go ahead and assume more of a role as time goes by.

Even when mothers do not explicitly ask for help with discipline, they can indirectly signal their willingness to allow stepfathers a disciplinary role. Eddie recounts a memorable experience of this kind with his stepdaughter Rhendy.

Only one time did she bring up, "You can't tell me what to do because you're not my daddy." Only one time, and that got corrected real quick, not by me, by Melissa, because Melissa was . . . I told her [Rhendy] to do something and Melissa was sitting right there and she said, "You can't tell me what to do because you're not my daddy.' Oh, that was a wrong comment. She got . . . first Melissa corrected her and then she got a few things taken away from her.

Children as Choreographers

Although we generally think of mothers as the primary choreographers of stepfamily life, children occasionally act as choreographers in their own right. Out of concern for their parents, some children monitor their parents' relationships, as happened when Harmony's stepfather John entered her mother Beth's life. Beth recalls Harmony's reaction to her forthcoming marriage to John: "Well, she [Harmony] told him at the beginning [of the relationship], if there's any violence, if there's any loud cursing, she laid it all out, she said, 'You're out.'" Harmony agreed to live with her mother and John, but on the condition that John agreed to treat her mother well. Harmony also made her mother agree to leave at the first sign of violence. As Beth describes it, the situation was "very solemn. Both John and I agreed to her terms and then from there, we were all living together."

DANCING ON A CROWDED FLOOR

Because mothers and their children commonly have continuing relationships with the children's biological father, stepfathers must learn to coordinate their dance styles knowing that another man is in the wings, or, perhaps, still on the floor. This can make for considerable awkwardness, as stepfathers coordinate their moves in relation to another man's rhythms. Stepfathers who aim to develop their own unique routines with stepchildren must often move on a crowded floor as they take account of potentially clashing partnerships (see Marsiglio 2004b).

Lingering Resentments

The family dance is complicated by the biological fathers' previous romantic involvement with the mother. The biological father may be jealous and
angry about the stepfathers' current attachment to the father's former lover,
his children's mother. Russ's case illustrates the emotional difficulty some
men face when dealing with biological fathers who harbor this form of
resentment. Asked how he felt when his stepson's biological father came into
his home to visit, Russ responded, "Well, I guess the fact that my wife and
him was once married and lived together . . . knowing he had been with my
wife before . . . I just felt kind of uncomfortable about the whole situation."

Fathers, in turn, may feel betrayed if their biological children decide
to view the stepfather as the primary dad in their lives. Stepfathers often
struggle with their own feelings of jealousy and loyalty, especially when
stepfamily members have regular interactions with the biological father.
Life can be stressful, if not turbulent, for children, who can be caught
between parents who harbor anger or resentment toward one another or
between a biological father and a stepfather who may, at best, view one
another ambivalently and, at worst, with distrust, anger, and contempt.

Clashing Decisions

The family dance becomes very complicated when the child's biological
mother and stepfather do not agree with the biological father's parenting
decisions. Disagreements may arise over the biological father's lifestyle,
including his dating or married life, living arrangements, religious beliefs,
and personal habits.

Brad's situation is a case in point, showing how difficult the family
dance can be and how disagreements over the biological father's lifestyle
can stir family tensions. His stepson Bobby's father lives out of town and,
as part of the divorce settlement, has visitation rights that call for Bobby to
visit him for a week three times a year. However, the biological father suf-
fered severe brain injuries from an accident, forcing him to live in a group
home. Because the father can't host Bobby at home, mother Nannette flies
the father in three times a year to spend a week with Bobby in their home.
Brad describes his uneasiness with the biological father's influence over
Bobby during these visits.

> His dad's got just some . . . how do I say . . . outmoded ideas of what men
> and women are and that kind of thing, in his mind. He makes comments like,

"Oh what do you expect from a woman?" That kind of thing. He's very chauvinistic and has this really . . . a woman's place is in the kitchen, women have no right to do this, or shouldn't be doing that. That kind of thing. He displays those attitudes frequently to Bobby. Like I said, I feel like we have to kind of deprogram Bobby after his visits sometimes because he gets this, a week's worth of this indoctrination from his dad and it's his dad. He looks up to him. I mean, it's only natural that a kid is going to look up to his dad and think, "Well, that must be the way things are, because Dad says so."

Who's the Dad?

The frustrations stepfathers and biological fathers sometimes have with one another can be compounded when open references figure into who the dad is. Zack, Terry's stepson, visits his biological father for a month each summer. Terry and the mother struggle to manage their dissatisfaction with the unhealthy environment the biological father provides, reflecting some of Brad's issues with his stepson Bobby's biological father. But these concerns are clearly accentuated when Zack refers to Terry as "Dad" in front of his biological father, as Terry describes.

> His father . . . he just lost it, lost it. He's a very, very ugly person, and called up threatening me and very demonstrative towards Zack and telling him he can't call me Dad, [saying] I'm not his dad. He's just an ugly person. I tried to speak with him and it's just impossible. He's just an ignorant redneck. I hate to use terms like that, but he's just so ugly. I tried as hard as I could, saying about, trying to think what's best for Zack. He has no care about what's best for Zack. All he cares about is himself. But that doesn't matter anymore. We went through that and he came back and it was very awkward for a couple of weeks. He was really confused. That's when we had a talk. I said, "Look, it's OK to have two dads. You have a couple sets of grandparents and whatever. It's OK to have two different fathers. I'm the one that's here with you all the time and he's the one up there. If he gets more involved in your life, then great! If he doesn't, nothing changes. I'm still here. I'm the one that's going to be here every day." So I said, "Don't be afraid to call me whatever you want to call me. If you want to call me Dad" . . . and he was cool with it. We haven't had any problems since.

While Terry's concern prompted him to sit down with Zack and reaffirm his commitment to him, later in the interview Terry continued to express alarm over the biological father's influence on his stepson, pointing to the seemingly neverending complications and crowdedness of the dance floor in question.

We're very pro-education. Her [Terry's wife] father is a professor. It's a completely different world up there in [a southern state with the biological father]. They're in the woods. They live in a trailer. They smoke fifty-nine thousand packs of cigarettes a day in the trailer. They drink beer. They . . . not that I mind drinking beer, but I mean, they drink a lot. They cuss all the time. He [biological father] has a different girlfriend every time [Zack's] around him. It's just a completely unsavory environment from what we try to foster down here.

SHARING THE FLOOR

Shared paternity works best when the biological father and stepfather cooperate, which is likely to extend to the children's mother and the children. Everyone is involved in the family dance; they act as allies. When this succeeds, the family members take a collaborative orientation to coordinating the troupe in a mutually satisfying performance.

Avoiding the Term "Dad"

One way this plays out is when stepfathers discourage the use of the term "dad" in reference to themselves. Stepfathers act as father allies when they suggest that the children reserve the label and its corresponding social con-notations for the biological father. Because issues of loyalty and betrayal are so emotionally charged in the family context, this simple move conveys the stepfather's respect for the biological father's place and rights in the child's life. Stepfather Robby's feelings about his own biological children from another marriage helped him imagine the situation from his step-child's biological father's perspective.

> 'Cause it's come up because when my daughter [stepdaughter Tracy] would call me Daddy. And one time when we were sitting at dinner and Tracy looked at me and said Daddy and I stopped and said, "Tracy, I'm not your daddy. Your daddy is Brad." I don't want my [own] daughter calling anybody else daddy and I know Brad must feel the same way. He doesn't want his kids calling anybody else daddy and I don't blame him.

Partnering Up

Taking a nonadversarial, friendly stance toward the biological father in front of the children is another way stepfathers can signify their willingness to act as supportive partners rather than competitors in the family dance. Eddie, thirty-five, cooperates with his stepdaughter Rhendy's biological father and spends time with him when he comes to the house to pick up Rhendy. He extends the cordiality into the workplace where both are employed. Eddie considers the biological father a friend, although the two don't interact outside of these house visits and their time at work.

> By that time, within the last year we really, really become good friends. I mean, we'll watch . . . he'll come over, he'll come to pick Rhendy up and the football game on . . . we'll sit there and watch football with him if he comes in on it, or something happen at work, we'll come in on that. He come . . . probably spend about thirty minutes which—it only takes about two minutes to come pick the kid up. He'll come and stay about thirty minutes and we'll chit-chat, laugh, joke. He comes back with her, chit-chat some more, laugh, joke and he's off. We come to work and we pass by each other, comments, little jokes, and keep going.

Sharing the dance floor sometimes extends to defensive partnerships, with stepfathers intervening on behalf of biological fathers to manage their missteps. Eddie's informal alliance with Rhendy's biological father, Dave, is illustrative. Dave often works late and occasionally has promised to pick up Rhendy at a specified time, only to break his word. This upsets his daughter. Eddie attempts to calm Rhendy when this happens, softening her frustration with her father.

> I try to soften the blow for her and put him and everybody [at ease]. It's OK. He [Dave] probably had to do something late at work. I understand he didn't call. There might be some reason he didn't call. Let's check that out first before we come unglued. He needs to explain it to you. If he's not going to call, let's just tell Rhendy, "Listen, maybe Dad had something important at work that he couldn't get away to call you. But you need to talk to your dad and ask him why. You just can't be mad at him. You've gotta find out why first, then you can get mad if you don't like the answer, but let's find out first before you get mad." If he don't call or he don't pick her up when he says he's going to pick her up, then I guess I kind of smooth things over for him. When he do bad things, whether he do it intentionally or not, I try to make him look like he . . . it's a mistake, nobody's perfect. Dad is going to make mistakes. It's OK for Dad to make mistakes. He's human. He doesn't know half the times I cleaned up his mess. He doesn't know half the things I do. I'm not doing it for him. I'm doing it for her.

Sharing the dance floor with the biological father generally includes the mother. For example, from the start, stepfather Keith encouraged his wife

Denise to use caution and not talk negatively about his stepchildren's biological father in front of them. In this case, Denise's anger at the biological father resulted from an extramarital affair that precipitated their divorce. Keith reports that Denise took this advice even while Denise still resents the betrayal.

Biological fathers themselves can collaborate on the choreography, reciprocating with cooperative or supportive gestures toward the stepfather. Recall that Eddie works with Rhendy's biological father. In fact, the biological father helped Eddie get a job at the store where they both work. The biological father was able to contribute directly to the economic support of his daughter by enabling her resident stepfather to secure paid employment.

SUMMING UP

The stepfather family is the most common type of stepfamily. Stepfamilies evolve over time as people share routines and rituals, make their respective moves, exchange emotions, and develop a shared sense of familial history (see Ganong et al. 1999; Marsiglio 1995, 2004a, 2004b). We adopted the metaphor of the family dance to characterize how individuals interact within a stepfamily and how this affects the complex rhythms of stepfathering.

Being part of the family dance means that family members influence each other on the dance floor. For some stepfathers, the floor may be crowded and contested; others share the floor supportively with biological fathers. The mother usually is the key choreographer of this dance, as she supplies direction to the stepfather in cultivating his relations with the children. Stepchildren can be choreographers too, as they shape their relationships with the stepfather. All are part of the troupe whose varied dance steps can make for successful or failed performances.

REFERENCES

Cherlin, Andrew. 1978. "Remarriage as an Incomplete Institution." *American Journal of Sociology* 84:634–50.

Ganong, Lawrence H., Marilyn Coleman, Mark Fine, and Patricia Martin. 1999. "Stepparents' Affinity-Seeking and Affinity-Maintaining Strategies with Stepchildren." *Journal of Family Issues* 20:299–327.

Marsiglio, William. 1995. "Stepfathers with Minor Children Living at Home: Parenting Perceptions and Relationship Quality." Pp. 78–101 in *Fatherhood:*

Contemporary Theory, Research, and Social Policy, edited by William
Marsiglio. Thousand Oaks, Calif.: Sage.
——. 2004a. "When Stepfathers Claim Stepchildren: A Conceptual Analysis."
Journal of Marriage and Family 66:22–39.
——. 2004b. *Stepdads: Stories of Love, Hope, and Repair.* Boulder, Colo.:
Rowman & Littlefield.

FURTHER READING

Bumpass, Larry L., R. Kelly Raley, and James A. Sweet. 1995. "The Changing
    Character of Stepfamilies: Implications of Cohabitation and Nonmarital
    Childbearing." *Demography* 32:425–36.
Hofferth, Sandra L., and Kermit G. Anderson. 2003. "Are All Dads Equal? Biology
    Versus Marriage as a Basis for Parental Investment." *Journal of Marriage and
    Family* 65:213–32.
Mason, Mary A., and J. Mauldin. 1996. "The New Stepfamily Requires a New
    Public Policy." *Journal of Social Issues* 51:11–27.
McDonald, William L., and Alfred DeMaris. 2002. "Stepfather-Stepchild
    Relationship Quality. The Stepfather's Demand for Conformity and the
    Biological Father's Involvement." *Journal of Family Issues* 23:121–37.
Phillips, R. 1997. "Stepfamilies from a Historical Perspective." Pp. 5–18 in *Step-
    families: History, Research, and Policy,* edited by I. Levin and M. B. Sussman.
    New York: Haworth.
White, Lynn, and Joan G. Gilbreth. 2001. "When Children Have Two Fathers:
    Effects of Relationships with Stepfathers and Noncustodial Fathers on
    Adolescent Outcomes." *Journal of Marriage and Family* 63:155–67.

Discussion Questions

1. The idea of the choreographer is a powerful way of viewing familial
   influence. How might it apply to other members of the family network,
   such as aunts, uncles, and grandparents in matters of stepparenting?

2. The concept of the dance floor suggests that a social location such as
   a household has boundaries, puts one's performance on public display,
   and can be empty or crowded. How useful has this been in illuminating
   the stepfathering experience?

3. What are the limitations of the "family dance" metaphor? What other
   metaphors might be applied to stepfathering? What additional insights
   do they offer for domestic relations in this circumstance?

INDEX